Tools for Thought

Tools for Thought

Graphic Organizers for Your Classroom

Jim Burke

HEINEMANN
Portsmouth, NH

Heinemann

361 Hanover Street
Portsmouth, NH 03801–3912
www.heinemann.com

Offices and agents throughout the world

The author and publisher wish to thank those who have generously given permission to reprint borrowed material:

Excerpt from "Hire Me First" by Linda Woo is reprinted by permission of the South County Journal.

Library of Congress Cataloging-in-Publication Data

Burke, Jim, 1961–
Tools for thought : graphic organizers for your classroom / Jim Burke.
p. cm.
Includes bibliographical references and index.
ISBN 0-325-00464-1 (alk. paper)
1. Lesson planning. 2. Effective teaching. 3. Teaching—Aids and devices.
I. Title.
LB1027.4 .B87 2002
371.3'028'1—dc21

2002011344

Editor: Lois Bridges
Production: Abigail M. Heim
Cover design: Judy Arisman, Arisman Design
Typesetter: House of Equations, Inc.
Manufacturing: Steve Bernier

Printed in the United States of America on acid-free paper

12 11 10 EB 9 10 11

This book is dedicated with gratitude to my friend and colleague Sam Intrator, whose friendship has been an essential tool and a great blessing.

A teacher is one who brings us tools and enables us to use them.

—*Jean Toomer*

Give me a lever long enough and I will move the world.

—*Archimedes*

Contents

Appendices

Acknowledgments

The ideas in this book come not from my own head but from the conversations I've had with colleagues and the lessons I've learned from my own students. In particular I would like to thank Sandy Briggs for all that she taught me about working with ESL students and the SDAIE methods that help such students succeed. Rebecca Shirley, through our friendship and conversations, has mentored me in the area of special education, telling me what works and why, asking the right question at the right time. My colleagues at Burlingame High School have been instrumental to the process of developing these tools. They have been patient and supportive of me as I ask what works and why, sharing with me their own insights into the teaching and learning process. Several colleagues merit special thanks for helping me improve these tools or suggesting ways to improve them: Elaine Caret, Diane McClain, Linda McLaughlin, and Marilyn Nelson (English); Matt Vaughn and Chris Balmy (science); Shelly Bischoff and Antonella Wemple (foreign language); Kevin Nelson and Frank Firpo, Steve Erle, and Steve Mills (social science).

During the summer of 2001 I worked with many teachers around California in a series of professional development institutes. That experience and comments from participants were invaluable and I thank these many colleagues for helping me better understand the use and value of the tools discussed in this book. In addition, these tools have been available on my Web site for some time now; users have routinely sent in suggestions about the format or function of the tools. These comments always improved the tools and inspired new techniques. Many thanks to the englishcompanion.com visitors for their guidance and support.

I had the blessing of the best student aides in the world during the time I wrote this book. Nicole Cinti and Nick Spillane offered help whenever I asked. I must thank Alice Lee separately. She invested uncounted hours getting student samples into shape so they would reproduce nicely; she ran the operation, leaving me free to concentrate on the writing.

Several other colleagues offer me so much guidance, teach me so much, I must always take the chance to thank them; their contribution to this book was no less than to others I have written: Carol Jago, Kate Kinsella, Regie Routman, and Sam Intrator.

No one teaches me more than my students. The material in this book comes from several different classes, but all students were freshmen or sophomores. You will notice repeated references to certain works; this is an unavoidable consequence of writing the book during the course of a single year. I trust you will be able to see from these examples how to use the tools for whatever your students are reading, writing, or thinking about.

Finally, I must thank the two people to whom I am always indebted and without whom my work could not be possible. My editor, Lois Bridges, encourages, guides, nurtures, challenges, teaches, and, ultimately, mentors me through the process. Her questions result in better thinking, improved writing, and more useful books. And to my wife, Susan: I can never say thank you enough. Every book I write we create together, accompanied along the way by our three wonderful children, Evan, Whitman, and Nora.

How to Use This Book

Books are, of course, one of the most powerful tools we use. I hope this book will prove no less useful to you than the tools provided here have been to me; the measure of its value and success will be determined by how much it helps you teach and your students learn. I use these tools myself for many projects; as a teacher, I use them to give structure to and ensure depth in my teaching. I choose which one to use by following a rather informal but nonetheless structured sequence that looks something like this:

The power of the unaided mind is highly overrated. Without external aids, memory, thought, and reasoning are all constrained.

—DON NORMAN, *THINGS THAT MAKE US SMART*

1. What verbs describe what I want people to do (e.g., compare, discuss, identify)?
2. What do I want students to be able to do with this information (e.g., write a paper, take an exam, give a presentation)?
3. From how many angles (i.e., perspectives, aspects) should students consider this subject?
4. Should students do this by themselves or with others?
5. Do students need me to model for them how to use this tool in general or on this specific assignment?
6. What will students do with their page of notes when they are finished?

I have included three different systems to help guide your own decision-making process as to which tool or technique to use. On the following pages you will find these support documents, two of which I created (Making Effective and Efficient Notes and Toolbox: A Visual Directory of the Tools) and one that others created (the Faciones' Holistic Critical Thinking Scoring Rubric).

The tools and techniques in this book support challenging work and improved academic understanding in all subject areas. Though most examples here come from my English classes, I have included where possible examples from social studies classes. These student examples are important because they come from my freshman academic literacy classes (I call them ACCESS—academic success—classes); students in these classes, whom you'll see at work in pictures throughout the book, found these tools very helpful as they learned to work as students and improve as readers. Their inclusion in the ACCESS program means these students entered high school reading two or more grade levels below freshman year. These tools have also proven very effective with students in the ESL classes and those in mainstream academic classes who needed help understanding what they were doing. During the year in which I was writing this book, I gave many workshops to teachers around California; these were all teachers whose students were not performing at grade level according to our state tests. I also gave several presentations on the use and value of such tools to Specially Designed Academic Instruction for English Learners (SDAIE) classes; here again, teachers found the tools helped students learn in different subject areas, including classes in foreign language, industrial technology, and health.

Those who have purchased my other books will find these tools and techniques consistent with and a useful complement to those books. The chapter on teaching and learning in *The English Teacher's Companion* (1999), for instance, identifies four aspects of effective learning: occupation, conversation, construction, and negotiation. The tools in this book extend and help to clarify further what such principles look like and how we can enact them in the diverse classrooms in which we teach. Those familiar with my book *Reading Reminders* (2000) will have seen some of these tools; it was during the writing of that book—a year when I had 165 sophomores, many of whom had learning difficulties or were still learning English—that I came to understand the power of such tools. This book builds and improves on those first tools. My book *Writing Reminders* (forthcoming), which currently exists as a draft, will demonstrate the effectiveness of such tools in writing.

Use the following three documents, then, to help you choose which tool to use as described:

- *Faciones' Holistic Critical Thinking Scoring Rubric*: Let this concise rubric help you evaluate your teaching and students' performance; then choose those tools that will help you address areas of need.
- *Toolbox: A Visual Directory of the Tools* (Figure 1): While every tool is not represented (how you do *draw* annotating?) this will help you quickly evaluate what you need for an assignment. This toolbox, combined with the table of contents, will serve as a menu of sorts.
- *Making Effective and Efficient Notes* (Figure 2): This page, which is designed to be run off for students, summarizes the different techniques common to taking good notes. Use this to introduce the habits of good note taking, and refer them to it as needed.

Finally, let me explain how each chapter works. You will find the tool identified in the chapter title (e.g., "Conversational Roundtable"). The chapter begins with a general description of the strategy; here I describe when, how, why, and with whom to use the tool. Then I have included examples of at least one, in some cases more, assignment from my students. To help you better understand how I use each tool, and how I got the results I did, I narrate what I did, how I did it, and why I did it. Blank, reproducible versions of each tool, as well as a few extra tools that did not merit their own chapter, are included in the Appendix.

HOLISTIC CRITICAL THINKING SCORING RUBRIC (FACIONE AND FACIONE 1996)

4 Consistently does all or almost all of the following:

- Accurately interprets evidence, statements, graphics, questions, etc.
- Identifies the salient arguments (reasons and claims) pro and con.
- Thoughtfully analyzes and evaluates major alternative points of view.
- Draws warranted, judicious, nonfallacious conclusions.
- Justifies key results and procedures, explains assumptions and reasons.
- Fair-mindedly follows where evidence and reasons lead.

3 Does most or many of the following:

- Accurately interprets evidence, statements, graphics, questions, etc.
- Identifies relevant arguments (reasons and claims) pro and con.
- Offers analyses and evaluations of obvious alternative points of view.
- Draws warranted, nonfallacious conclusions.
- Justifies some results or procedures, explains reasons.
- Fair-mindedly follows where evidence and reasons lead.

2 Does most or many of the following:

- Misinterprets evidence, statements, graphics, questions, etc.
- Fails to identify strong, relevant counterarguments.
- Ignores or superficially evaluates obvious alternative points of view.
- Draws unwarranted or fallacious conclusions.
- Justifies few results or procedures, seldom explains reasons.
- Regardless of the evidence or reasons, maintains or defends views based on self-interest or preconceptions.

1 Consistently does all or almost all of the following:

- Offers biased interpretations of evidence, statements, graphics, questions, information, or the points of view of others.
- Fails to identify or hastily dismisses strong, relevant counter-arguments.
- Ignores or superficially evaluates obvious alternative points of view.
- Argues using fallacious or irrelevant reasons, and unwarranted claims.
- Does not justify results or procedures, nor explain reasons.
- Regardless of the evidence or reasons, maintains or defends views based on self-interest or preconceptions.
- Exhibits closed-mindedness or hostility to reason.

Note: Visit <www.insightassessment.com> to read instructions for using the Holistic Critical Thinking Scoring Rubric.

Toolbox

Character Directory	Conversational Roundtable	Decision Tree	Episodic Notes (3-Square)	Episodic Notes (6-Square)	Idea Cards
Interactive Notes	Linear Array	Outline Notes	Plot Notes	Pyramid Notes	Q Notes
Reporter's Notes	Spreadsheet Notes (3-column)	Spreadsheet Notes (Multicolumn)	Story Notes	Summary Notes	Summary Sheet
T Notes	Target Notes	Think in Threes	Time Line Notes	Venn Diagram	Vocabulary Squares

FIGURE 1 Toolbox: A Visual Directory of the Tools

Making Effective and Efficient Notes

Overview

Good notes must be complete, coherent, and concise. Whether you are reading, listening, or watching, you must be able to make notes quickly in a format that will be helpful later on when you prepare to write, speak, or take a test.

Lay Out Page

Divide the page into sections that serve different purposes. There are four primary spaces you can use to arrange information on the page, as the sample page shows:

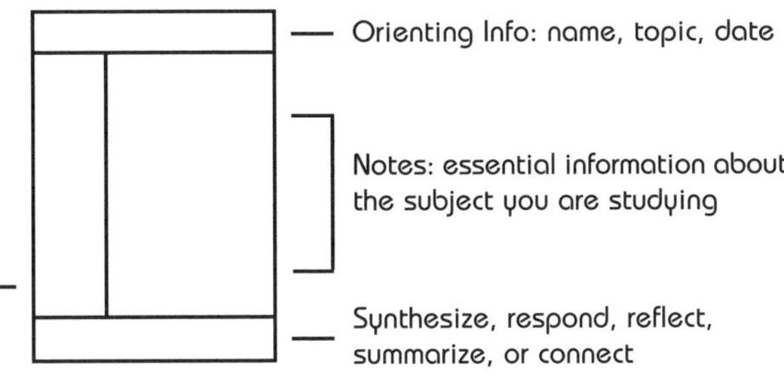

Organize Information

Organize information into a visual format that you find helpful. This might include bullets, dashes, or numbers. Though an outline format is helpful, keep it loose so that you don't get confused as you make notes. Identify and organize information into categories that align themselves with chapters, headings/subheadings, major themes, or chronological events; such organization gives your notes structure and coherence. Use additional techniques such as underlining and ALL CAPS to quickly orient your eyes.

BENEFITS OF GOOD NOTES

- Improve Recall: Info is better organized, which aids the memory when tested.
- Increase Understanding: Organizing info forces you to digest it and establish connections between different ideas.
- Increase Attention: Whether you are reading or listening, taking good notes forces you to pay close attention to what you are studying. It does this by:
  - Establishing a purpose
  - Giving you a focus
  - Determining what is important

Abbreviate

You are the only one who must be able to use and read your notes. Each class or topic has words and ideas that come up repeatedly. Using symbols, abbreviations, acronyms, or other tricks to condense your notes helps you get down more information in a useful format. Here are some samples and suggestions:

- **Shorten familiar words:** *info* for information; *NY* for New York; *WW2* for World War Two
- **Use symbols to represent words or ideas:** + for add; = for equal; *w/o* for without; & for and; *b/c* for because
- **Use acronyms to abbreviate familiar terms:** *MWH* for Modern World History; *NATO, GNP, USA, UN, WWI*
- **Shorten words through omission:** *gov't* for government; *bldg.* for building; *pps* for pages; *prob* for problem
- **Abbreviate names:** *A* = Atticus; *BR* = Boo Radley; *BE* = Bob Ewell; *FDR* = Franklin Delano Roosevelt
- **Shorten common terms:** *RJ* = Romeo and Juliet; *Eng* = English; *OLine* = outline; *BStorm* = brainstorm

Telegraph

You do not need to write down *every* word you read or hear. Cut out unnecessary words. Example: "Atticus takes case" or "Germans lose battle; morale worsens."

Use White Space

Don't crowd your page! Leave space between ideas (e.g., leave an extra space between main ideas). This leaves room to add more information later on and makes your notes easier on the tired eyes trying to read them.

Set Purpose

Decide *why* you are taking notes so you know how to organize your information and evaluate what you should write down. If, for example, you are making notes for a paper on consequences of a particular historical event, you need to pay special attention to information about what followed that event. Keep asking yourself: What is the question these notes are trying to help me answer (e.g., What are the primary consequences of . . .?)?

FIGURE 2 Making Effective and Efficient Notes

Introduction: Tools for Thought

I use the tools in this book every day to help me "enter the house" of my own ideas and those found in the different texts I read and teach to my advanced and struggling students. I use them to help my students generate and organize their ideas when reading and writing. They have become a vocabulary of shapes I use to think about teaching and learning, reading and writing. However, that is not all; I use them to design my Web site (<www.englishcompanion.com>) and explain ideas to myself and others.

While some of them are familiar "graphic organizers," I prefer the term *tools*. Usually I resist such semantic hairsplitting, but the difference here is important: I use them for so many different purposes, in so many ways, I can only understand them as tools, for they do not only *organize*. Like the telephone repairperson whose worn leather belt sags with different instruments that help him connect, hear, and assess, I use these tools to meet my many personal and professional needs. My students also learn to use these tools to:

- Generate ideas, solutions, information, details, possibilities
- Evaluate events and texts
- Identify what is important and why it is important
- Prepare to write
- Develop their capacity to read different texts critically
- Organize ideas and information when reading, writing, speaking, or thinking
- Connect or compare different ideas, texts, characters, or events
- Explain different ideas, relationships, and patterns
- Focus on specific aspects of different texts
- Assess their understanding of texts and concepts
- Facilitate whole-class, small-group, and one-on-one discussions
- Synthesize information from a variety of sources

Such tools and their associated techniques allow me to create a classroom "in which the teacher searches for students' understanding of concepts, and then structures opportunities for students to refine or revise these understandings by posing contradictions, presenting new information, asking questions, encouraging research, and/or engaging students in inquiries designed to challenge current concepts" (Brooks and Brooks 1999). Such a classroom is consistent with the five principles of a "constructivist classroom":

- Teachers seek and value their students' points of view.
- Classroom activities challenge students' suppositions.
- Teachers pose problems of emerging relevance.
- Teachers build lessons around primary concepts and "big" ideas.

When we enter a house for the first time, we of course find it unfamiliar. By walking around for a while, however, looking into various rooms and peering into cupboards, we quickly get to know it. But what if we cannot enter the house, and our own knowledge of it comes from the instructions and plans that were used to build it? Moreover, what if those instructions and plans are written in a highly technical language that we find intimidating and incomprehensible? What if, try as we may, we cannot form any mental picture of the house? Then we are not going to get much of a sense of what it is like to live there. We are not going to be able to enter the house even in our imagination.

—KEITH DEVLIN, "DO MATHEMATICIANS HAVE DIFFERENT BRAINS?" IN *THE MATH GENE*

- Teachers assess student learning in the context of daily teaching. (Brooks and Brooks 1999)

The tools share several traits that make them effective. Their designs are intuitive, often based on familiar patterns (e.g., a target) or concepts (e.g., the standard reporter's questions). This familiarity helps students adapt them to various uses, as compared with many traditional graphic organizers, which often have specific uses and require detailed instruction in how to use them. Another feature is the one just mentioned: adaptability. A tool like the Conversational Roundtable serves many purposes in my class, preparing kids to write and helping them to read. The tools are also adaptable to all grade and ability levels. While I might use a tool like Think in Threes in different ways, the same tool works equally well in both advanced and remedial classes.

The tools included here have evolved into a canon of methods from which I can draw quickly and with confidence, knowing the benefits each one provides to the user. In fact, another outcome of designing and learning to use these tools has been the emphasis on *user* as opposed to *reader* or *writer*. This shift in focus challenged me to think less about reading and writing and more about teaching and learning. As students *use* books and curricula, computers and different media to gather information and ideas, they need tools to help them evaluate and organize what they learn. We now have a much wider range of users than previous generations of teachers. Students learning English and those with learning differences often need and always benefit from tools that help them *see* what they read, that make the abstract more concrete. To this end I have made sure the tools and techniques discussed in this book are aligned with the best practices discussed in books for Specially Designed Academic Instruction in English (SDAIE) classes and students with learning differences. As SDAIE emphasizes content area literacy, I have worked hard with teachers in all subject areas, even industrial arts and foreign languages, to learn how these tools can support their work in the classroom.

This book is based on the simple assumptions that kids cannot read or write about what they cannot understand, and that they cannot understand what they cannot "see." Books such as Howard Gardner's *Disciplined Minds* (2000) and Robert Sternberg's *Thinking Styles* (1997) emphasize the importance of providing students with multiple entry points and a variety of means for communicating what they know or have learned. Other books—*Things That Make Us Smart* (Norman 1993), *Making Connections* (Caine and Caine 1994), *Classroom Strategies for Interactive Learning* (Buehl 2001), and *The CALLA Handbook* (Chamot and O'Malley 1994)—stress the interactive nature of learning and the importance of making connections during the learning process. Over time, however, students must learn to make such connections on their own; thus another core belief in this book is the need for scaffolding and inevitable independence. The tools in this book include directions and examples, but eventually students must learn when and how to use them on their own so they can develop the independence that all successful adults acquire over time. The tools included here for literature circles, for example, develop students' ability to think and work in specific roles (e.g., Discussion Director); once students have learned the skills, however, the tools become intrusive and should only be used if students need reminding.

Some tools for thought should but cannot be represented here. These additional tools include computer programs and video cameras. This might seem an odd assertion, but both provide powerful means of thinking that, typically, we may not consider. Computer programs are powerful tools for thought in several ways. Bullets force us to evaluate what is *worth* a bullet (i.e., what is an important, discrete item worth singling out). Fields in databases teach us to identify, prioritize, and organize information; they invite us to ask, "What are the types of information I need to gather?" and "How can I best organize that information?" Spreadsheets, while similar to databases, challenge us to identify the essential fields and examine the relationship between the data in one and that in another. Video, which we are just beginning to learn to use for instructional purposes, offers a powerful means of recording, processing (through the editing process), and improving on ways of working and thinking, thanks to the visual feedback. All of these tools serve, in respects, the one great tool through which we have achieved so much over time: stories. Gardner (1996) found that one of the common traits among all great leaders in any field was their ability to use stories to inspire, explain, and teach.

Feedback gained through watching, comparing, and evaluating data is crucial to the learning process, which relies on information about what works and what does not (Schmoker 1999; Norman 1993). Kids learn, by using these tools, for instance, what to pay attention to and what to ignore. The tools direct kids' attention and provide a focused task that yields immediate rewards to students, especially those with attention and processing differences (Levine 1994). They provide the additional benefit of being easy to assess and quick to score, even as they provide students the support they need to advance their thinking.

In her study, "Beating the Odds: Teaching Middle and High School Students to Read and Write Well," Judith Langer (1999) found six traits common to schools that succeed with such students:

- Students learn skills and knowledge in multiple lesson types
- Teachers integrate test preparation into instruction
- Teachers make connections across instruction, curriculum, and life
- Students learn strategies for doing the work
- Students are expected to be generative thinkers
- Classrooms foster cognitive collaboration

These principles, along with those previously mentioned, inform the ideas in this book and, of course, my own classroom teaching. I hope you find the tools included here as helpful as I do. I struggle, as we all do, to meet the diverse needs of my students, who must learn to do challenging academic work. I also struggle with the workload. These tools have allowed me to narrow my teaching repertoire to a set of tested, adaptable tools from which I can draw one or more to do the job. The days of creating an endless number of discrete lesson plans as part of a novel unit are over for me. Instead, I simply ask which tool is the right one for the job and work to help students master the intellectual habits they need to use such tools on their own. No tool or technique will ever meet all our needs, something I long ago realized. These tools have done all I can ask of them, and have done it well: they have made me a better teacher. For this I am grateful. I hope they will do the same for you as you continue your own quest to be the teacher all your students need.

Jim Burke

Tools for Thought

Annotations

1

DESCRIPTION

Annotating looks a little different from the other tools discussed in this book; yet it is no less a tool—one that comes complete with its own set of implements. These Annotation tools include such things as crayons, highlighters, pencils, colored pens, sticky notes, and codes. To annotate is to make marks, critical or personal, on a text; when made in the margins of a text, such notes are called marginalia. These marks, which include words, codes, patterns (e.g., circled versus underlined), colors, and illustrations, transform the reading experience into a conversation, an interaction between the reader and the text. Students often gravitate toward the colorful highlighters to do such work, yet a pencil is often much more beneficial, as it allows them to both underline and explain why they underlined that word or passage. Too often we return to a page of highlighted words and have no idea why the highlighted sections are significant.

What we annotate and how we annotate depends on our purpose, of course. If students are learning about different human needs, they might be asked to underline examples of different needs discussed in an article and then, in the margin, write down the type of needs they identified. Students reading a poem for style or, more specifically, aspects of sound, might indicate different sound patterns. Or, to extend the literary emphasis, students reading to analyze a character's motives might highlight or otherwise indicate examples they want to use in their subsequent paper. In the margin they could jot down code words that would help them navigate the text and find their examples later. Aside from forcing us to read more closely, annotating is, ultimately, a navigational strategy. After all, I don't mark up texts I do not intend to use in one way or another. To this end it is useful to indicate—in the header or on a sticky note—big events or important information you want to be able to find quickly.

NOTES AND EXAMPLES

Example One: Sticky Note Annotations

The nice textbooks I worked so hard to get money for will not stay nice if we write in them. But I want my kids to be active readers, especially those learning to read more challenging texts. In Figure 1.1 you see a method that works very well: Sticky Note Annotations. Kids keep

STANDARDS

- Reading
  - ☐ Analyze organizational patterns of information
  - ☐ Compare ideas, texts, or authors
  - ☐ Evaluate the arguments presented in a text
  - ☐ Extend ideas
  - ☐ Generate relevant questions
  - ☐ Identify and analyze recurring themes
  - ☐ Prepare to read
  - ☐ Synthesize information from multiple sources
- Writing
  - ☐ Establish a main or controlling idea
  - ☐ Integrate quotations and examples in written response
  - ☐ Prepare to write
  - ☐ Use sensory, concrete, or illustrative details to support claims
- Language Study
  - ☐ Distinguish between denotative and connotative meaning
  - ☐ Examine and use different Greek and Latin roots of words
  - ☐ Know and use different parts of speech
- Listening
  - ☐ Improve note-taking skills
  - ☐ Examine author's use of style
- Test Preparation
  - ☐ Comprehend information
  - ☐ Organize ideas
  - ☐ Prioritize information
  - ☐ Remember information

SUBJECT AREAS

- English language arts
- Health
- Humanities
- Mathematics
- Science
- Social studies

USES

- Ask useful questions
- Assess student performance
- Compare two or more items, aspects, or people
- Develop academic literacy
- Evaluate ideas
- Extend ideas beyond obvious
- Facilitate discussion
- Gather evidence to support claims
- Identify themes
- Make connections
- Narrow or refine subject
- Observe patterns
- Prepare to read
- Prepare to write
- Respond to reading
- Support critical reading
- Synthesize ideas
- Take notes while reading

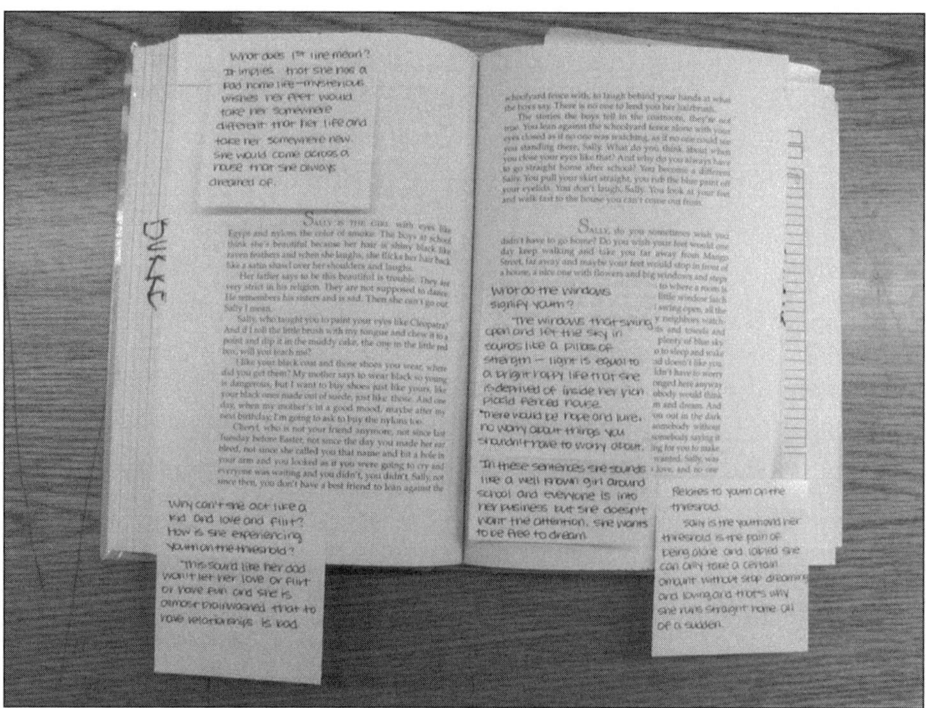

FIGURE 1.1 Sticky Note Annotations

a few sticky notes handy as they read. When they get confused or want to respond, they put the note right on the relevant spot in the text. This is very helpful for improving comprehension because the reader, in order to make the note, must diagnose their own problem (Tovani 2000). The reader might determine, finally, that there are a couple of words that are the source of their confusion. This method then allows the teacher to work efficiently and help the student "fix up" the problem and keep on reading.

Alternatives to this technique include having students write:

- A summary of a passage or section in a textbook
- Notes that connect this text to others they are reading (e.g., for a research project)
- Questions to ask the teacher or use for further inquiry

Example Two: Annotated Poem

Students in my English classes read a weekly poem. I favor the annotation approach for poems because students can read them many times and mark up the text, as Figure 1.2 shows. When first introducing the technique, I give them a copy of the text and put a copy on the overhead so we can work through it together. We discuss what to do when we annotate. We always start, as you can see, by clustering the title and using that to prepare us for the reading. Kids are not always sure what to write when they annotate. Options include questions, comments, definitions, and connections to the readers' own experiences or other texts they have read. Before they begin reading and annotating, remind students of their purpose, as this will help determine what they annotate. In

Weekly Poem | Your Name:______________________
Mr. Burke/English | Period:___________

Overview: Read the poem first to enjoy it. Read it straight on through, *preferably* aloud. Then read it again (and again), looking for any of the following literary devices or features:

- ❑ *Language*: tone, style, diction (word choice)
- ❑ *Conventions*: punctuation, grammar, poetic forms
- ❑ *Devices*: imagery, metaphor, symbols, repetition, and more.
- ❑ *Design*: structure, organization of content (e.g., stanzas, past-to-present)
- ❑ *Themes*: ideas that run throughout the poem
- ❑ *Connections*: how might this relate to the other works we are reading, conversations we are having in class lately?
- ❑ *Purpose*: is the poet trying to explain? Define? Persuade? What, why, and how do they do this?

The front *must* show evidence of close reading—e.g., underlined words, comments, questions, connections, suspected patterns. Your written response (on the back or on a separate sheet of paper), should be **one perfectly written paragraph** (not a loosely written journal-type response) with a clear assertion, supporting details, and examples or quotations from the poem. *Your paragraph must include quotations from the poem.* These quotations must be *embedded*, not left to stand alone.

Remember to consult the Literary Analysis sheet I gave you this week. Pay attention to the verbs. Begin your paragraph: In her poem "I'm Nobody!" Emily Dickinson (pick a verb from the lit analysis list______...."

There is a wonderful video profile of this poem at http://www.favoritepoem.org/archive/liang.html

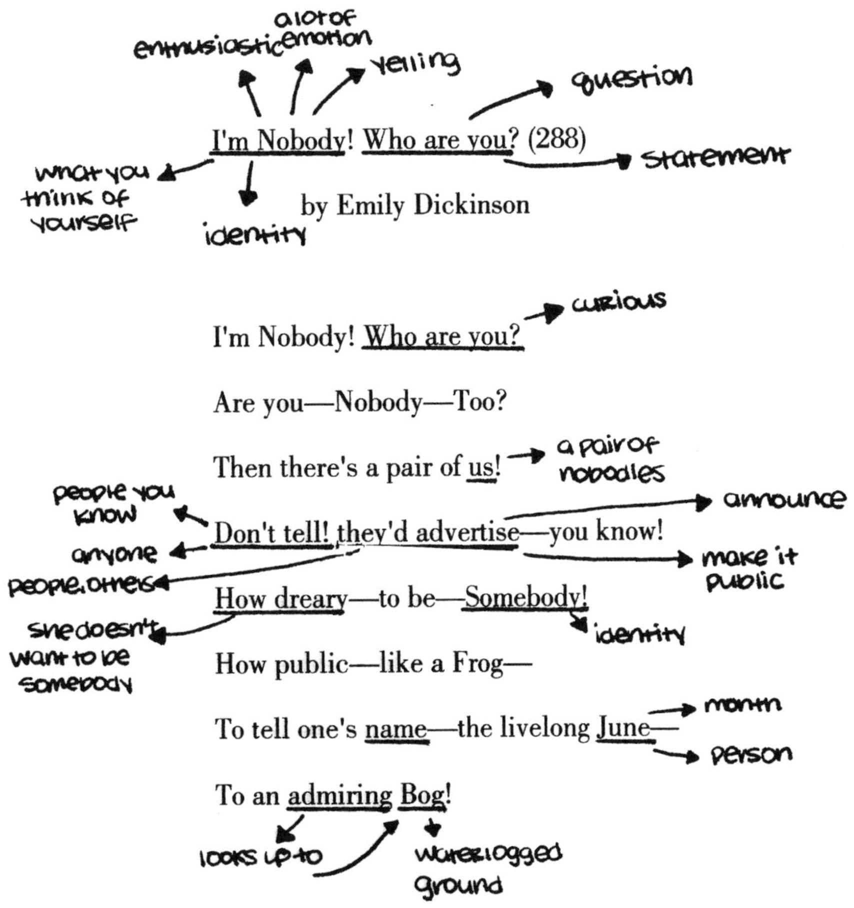

I'm Nobody! Who are you? (288)

by Emily Dickinson

I'm Nobody! Who are you?

Are you—Nobody—Too?

Then there's a pair of us!

Don't tell! they'd advertise—you know!

How dreary—to be—Somebody!

How public—like a Frog—

To tell one's name—the livelong June—

To an admiring Bog!

FIGURE 1.2 Sample annotated poem

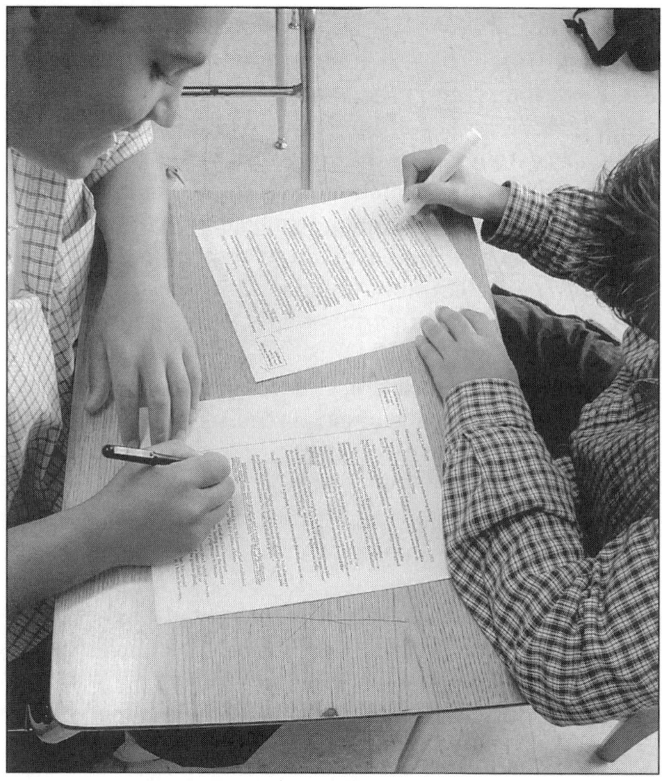

FIGURE 1.3 Sutton and Mike use collaborative annotation to read an article about Islam for their Modern World History class. I copied the text from the Web to format the document with a wider margin for better annotating.

the early stages of introducing this technique, I take the better examples of student work and copy those to paper or overhead transparency film so we can learn from their example. Another option is to have students huddle up after annotating and discuss the text by asking, "What did you underline and why?" This provides an effective context and structure for good academic discussion while at the same time developing their ability to participate in such discussions. Students can also, prior to such discussions, read the text together and make their annotations collaboratively (see Figure 1.3), discussing with each other what they should mark and what they should write down. Such an approach is ideal for English language learners or students with reading difficulties; you can pair them with stronger readers who can explain why they do what they do. This last demand, that they explain their thinking or annotations, is crucial. E.B. White wrote that "a sentence should contain no unnecessary words, a paragraph no unnecessary sentences, for the same reason that a drawing should have no unnecessary lines and a machine no unnecessary parts" (Strunk and White 1999, 23). So it is with annotating: you should always underline/highlight only as much as you *need* to help you accomplish your purpose. Here Melissa Glass uses her Annotations of Dickinson's poem in Figure 1.2:

> In her poem "I'm Nobody!" Emily Dickinson implies that it is better to be a nobody than somebody. Emily Dickinson says, "How dreary—to be—somebody." She is implying that she would rather be a nobody because in the following lines she replies, "How public—like a frog," and "To tell one's name." Those are all really saying that she chooses

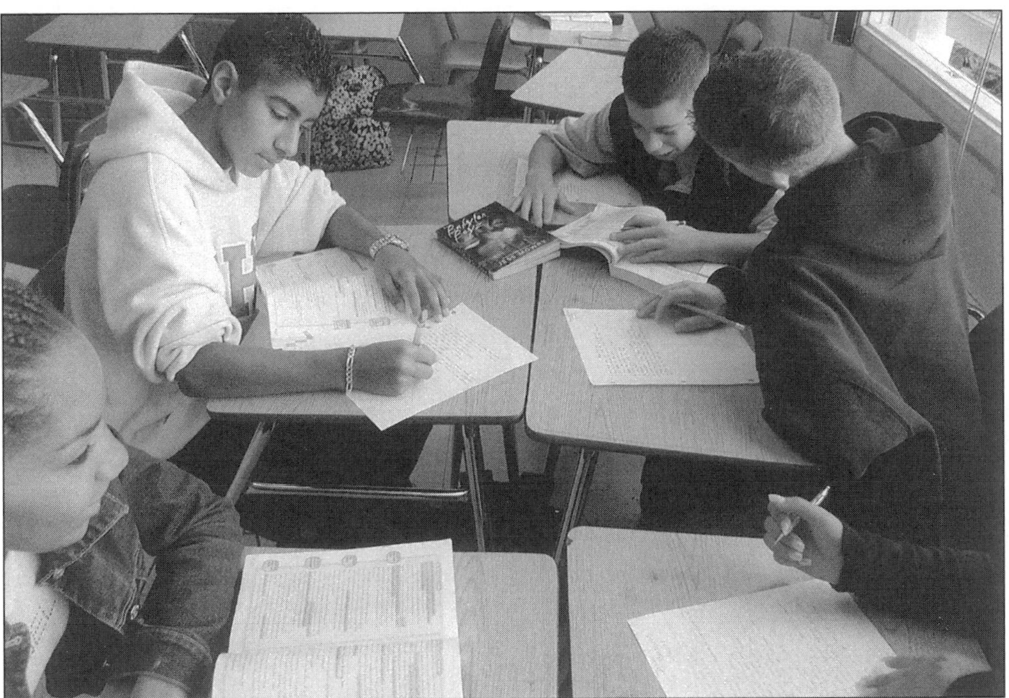

FIGURE 1.4 Students read *The Reader's Handbook* (Robb et al. 2001). The book models how to annotate; thus my students explain why the authors of the book highlighted certain portions of the text. In other words, they annotate the author's annotations.

to be a nobody because she thinks it is better. Just the title of the poem alone gives you a sense that she is passionate about being a nobody, almost in a proud sense. Her language also gives me the feeling that she is standing up for herself by adding an exclamation point after "I'm Nobody!" An exclamation point really means you are claiming something, and she is trying to exclaim that she *is* nobody.

Example Three: Coding the Text: Reading for Changes

While Reading for Changes is a powerful technique (see Figures 1.5 and 1.6 for an overview and example of this strategy), coding the text is the key aspect of this annotation strategy. What codes you use, how you apply them, all depend on what you are reading and why you are reading it. You can adapt this technique to any type of text or discipline. I suggest providing the codes to students at first so they can learn how to use them. In one assignment, for example, students in a social studies class learn about Maslow's hierarchy of needs; they apply these needs to their reading by creating a set of codes that they apply to the text. Thus when a student reads a passage, she asks, "Which of Maslow's needs is that an example of?" and then, depending on the answer, she jots down the appropriate abbreviation in the margin. Depending on the goal of the assignment and the amount of time, I might have students underline the portion of the text that illustrates their code. If, for example, the student wrote an F (for "friendship") in the margin, I would ask him to underline the passage that refers to friendship. Figure 1.6 offers an example; notice how I have reformatted the text to create a dedicated (and adequate) space for explaining the students' codes.

Reading for Changes: Fiction

<table>
<thead>
<tr><th>SYMBOL</th><th>DESCRIPTION</th><th>WHAT TO LOOK FOR</th><th>IMPLICATIONS/CAUSE/
IMPORTANCE OF THE CHANGE</th></tr>
</thead>
<tbody>
<tr><td>Δ^{A}</td><td>Change in the Action: "Action" refers to what the character(s) is doing or what is happening in the story.</td><td>Verbs that describe actions.</td><td rowspan="8">Use the following questions to help you determine if something has changed:
■ What is the situation?
■ Did something change?
■ What changed?
■ How did it change?
■ What caused it?
■ Is this change important?
Ask the following questions to help you evaluate the consequence of the changes you observe:
■ What or whom did this change affect?
■ To what degree or in what way did this change affect others?
■ What is the cause of this change?
■ What questions might help you determine the importance of this change?
■ What evidence of this change can you provide?
■ How has the character/situation changed from the beginning to the end of the story? (What evidence can you provide?)
■ What helped you identify this change (e.g., if the change is in time, you should look for changes in tense or language like, "Several hours later . . .")?
■ Use the following prompts to help you write about or discuss any changes:
□ This change is important . . .
□ The author's language creates a dark tone . . .
□ The change in point of view allows us to see . . .</td></tr>
<tr><td>Δ^{T}</td><td>Change in Time: The story skips ahead or back.</td><td>Language that signals such shifts: Days later . . . After some time had passed . . . Twenty years before . . . Immediately . . .</td></tr>
<tr><td>Δ^{F}</td><td>Change in Focus: Imagine a camera's lens shifting to a new object or event. Or the story might shift from a focus on a character's feelings (internal) to how he or she is responding (external).</td><td>Language that signals directional shift; movement from one place or point of reference to another.</td></tr>
<tr><td>$\Delta^{T/M}$</td><td>Change in Tone or Mood: Sound or feeling that the word brings to the reader's mind. Also associated with colors and emotions.</td><td>Language that intensifies (suddenly, slowly, faster); imagery that paints the scene (e.g., shift from light to dark).</td></tr>
<tr><td>Δ^{S}</td><td>Change in Setting: Where and when the action takes place.</td><td>Language that signals change in time or place. Books sometimes use ¶ breaks and extra space between ¶s to signal such shifts.</td></tr>
<tr><td>Δ^{POV}</td><td>Change in Point of View: Story shifts from one character's point of view to another; or, from one time (e.g., when young) to another (when older).</td><td>Shift in time; shift in pronouns or other referents. Books sometimes use ¶ breaks and extra space between ¶s to signal such shifts.</td></tr>
<tr><td>Δ^{D}</td><td>Change in Direction: Related to but not the same as focus. The plot is headed in a certain direction, perhaps a predictable one, when suddenly the entire story's direction changes in a way you could not have predicted.</td><td>Look for structural signals like extra space between ¶s; new chapters; or language that signals significant shift in plot.</td></tr>
<tr><td>$\Delta^{C/S}$</td><td>Change in Condition or Status: Refers to a significant change in the character's physical, emotional, or social situation.</td><td>Look for changes in behavior or circumstances compared with earlier portions of the story.</td></tr>
</tbody>
</table>

FIGURE 1.5 Reading for Changes overview

EXPLAIN THE CHANGE | CHANGES

Change in his condition: he is ill; I know this because he is described as "white," "walked slowly as though it ached."

Change in time as indicated by "when I came downstairs" signals a shift in time (when) and place (downstairs).

Change in tone—the words "miserable" suggests a change.

Change in action: doctor arrives; change in time ("when dr. came")

Focus shifts from boy to treatment + medications

Change in setting—"back in the room."

Focus shifts back to boy + his illness

Change in action signalled by Q "want me to read?"

A Day's Wait

by Ernest Hemingway

mom + dad?

HE CAME INTO THE ROOM TO SHUT THE windows while we were still in bed and I saw he looked ill. He was shivering, his face was white, and he walked slowly as though it ached to move.

"What's the matter, Schatz?"

"I've got a headache."

"You better go back to bed."

"No. I'm all right."

"You go to bed. I'll see you when I'm dressed."

But when I came downstairs he was dressed, sitting by the fire, looking a very sick and miserable boy of nine years. When I put my hand on his forehead I knew he had a fever.

"You go up to bed," I said, "you're sick."

"I'm all right," he said.

When the doctor came he took the boy's temperature.

"What is it?" I asked him.

"One hundred and two."

Downstairs, the doctor left three different medicines in different colored capsules with instructions for giving them. One was to bring down the fever, another a purgative, the third to overcome an acid condition. The germs of influenza can only exist in an acid condition, he explained. He seemed to know all about influenza and said there was nothing to worry about if the fever did not go above one hundred and four degrees. This was a light epidemic of flu and there was no danger if you avoided pneumonia.

Back in the room I wrote the boy's temperature down and made a note of the time to give the various capsules.

"Do you want me to read to you?"

"All right. If you want to," said the boy. His face was very white and

332

FQ: by end of pg. 1 what do we know about the situation?

FIGURE 1.6 Sample passage modeling Reading for Changes using Ernest Hemingway's story "A Day's Wait." Source: Hemingway, Ernest. 1998. *The Complete Short Stories of Ernest Hemingway: The Finca Vigia Edition*. New York: Scribner.

Schools Try Rating Kids' Employability

Program assesses students' readiness for work world

By Linda Woo
SOUTH COUNTY JOURNAL

KENT, Wash. – When Kentridge (Wash.) High School student Peter Than goes job hunting next spring, he will be armed with a new tool that could help him land his ideal job.

> What's the tool? How can it help him in lift

The Hire-Me-First Card, which looks like a business card, tells prospective employers that Than has the skills and qualities – such as good attendance, preparedness and cooperation – they want.

> This card can tell people your skills & qualities that they may want.

"It shows I'm responsible and I've taken the steps that'll help me at work," said Than, 15, the first Kentridge student to earn the card. "It's just part of my ID, and I carry it everywhere."

Than, who plans on becoming a doctor, will use his card when applying for work in a medical office next spring or summer.

> Will we really benefit from having this card?

The card is available to students at Kentlake, Kentridge and Kentwood high schools; Kent-Meridian may offer the program next year. It's just one of the moves the Kent high schools are making to help prepare their students for the workplace.

> We are moving very quickly into the world of technology

This fall, school officials added an employability grade to report cards to measure skills crucial for landing summer jobs and building careers. Teachers rate each student's work habits and attitudes, cooperation, commitment to quality, quantity of work, attendance and punctuality.

> Why do students need to be graded on their employ ability?

Kent's program is a spin-off of Enumclaw High School's Learning and Employability Profile program, which started in the fall of 1997. The program has received good reviews from businesses that have hired Enumclaw High students.

> Employers are happy with employees with hire-me-first cards

The LEP is a grade reflecting five traits Enumclaw educators believe are important in and out of school. School and business officials say those traits can spell the difference between success and failure in high school, college and the workplace.

> Some say card will help you benefit in school, college, and workpla

"It's really talking about a quality, productive citizen, whether it's work, school or home," said Joe Kristof, assistant principal at Enumclaw High.

In both districts, students rate themselves first. Then their teachers make an assessment and there's room for discussion. The LEP grade shows up on student progress reports; at the end of each school quarter, it accounts for 20 percent of a student's grade in each subject. In Kent, the employability grade isn't factored into the student's academic scores and doesn't show up on the student's official transcript.

> Why should you let the kids rate themselves? Why not just the teachers.

Gregg Fugate, a partner in Enumclaw's Fugate Ford-Mercury-Mazda dealership, worked on the high school committee that helped initiate the Enumclaw High program. He looks at LEP grades when hiring high schoolers at the dealership and said the profile often sets the tone of the job interview.

> By having the card employers say its easier at job interviews.

"With everything being equal, we lean toward the higher scores," said Fugate, who even reviewed his daughter's LEP before hiring her. "The student needs to know I'm looking at those."

So far, Fugate said, he has seen a correlation between high LEP scores and high work ethics and consistent job performance.

> Positive association between scores / work ethics / job performance.

When 17-year-old Audrey Milliken applied for her first job at Fugate's business, she noted on her resume that she had never received less than 90 percent on her LEP.

> Kids are more confident with themselves b/c of the card

"I was confident with the grades I received," said Milliken, who has been working as a receptionist at the dealership for more than a year.

The Enumclaw High senior acknowledged that some students don't care about the LEP grade and said she probably wouldn't volunteer the information if she received a poor report.

> What do you do about the kids that don't care

Jeff Iunker, owner of Enumclaw Travel, has turned some students

FIGURE 1.7 Newspaper article we used as part of the final exam for the freshman ACCESS class

Example Four: Explain Your Annotations

Figure 1.7 shows an article that we used as part of the final exam in my freshman ACCESS class. I wanted my students to show me all that they could do by semester's end. Among the different tasks they were responsible for was annotating the text. They then needed to use their annotations to respond to the article. Here is Jessica Batchelor's summary and her subsequent response:

> SUMMARY
>
> The Hire-Me-First program tells employers how a student will perform in the working world. It reveals their skills and qualities and makes the student feel responsible. Employers rave over the card, saying things like, "It helps me with job interviews and whether I can count on them or not." Many say it will help students succeed in high school, college, and the work place. Many high school students today don't care about the card. Tests were done and findings showed many did not dress properly, fill out applications, or have the spelling, math, or writing skills needed. Many graduates say high school was lenient and had too many loop holes. They say they were very unprepared for college.
>
> PERSONAL OPINION
>
> My opinion is that I think this card would be a benefit if it could gain interest to all students in high school, not just some. I would use the card if provided because I see it as a better way to learn and develop the skills I need for the real world. Some may see it different, but it will pay off when you see the associations between card holders and money makers.

2 Conversational Roundtable

STANDARDS

- Reading
  - ☐ Analyze organizational patterns of information
  - ☐ Compare ideas, texts, or authors
  - ☐ Evaluate the arguments presented in a text
  - ☐ Extend ideas
  - ☐ Generate relevant questions
  - ☐ Identify and analyze recurring themes
  - ☐ Prepare to read
  - ☐ Synthesize information from multiple sources
- Writing
  - ☐ Establish a main or controlling idea
  - ☐ Integrate quotations and examples in written response
  - ☐ Organize information and ideas in logical, appropriate format
  - ☐ Prepare to write
  - ☐ Use sensory, concrete, or illustrative details to support claims
  - ☐ Use writing for a variety of purposes
- Speaking
  - ☐ Analyze devices used in others' speeches
  - ☐ Compare events or ideas
  - ☐ Organize information for desired effect on audience
  - ☐ Prepare and deliver multimedia presentations
  - ☐ Prepare to speak
- Language Study
  - ☐ Examine and use different Greek and Latin roots of words
  - ☐ Know and use different parts of speech
- Listening
  - ☐ Improve note-taking skills
  - ☐ Organize information
- Viewing
  - ☐ Assess different techniques or devices used
  - ☐ Gather details and examples for subsequent analysis of text

SUBJECT AREAS

- English language Arts
- Health
- Humanities
- Science
- Social studies

USES

- Ask useful questions
- Assess student performance
- Compare two or more items, aspects, or people
- Develop academic literacy
- Evaluate ideas
- Extend ideas beyond obvious
- Facilitate discussion
- Gather evidence to support claims
- Generate ideas
- Identify themes
- Make connections
- Narrow or refine subject
- Observe patterns
- Organize information
- Prepare to read
- Prepare to write
- Respond to reading
- Support critical reading
- Synthesize ideas
- Take notes while reading

DESCRIPTION

Bill Clawson, a master teacher for many years and one of my mentors, led me to create this tool. His final exam asked his students to write an imagined dialogue between the main characters from the different books they had read that semester. Kids had to think about what the characters could talk about, and how other characters would, from their own perspectives, react to something Hamlet, for example, might say. At the time I was teaching freshmen; they had by this time read four books that had many interesting similarities. The books were Homer's *Odyssey*, Harper Lee's *To Kill a Mockingbird*, Rudolfo Anaya's *Bless Me, Ultima*, and Larry Watson's *Montana 1948*. We began by writing in the middle of the page those subjects each book would allow the characters to discuss. All four books, for instance, have sons who are struggling to figure out their place in the world. By the time they were finished, the students had abundant notes, all organized around important ideas and within a tool that prepared them now to write well.

Begin by asking what is at the center of your inquiry or, depending on what you are doing, what you want to consider from the four different perspectives. The whole concept of the Conversational Roundtable is that four perspectives, four characters, four anythings can sit around the table and discuss what is on the table between them.

The Conversational Roundtable (CRT) works equally well as a note-making tool while reading or a generating device to prepare you to write or speak. I will often put a blank CRT on the overhead projector and use it to simply support our discussion. I might ask, "What is the question we are trying to answer about this character?" and put that question in the middle. Or I might ask, "What is one of the central themes (or events) in the book?" We will then generate responses in the four domains from different characters. When we finish, students are then ready to begin drafting a paper, outlining a presentation, or reading with greater attention to the organizational pattern and themes in the story. If I have used a transparency, we can resume the next day by reviewing the CRT and thereby ensure greater continuity in the class.

Other tools, most notably Think in Threes and Target Notes, have a circle at the center. The main difference between these is the amount of space each provides the student and the number of domains that apply to the subject. I always begin by asking, "How many domains do I need?" or "How many perspectives do I need to represent when I take these notes?" Four is a good number; it often forces the reader or writer to think beyond the obvious characters or ideas and often allows her to include herself in the comparison, as some of the examples that follow show. The CRT is, in the end, a powerful tool for the very reason suggested by its name: it helps create essential conversations within the classroom and the student's mind, conversations that invite more than one perspective to the table, that make room for more than one important idea, but which always keep students focused.

This tool offers help to teachers in many subjects. History teachers, for example, could put a specific movement, era, or event in the center and take notes on four different aspects of or perspectives on the subject. Science teachers can generate or organize information in four domains or four stages of development; they could also put a controversial topic like cloning in the center and take notes on four different perspectives on that subject. Language teachers could put a topic in the center (e.g., food) and have students generate different nouns, verbs, adjectives, and adverbs in the different squares by way of preparing them to discuss the subject. English teachers, naturally, can use it in more ways than I can describe. Several examples on the following pages will illustrate what you can do in an English class.

NOTES AND EXAMPLES

Example One: Soto Story

Students used this CRT to take notes while reading a Gary Soto short story in *Living Up the Street.* (See Figure 2.1.) The first step asked them to write down details about Gary Soto's neighborhood in the top right-hand box, then, in the lower right-hand box, describe things people in his neighborhood did or stories about Soto's neighborhood in the left-hand boxes. Then students had to do the same for their own neighborhood in the left-hand boxes. This prepared them to write their own story about their neighborhood. This CRT thus helped them read better and prepared them to write well. The space at the bottom of the page is not always appropriate; in this case, for example, students' notes prepared them to write a much longer piece than the box would allow.

Examples Two and Three: Meral and Ralph

The tool shown in Figure 2.2 was the first of two CRTs used for this assignment. Because the second phase (about *Lord of the Flies*) was more abstract, I needed to prepare the students for it. Besides, Golding's book is remote from most kids' experience; anything I can do to make it more familiar will increase the chances of their success. Putting "Meral" (the student's name) in the center gave her a chance to get some distance on herself, to see herself as a character in her own story. She was a freshman when she did this, so she needed to sit down at the Conversational Roundtable with herself: it's an important transitional year. Having completed phase one about herself, she was prepared to write about Ralph, a character in *Lord of the Flies.*

The addition of "Why," in the little box in the second CRT (see Figure 2.3), was an ill-conceived attempt to extend the tool for other purposes. I had imagined that students would explain "*what* the character does," then go on to explain "*why*" he did it. I include this example to emphasize the adaptable nature of these tools and to encourage you to find ways to try to extend them, even if you must ultimately change your mind and tell students to ignore the idea.

Name Paulina Gavilanez	Date 3/22
Project/Topic	Period 2°

	Yours	Soto's
Neighborhood	Huron: cookie lady butterfly mean lady Nick gets runover steal candy playing with fire burned the carpet	• Brad N streets, Fresno • Across street Coleman Pickles. • Rightside junkyard dealt in metals. • Downside Sun-Maid Raisin • Many relatives worked S-M-R • Stolle soda from a 7-up company. • Futer step father worked at Western Book Distributor, place books in boxes • Played with the Molinas live down side. • Wrestle, eat raw bacon, jump from the couch, sword fight, steal from neighbors, kick chickens, through rock at passing cars. • Sottor are inherently violent.
Actions/Stories	Dog that died (killed) Build a playhouse Cudys Througheggs at the mean ladys Corner store the guy would always give me candy Play football.	• Aunts would fight men would just watch. • He would chase Rick with rocks, pans, or any other thing. • He through bottle at Rick and it cut his leg open. • He through a bottle and missed and an older kid punched him. made his house blid. • They got in a fight with some new neighbors molinas ran off. • They got some cats put it in a sack were going to through it at the new kid. They just kick their garbage down. • Burn boxes, crayon, windows. • They would lite up the house than get the hoses and turn it off.

FIGURE 2.1 Paulina's Conversational Roundtable for Gary Soto story from *Living Up the Street*

Conversational Roundtable

Name Meral Sovsou

Date March 19

Topic Reading and my life

Period 1°

Suggestions for Use: Ask yourself what is the focus of your paper, discussion, inquiry. Is it a character, a theme, an idea, a country, a trend, or a place? Then examine it from four different perspectives, or identify four different aspects of the topic. Once you have identified the four areas, find and list any appropriate quotations, examples, evidence, or details.

How Meral acts and feels:
- Shy when don't know a person
- confused as a teenager
- independent in my studies
- I feel that I could never hold in my feelings. I have to let someone know I feel.
- I'm most of the time happy with my friends.

How other people feel about or react to me:
- Friends respect my differences.
- Teachers respect me & how I work.
- My parents listen when I have something to say
- Friends & family never let me down.
- Fun to be around.
- Mr. Burke sees me as a hard worker.

Meral

How I look:
- Brown hair, Blonde streaks.
- Brown eyes
- sholder length hair
- 5' 4" tall
- average
- Straight hair
- Ears pierced

What I think about myself:
- I am happy with the way I am.
- I try to be myself & not to act like other people.
- I would not want to change.
- My grades need to improve.

My name is Meral, I am many different people, my teachers for example, see a 14 year old who is honest, if I do not understand what I am supposed to be doing then I tell them & ask for help. I am also very caring I want to hear what people say. My friends on the other hand think I am outgoing in the fact I alway want to go out & hangout. I am also very sensitive I feel that is my toughest weakness. If someone tells me something that is sad I can't help but crying. People tell me it makes the situation worse but I feel it is better to let it out than hold it in.

FIGURE 2.2 Meral's Conversational Roundtable about herself

Conversational Roundtable

Name	Date
Topic	Period

Suggestions for Use: Ask yourself what is the focus of your paper, discussion, inquiry. Is it a character, a theme, an idea, a country, a trend, or a place? Then examine it from four different perspectives, or identify four different aspects of the topic. Once you have identified the four areas, find and list any appropriate quotations, examples, evidence, or details.

WHO — what the character thinks:

- Ralph thinks that the fire is important because they could get rescued.
- Ralph thinks that Jack and his tribe are being unfair.
- Ralph thinks that he should be chief.
- Ralph thinks that all Jack wants is meat.
- Ralph thinks that they murdered Simon

HOW — what the character feels:

- Ralph feels that no one understands the importance of the fire.
- He feels betrayed by others who followed them.
- He feels that other things are more important.
- He feels betrayed and disrespected by the others who voted for him.
- He feels guilty about Simon's death.

Ralph

WHY — what the character does:

- He builds a fire and encourage what's left of his tribe to keep the fire going.
- He keeps the people in his group and doesn't go with Jack.
- He tries to persuade everyone to follow him.
- He worries about Simon's death.

WHEN — what the character says:

- He tells Sam and Eric to continue to collect wood even though they are tired.
- He tells Jack how he feels.
- Ralph tells Sam and Eric and Piggy that meat isn't everything and being scavengers isn't good.
- He tells the others that he is chief but none listens to him.
- He tells Piggy that it was murder.

FIGURE 2.3 Meral's Conversational Roundtable about Ralph from *Lord of the Flies*

Conversational Roundtable

Name	Date
Topic	Period

Suggestions for Use: Ask yourself what is the focus of your paper, discussion, inquiry. Is it a character, a theme, an idea, a country, a trend, or a place? Then examine it from four different perspectives, or identify four different aspects of the topic. Once you have identified the four areas, find and list any appropriate quotations, examples, evidence, or details.

Telemachus
- brave (goes out to look for his father without any knowledge)
- acceptant (accepts the fact that he has to grow up and earn his family respect.)
- sensitive (weeps for father, though he barely knows him.)
- strong (overcomes his child-like fears)
- caring (doesn't want mom to find out he left or she will worry)

Penenelope
- cunning (tricks suitors)
- faithful (doesn't desert Odysseus)
- caring (worries about Telemachus after he leaves.)
- powerless (has no power to drive away suitors, is a woman)
- remorseful (wishes Odysseus was with her and not gone)
- strong (refuses to marry suitors no matter what.)

CHARACTER
Q: What kind of person are these characters?

Odysseus
- wise (questions Calypson why he is being set free)
- strong (survives the terrible storm on sea)
- determined (wants to go home with no dawdling)
- faithful (does not marry Nausicaa)
- pleading (both Nausicaa and Areles give into his cry)
- trusting (trusts Nausicaa to tell him the truth)

Suitors
- disobidient (refuse to leave Odysseus' house)
- stupid (do not realize Penenelope is unwinding the rug until they are told.)
- disrespectful (make fun of Telemachus for becoming so "wise" and "grown-up")
- revengeful (want to kill Telemachus for being so powerful and manly towards them)

There are two main ways by which one can generally tell another person's qualities and ideals. These two ways are by speech and actions. For example, one could say that Penelope is whinning because of how she holds off the suitors. Once these tools for recognition are impling one can more thorogYly grasp the concept of a story.

FIGURE 2.4 Conversational Roundtable examining the main characters in Homer's *Odyssey*

Example Four: Homer's *Odyssey*

After the first few books of *The Odyssey*, kids need to be clear about who is who and what kind of person each character is. The CRT offers the perfect structure to get kids focused on one question (What kind of person is each character?). If I wanted to extend it into a longer writing assignment, I could easily do so. As it is, I decided to have them synthesize their ideas at the bottom of the tool. (See Figure 2.4.) A variation on this approach would be to put one person, event, or idea in the center and describe what four different characters would think or do about it, then use the space in each box to have students list examples and explain their thinking.

Decision Tree

3

DESCRIPTION

Everyone makes decisions: writers, designers, leaders, scientists, teachers, readers. To be effective in any of these domains, one must recognize the different decisions made during the creative process. Each decision leads to different outcomes, some of which are foreseeable and others of which are a complete surprise. Thus the Decision Tree helps us think about the factors involved in each decision; it does this by providing a visual means of representing this process and its various outcomes.

There are many ways to use this tool, all of which depend on your objective. A writing class, for example, could examine the different possible decisions a writer made when writing a book, and how each choice affected the meaning and style of the book. Teachers of any class could give the students this tool on an overhead transparency (or give them a big sheet of butcher paper) and have them present their ideas to the class, explaining their thinking as they do so. Teachers themselves can put this up on the overhead and use it as a tool to visually organize a class discussion of a text. This is what I do when, for example, I put it up on the overhead and ask kids what Odysseus' choices are once he has won the contest against the suitors in Homer's *Odyssey*. We easily come up with five different possible choices for Odysseus; we use the tool to examine each one and the possible consequences, then focus on the decision he makes and how that affects the story's outcome.

The tool itself demands precise use. Here are several suggestions about how to use this tool:

- *Before*: You must take time to frame (or help students frame) the question you are trying to make a decision about. As in any decision-making situation, the answers can only be as clear as the question. You might ask, for example, what President Roosevelt's options were when the Japanese attacked Pearl Harbor. Having decided beforehand what to ask, you could be assured of having five (or more!) different outcomes to compare. If you are just introducing this tool, you might want to provide them with a range of questions, some excellent and others vague, so students can get a sense of what a good question in this context sounds like. Related, but different: before you begin, you must determine the

STANDARDS

- Reading
  - ☐ Analyze organizational patterns of information
  - ☐ Compare ideas, texts, or authors
  - ☐ Evaluate the arguments presented in a text
  - ☐ Extend ideas
  - ☐ Generate relevant questions
  - ☐ Prepare to read
  - ☐ Synthesize information from multiple sources
- Writing
  - ☐ Prganize information and ideas in logical, appropriate format
  - ☐ Prepare to write
  - ☐ Use sensory, concrete, or illustrative details to support claims
- Speaking
  - ☐ Analyze devices used in others' speeches
  - ☐ Compare events or ideas
  - ☐ Organize information for desired effect on audience
  - ☐ Prepare to speak
- Language Study
  - ☐ Distinguish between denotative and connotative meaning
  - ☐ Study the author's use of language
- Viewing
  - ☐ Assess different techniques or devices used
  - ☐ Gather details and examples for subsequent analysis of text
  - ☐ Identify organization of information

SUBJECT AREAS

- English language arts
- Health
- Humanities
- Mathematics
- Science
- Social studies

USES

- Ask useful questions
- Compare two or more items, aspects, or people
- Develop academic literacy
- Evaluate ideas
- Extend ideas beyond obvious
- Facilitate discussion
- Gather evidence to support claims
- Generate ideas
- Make connections
- Observe patterns
- Organize information
- Prepare to read
- Prepare to write
- Respond to reading
- Support critical reading
- Synthesize ideas
- Visualize what is read

purpose of the tool, as this will influence how it works and how students use it in the class.

- *During*: Once you begin using the tool—for whatever purpose—other questions arise. No decision path is free of subsequent decisions. Students should look out for those junctures when an additional decision must be made. They should identify or infer the questions those parties involved asked in order to make their decision.
- *After*: Having completed your Decision Tree, you may use this to facilitate a discussion or write a paper. You might use it to take further notes as to the consequence of (making and not making) certain decisions, picking up examples or quotations to support your ideas. Students could, for example, explain why one decision is the best; or, in the case of a situation in which a decision was actually made (e.g., to enter into World War Two), students might explain why that was (or was not) the best decision, taking examples from their studies to support their analysis. One other possibility would be to discuss how making a different decision than the one that was actually made would have changed the final outcome.

The tool offers teachers in many subjects a range of possibilities:

- *History*: Examine the different possible decisions and subsequent outcomes in a major historical event. Have students imagine they are President Lincoln, for example, and examine the different decisions he could make. Then have them follow through with the decision he did make and explain why they think he did (or did not) make the right decision.
- *Psychology*: Examine the process whereby an individual makes a decision. Use the Decision Tree to examine the other options and what ultimately influences one's decisions.
- *English*: You could use this tool to facilitate a discussion of a writer's different choices and why he chose the one he did. You could put five different possible narrators the author could have chosen and examine the outcome of each one. Then explain why you think the author did (or did not) make the right decision. Another option is to use the tool to examine the different choices a fictional character has and what the outcome of those different choices would be.
- *Science*: You could examine the different potential outcomes of different interventions during a scientific experiment. In this way the teacher and students can narrow their focus to the variables that most affect students' behavior or performance.

NOTES AND EXAMPLES

Two very good examples of how to use the Decision Tree, which are not represented here, are discussing grades and Homer's *Odyssey*. Students rarely have a sense of how their academic decisions affect their final outcome. I will periodically (e.g., around progress report time) put up the Decision Tree and write A, B, C, D, and F in the five Outcome spaces. We then walk through the decision-making process that leads to each outcome. I ask, "What's the first decision you make on day one?" Eventually, sometimes with a bit of prompting,

Decision Tree

Name Alex Montalvo	Date
Topic	Period

Suggestions for Use: Use this Decision Tree diagram to examine the possible outcomes of different decisions. You might consider the different consequences of a character's possible choices; or you might consider how it would change the story to tell it from different points of view. In Health, History, or Business, you might consider the ramifications of different choices. Provide arguments for and against each decision.

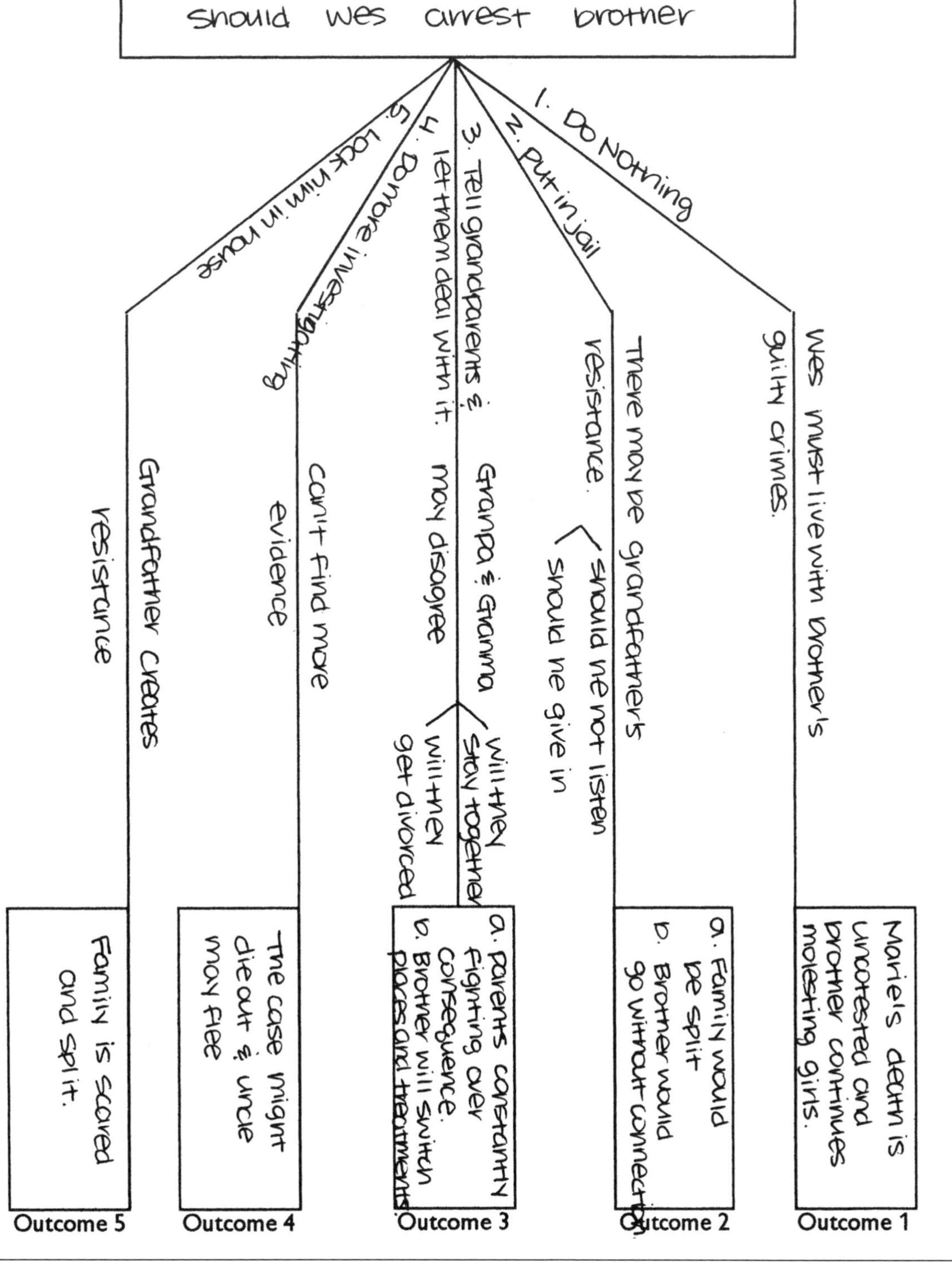

FIGURE 3.1 Alex Montalvo's analysis of the novel *Montana 1948*

we arrive at the decision of "whether to do your work or not." If students decide to do their work, they immediately face a second question: "Will I do my best, or will I simply do the minimum?" Each leads to a different outcome, as the tree clearly shows them.

With the *Odyssey*, we discuss Odysseus' five different choices near the end of the book:

- Kill all the suitors.
- Kill Antinuous, the self-proclaimed leader of the suitors; then let that be a lesson to the others who followed along.
- Kill all the men however he wants, but do not harm the women servants.
- Banish them all, but kill none.
- Do nothing; having seen his house and community, he could just leave them all behind and continue traveling.

Example: *Montana 1948*

The sheriff's son faces difficult decisions, as does his father, in this novel by Larry Watson. Each one leads to other complications. Since the main decision is a moral one, it is crucial to make the right one. In this assignment, students plotted out the different decisions Wes, the sheriff, could have made; then they explained why the one he chose was the right (i.e., best) solution. (See Figure 3.1.) This tool and Alex's notes then served as the basis for a class discussion in which others compared how they responded to the same assignment. In his explanation, Alex wrote:

> Wesley decided to prosecute his brother. It was the best decision because if he hadn't he wouldn't have been able to live with himself morally. Also, if he had let him go, his brother might have kept doing what he was doing until he either retired, died, or was convicted.

Episodic Notes

4

DESCRIPTION

Episodic Notes originated from the traditional storyboard technique filmmakers use to sketch out a scene. The concept of episodes or scenes has much broader applications, however. Each box just as easily represents a computer screen or a stage in a scientific process. And the space between the boxes, which means nothing in storyboards, can be used to examine the transitions or events that cause objects or people to change from one phase to another. Moreover, the users must evaluate the events or process in order to determine where one stage leaves off and the next one begins. Such thinking asks the users to examine what they are reading, observing, or creating with a careful eye, one able to determine which moments matter most.

The tool asks users to think both in words and images, with one commenting on or illustrating the other. These combined modes of thought access different ways of thinking and help students, especially when reading or observing, to visualize what is happening, since they must be able to draw and explain the action.

While most teachers will find it useful to give the students the tool on paper, other uses are possible. Giving kids the tool on transparency film with different colored markers, for example, allows them to publish their thinking to the overhead, where they can stand and practice their public speaking. Groups or individuals can stand up before the class and explain their Episodic Notes as they apply to whatever text, process, or events the class is studying. In this case, the tool is used to help illustrate what the student is saying.

Because of the visual aspect of the tool, Episodic Notes is ideal for use with special needs and English-language learners; in short, it helps anyone visualize the text or identify the important moments in a process. The organizational structure of three discrete boxes helps such students organize information or events into a sequence; moreover, the visual illustration combined with the written description allows them to process the ideas through multiple modalities, especially if they then use these notes to participate in a group or class discussion. Finally, having students compare their Episodic Notes with one another allows them to see how other students approached the same text or problem. If one student does something unique or exemplary, try to put it up on the

STANDARDS

- Reading
  - ☐ Analyze organizational patterns of information
  - ☐ Compare ideas, texts, or authors
  - ☐ Extend ideas
  - ☐ Generate relevant questions
  - ☐ Prepare to read
  - ☐ Synthesize information from multiple sources
- Writing
  - ☐ Establish a main or controlling idea
  - ☐ Integrate quotations and examples in written response
  - ☐ Organize information and ideas in logical, appropriate format
  - ☐ Prepare to write
  - ☐ Use sensory, concrete, or illustrative details to support claims
  - ☐ Use writing for a variety of purposes
- Speaking
  - ☐ Compare events or ideas
  - ☐ Organize information for desired effect on audience
  - ☐ Prepare and deliver multimedia presentations
  - ☐ Prepare to speak

SUBJECT AREAS

- English language arts
- Health
- Humanities
- Science
- Social studies

USES

- Ask useful questions
- Assess student performance
- Compare two or more items, aspects, or people
- Develop academic literacy
- Evaluate ideas
- Extend ideas beyond obvious
- Facilitate discussion
- Gather evidence to support claims
- Generate ideas
- Identify themes
- Make connections
- Narrow or refine subject
- Observe patterns
- Organize information
- Prepare to read
- Prepare to write
- Respond to reading
- Support critical reading
- Synthesize ideas
- Take notes while reading
- Visualize what is read

overhead for others to see and learn from so they can improve their knowledge and use of the tool.

Here are some possible uses for Episodic Notes in your class:

- *English*: Identify the three main scenes (see Figures 4.3 and 4.4) in a story, poem, or play. After drawing them, explain what is happening and why it is important. You could also draw three aspects of the story—a character in the past, present, and future; three different settings; three main characters with character details in the space next to the boxes.
- *Science*: Each box could represent a stage in a process that the student describes (or records observations of). The student could also use the tool to take notes on a reading that focuses on a series of changes or some other process. The tool would work well for anything that focuses on a sequence.
- *History*: Kids could use the boxes to draw a visual explanation of different stages in a war (e.g., three different maps representing the shifting front), which they could then explain in the text box area.
- *Presentations*: This tool is ideal for sketching out Microsoft PowerPoint (or similar) presentations; each box represents a screen. This allows students to do their thinking "in bullets" on paper and spend time thinking about what the real focus of their presentation is. They can concentrate on design or graphic elements when they get on the computer; thus, this tool allows them to focus on content.
- *Web Design*: Again, each box represents a screen or a Web page. Users can sketch out the general ideas—content, rough design layout, placement. They can jot down notes or ideas in the text boxes.
- *Video Production*: Too many student videos waste time and video; have students use this tool before they shoot to ensure a balanced, well-organized production. This helps them see what they want to create; it also helps them think of how the story or information might best be arranged to achieve the desired effect.
- *Visual Explanations*: While there is a separate chapter on this technique, this tool itself is ideal for visually describing a situation, as the *Othello* example in Figure 4.1 shows. In the box the user uses symbols, images, or patterns to explain what is happening. Additional uses include adding color to provide another level of representation.

NOTES AND EXAMPLES

Example One: "Pain for a Daughter"

Poems are difficult for some students. They can be so abstract and, while they often have a narrative aspect, students rarely see them as organized into scenes. Anne Sexton's poem "Pain for a Daughter" is arranged into different scenes, though which are the most important scenes is not so obvious to some students. We begin by analyzing the poem's title. (See Figure 4.2.) After reading the poem aloud to students and having them annotate it, I have them identify those points where the poem changes in time, place, or emphasis. We then discuss which of these shifts is most important. As Cassie's example (Figure 4.3) shows, art is not an important aspect of the assignment. Though it can

Name Jacqui de Borja	Date 5/2
Assignment/Topic Othello Visual Explanation	Period 5°

Episodic Notes

Purpose: Identify most important moments; show cause-effect and organization (sequence).

1. Determine the three most crucial stages, scenes, or moments in the story or process.
2. Draw in the box what happens and what you "see" in the text. Be as specific as possible.
3. Remember: these are *notes* not works of art: Try to capture the action and important details of the moment.
4. Explain (in the notes section) what is happening and why it is important.

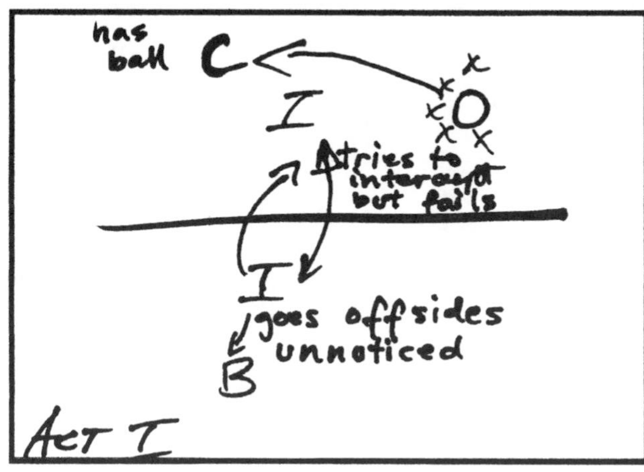

B = Brabantio

Caption I = Iago C = Cassio D = Desdemona O = Othello

O is QB; I really wants the ball. O passes to C instead. I betrays O by crossing to other side to tell O's father about O's secret wedding to his daughter.

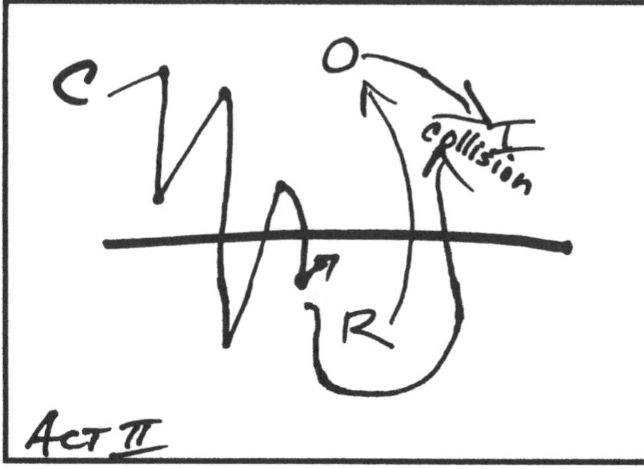

Caption R = Roderigo

Roderigo subs for Cassio. Cassio runs on field to distract players while Roderigo tries to sack Othello. Roderigo and Cassio both head for Desdemona, but collide. Cassio kicked out of the game.

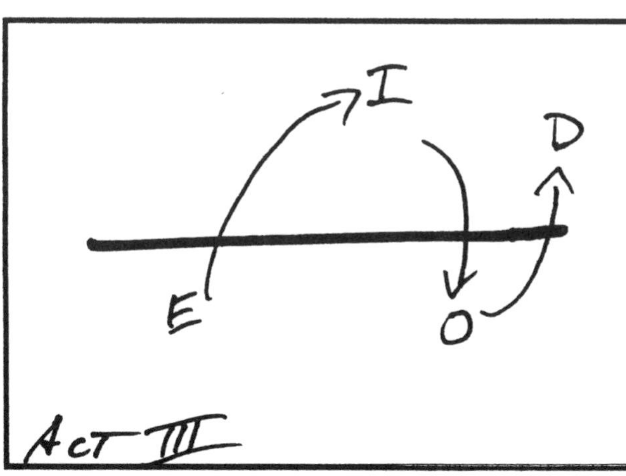

Caption E = Emilia

E intercepts the ball by giving hanky to I. I tries to tackle O by giving hanky to C, knowing O will go after D.

FIGURE 4.1 Combining Episodic Notes and Visual Explanations

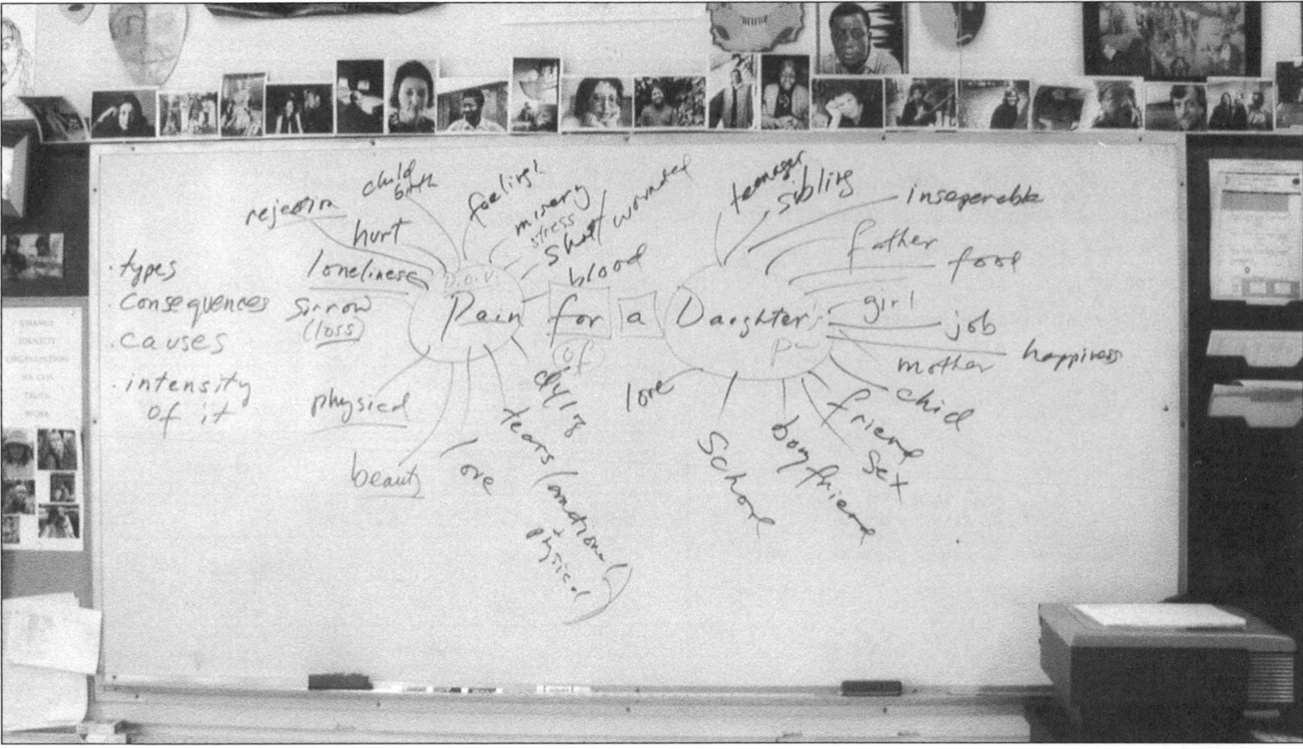

FIGURE 4.2 This is what my whiteboard looks like after we get done discussing possible meanings of the title of Anne Sexton's poem "Pain for a Daughter." In my class the whiteboard is an essential tool for thought; it captures what we think and challenges us to explain why we think it.

be nice to turn it into a more artistic creation, I prefer to use the tool for thought instead of art. In this case, Cassie's three scenes perfectly illustrate the poem. What's more, they provide a succinct assessment of her reading performance, as they show me what she thinks is important and why she thinks this. The visual depiction of the poem helps her to see what is happening. Our class discussion allows us to focus on why the poet designed the poem this way and how she shifts from one scene to the next.

Example Two: Short Story

A variation on the previous example, this one shows a student making notes on a short story. (See Figure 4.4.) In this class for struggling readers, kids often have trouble seeing what they read. Here Marcy turns to the story for concrete details to include in her drawing. I tell them that they cannot include it in their drawing if they cannot point to it in the story. This forces them to read closely and with a specific purpose. Again, they must also evaluate what the three most crucial scenes are in the story and explain not only what is happening but why and why it is important. Such compact explanations challenge students to think and allow me to assess on the run, something that is essential in my classes, which can have as many as thirty-five students. When appropriate (or necessary), I can even have them huddle up into groups to collaborate on such assignments. Talking about what should be included and why—while the most talented artist in the group translates others' words into images—allows them to process ideas more effectively while improving students' oral communication skills. (See Figure 4.5.)

Episodic Notes

Name Cassie Zakatchenko	Date 12/5
Topic "Pain for a Daughter"	Period 6°

Purpose: **Identify most important moments; show cause-effect and organization (sequence).**

1. **Determine the three most crucial stages, scenes, or moments in the story or process.**
2. **Draw in the box what happens and what you "see" in the text.Be as specific as possible.**
3. **Remember: these are *notes* not works of art: Try to capture the action and important details of the moment.**
4. **Explain (in the notes section) what is happening and why it is important.**

Caption Girl taking care of pony.

The girl was "too squeamish to pull a thorn from the dog's paw," but she loved her pony so much that she "drained the boil and scoured it with hydrogen peroxide." She faced her fear in order to help the animal she loved. This moment is important because it represents the girl's emotional pain, (pained her to see her horse sick).

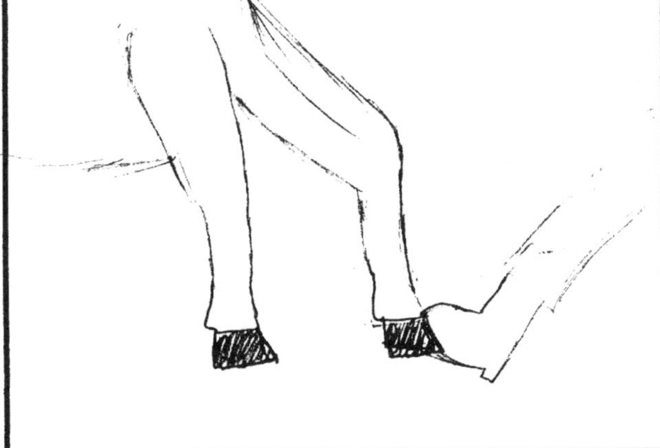

Caption Horse steps on girl's foot.

The same horse she nurtured and cared for like her own child stepped on her foot, making her "blind with pain." This is an important moment because it shows a change and represents the physical pain of the girl, (her foot hurt)

Caption Girl's foot being cleaned

When her father begins cleaning her foot, the girl yells in pain saying, "Oh my God, help me!" While this is happening, her mom is standing in the doorway. Her daughter's cry brings her pain because the girl is growing up and no longer comes to her mom in her time of struggle.

FIGURE 4.3 Cassie's Episodic Notes from "Pain for a Daughter"

Episodic Notes

Name	Date

Purpose: **Identify most important moments; show cause-effect and organization (sequence).**

1. **Determine the three most crucial stages, scenes, or moments in the story or process.**
2. **Draw in the box what happens and what you "see" in the text. Be as specific as possible.**
3. **Remember: these are *notes* not works of art: Try to capture the action and important details of the moment.**
4. **Explain (in the notes section) what is happening and why it is important.**

Caption

This is where they are relling in the line, and the truttle appears.
This is important because it shows how good of a relationship the father has with his son.

Caption

This is the part where they start cleaning the house and trying to fix it before the rest of the family gets there.
This is important because it shows how far the bond between father and son will go before the rest of the family gets there.

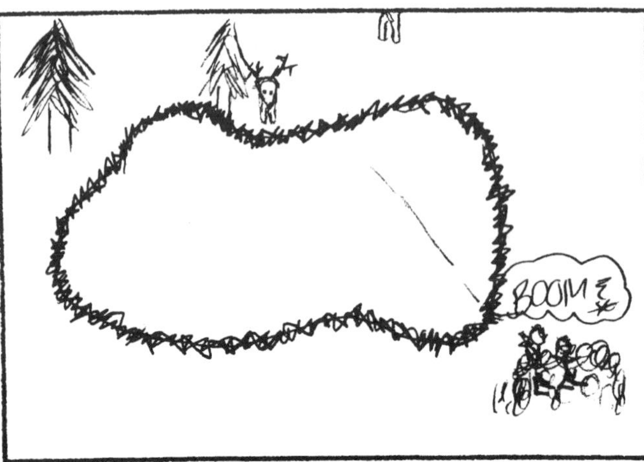

Caption

This part is when the father & son are out to shoot the deer they're going to eat.
This is important because this is the last activity they do together before they go home with the rest of the family.

FIGURE 4.4 Marcy Vega's Episodic Notes about a short story

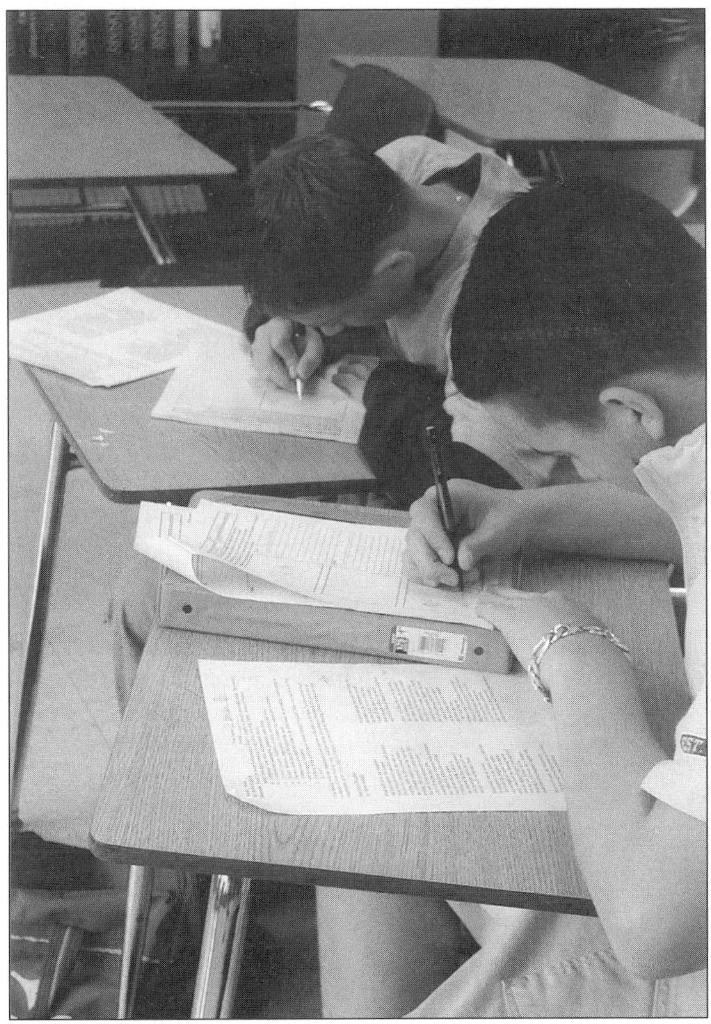

FIGURE 4.5 Spencer and Danny work together to complete their Episodic Notes on Anne Sexton's poem "Pain for a Daughter."

5 Idea Cards

STANDARDS

- Reading
  - ☐ Analyze organizational patterns of information
  - ☐ Compare ideas, texts, or authors
  - ☐ Extend ideas
  - ☐ Generate relevant questions
  - ☐ Identify and analyze recurring themes
  - ☐ Prepare to read
- Language Study
  - ☐ Distinguish between denotative and connotative meaning
  - ☐ Examine and use different Greek and Latin roots of words
  - ☐ Know and use different parts of speech
- Test Preparation
  - ☐ Organize ideas
  - ☐ Prioritize information
  - ☐ Remember information

SUBJECT AREAS

- English language arts
- Health
- Science
- Social studies

USES

- Ask useful questions
- Compare two or more items, aspects, or people
- Develop academic literacy
- Evaluate ideas
- Extend ideas beyond obvious
- Facilitate discussion
- Generate ideas
- Identify themes
- Make connections
- Narrow or refine subject
- Observe patterns
- Organize information
- Prepare to read
- Synthesize ideas
- Visualize what is read

DESCRIPTION

While they can be used as simple mini flashcards, Idea Cards are best used to manipulate ideas and explore relationships. Students write the names of characters, places, eras, objects, or ideas on the cards. After students cut them up, they can then manipulate the cards to examine how they relate to one another. Those studying language or, more specifically, grammar, can write different parts of speech or roots on the cards, then manipulate the cards to create words or sentences. History teachers could have students write down different groups involved in a conflict or event, then have them organize the different players to indicate the relationships among the different sides. They might also use the cards to examine the organizational relationships of different branches of government.

NOTES AND EXAMPLES

Example One: *Jasmine*

The example in Figure 5.1 comes from an English class in which students read Bharati Mukherjee's novel *Jasmine*. The novel's main character assumes six different names, lives in four different places in two different countries, and is involved with three different men by the novel's end. All of this gets pretty confusing for kids as she maneuvers between the past and present, one country and another, one name and another. Putting the names of the different people and places on Idea Cards and then cutting them up allows kids to visually organize the different relationships in the story. This technique is best done with Idea Cards because they allow the student to rearrange the cards to see different connections or configurations. Writing them down on paper implies there is only one arrangement, which is rarely true.

Example Two: Visual Note Cards

Aliye combined several different note-taking techniques in the study cards shown in Figure 5.2. She created them to prepare for tests, breaking the units into economic theories or principles, each one of which got its own card and graphic explanation to help her visualize the concept.

Idea Cards

Name JASMINE CHAR. RELATIONSHIPS

Date

PRAKASH | TAYLOR | JASE | LAHORE | INDIA

JANE RIPPLEMEYER | KARIN | JYOTI VIJH | HASNAPUR | NEW YORK

DUFF | WYLIE | DU THIEN | MASTERJI | IOWA

MATAJI | BUD | YOGI | JASMINE | AMERICA

FIGURE 5.1 Sample Idea Cards for the novel *Jasmine*

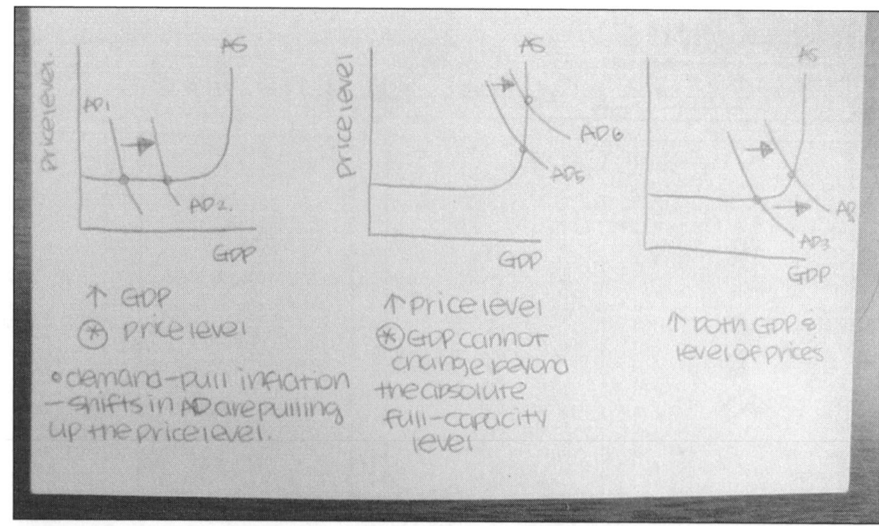

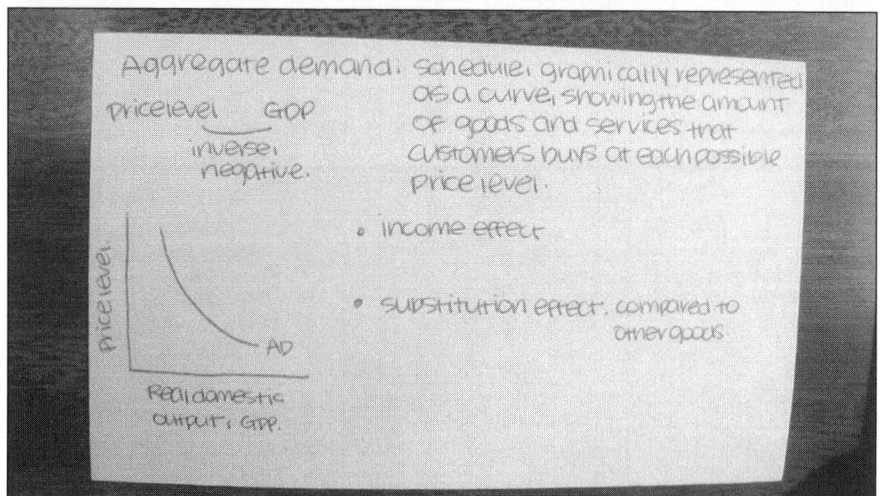

FIGURE 5.2 Sample Idea Cards; Aliye used these concept cards to study different ideas in her economics class.

Example Three: Interpretive Cards

This technique comes from Fran Claggett and Joan Brown's book *Drawing Your Own Conclusions: Graphic Strategies for Reading, Writing, and Thinking* (1992). Their emphasis on this assignment is the difference between what a text *says* and what it *does* or *means*. (See Figure 5.3.) This tool helps students see beyond the plot and its basic facts. Here are Claggett and Brown's instructions, which my colleague Linda McLaughlin followed with her seniors as they read Ken Kesey's novel *One Flew Over the Cuckoo's Nest.*

Choose an event or quotation from the assigned reading. Follow these steps using a 5-by-8-inch card:

1. Note the page number, and record the quotation or give a brief explanation of the event or section you will focus on, placing it in the context of your work.
2. Sketch a quick-draw that uses a symbol to indicate what your selection from the text *does* in the context of the story.
3. Add quotations from the section of text you are explicating to show how the event or quotation functions.

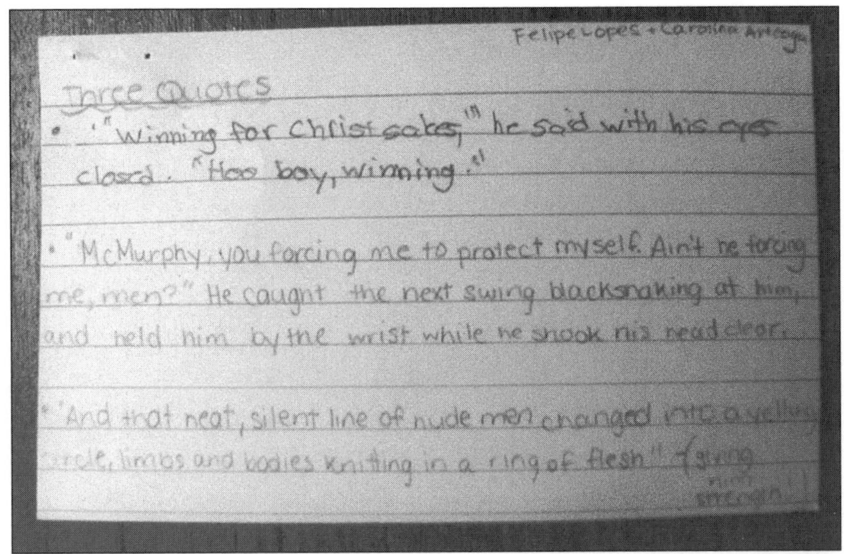

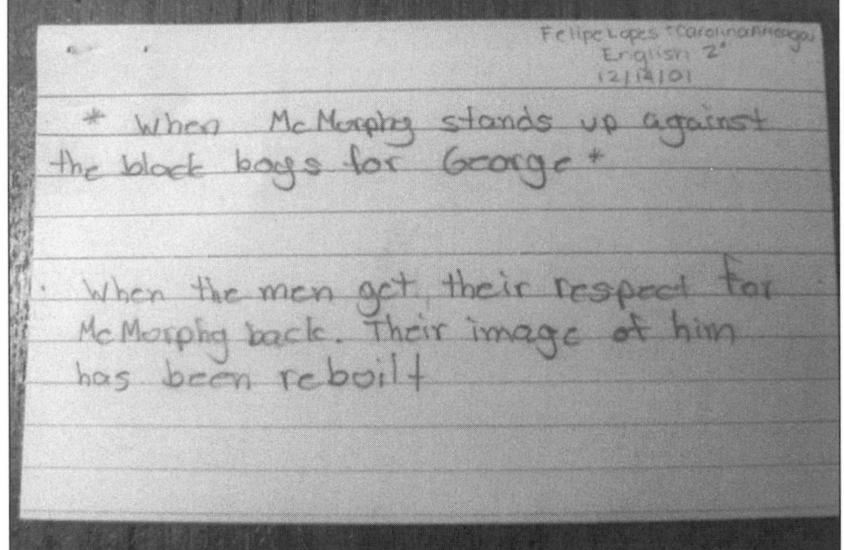

FIGURE 5.3 Carolina and Felipe used these Idea Cards to help them understand the symbolism and themes in Ken Kesey's *One Flew Over the Cukoo's Nest.*

4. Write a claim, stating what your event or quotation does to contribute to the meaning of the whole.
5. Explain the graphic tie-in by developing an analogy between your symbol and the quotation or event (e.g., not "I drew this wrapped package because it answers all the remaining questions," but "Like a neatly wrapped package, the epilogue ties up all of the loose ends"). (Claggett and Brown 1992)

Interactive Notes

6

DESCRIPTION

Interactive Notes recognizes the active process of reading, during which a reader makes meaning. We do not passively take in the words; we impose our will on them, questioning them, connecting them, wondering about them. We do these things throughout the reading process, which has three main phases: before, during, and after.

The Before phase of the tool prepares us to read by asking us to make decisions about how and why we will read. We also establish the criteria of importance, which is essential if we are to know what to write down, what to pay attention to while we read or watch a film. In this section of the tool, the readers can answer these questions on their own, or the teacher can work with the students to get them set up. This is preferable if the text is a new type or a very difficult one. The During phase begins once you start reading the text, listening to the lecture, or watching the film. The Interactive Notes template includes sample prompts to help students develop their academic language and direct their attention to those things most appropriate to discuss. After they finish reading or viewing the text, they need to synthesize or respond to it to make the necessary connections that will improve comprehension and memory. In this part of the template, students find more prompts to develop not only their response but the language needed to frame that response.

Encourage (or even require) students to "think in bullets" as they use the form. This added demand asks them to provide an additional level of organization and evaluation to their notes, as they must ask, "What is so important that it deserves to be singled out with a bullet?"

When introducing the tool, be sure to use examples from similar assignments, preferably done by students, to show them what good work looks like. If you do not have such examples, or if you are introducing the tool for the first time, put it up on the overhead and think aloud with them as you model its use, explaining why you chose to write something down. Setting a purpose so they know what to look for is essential at this phase.

This tool works equally well for literary (e.g., poetry, fiction, drama) and nonfiction or informational texts. It will help students "read a film" as well as a primary source document like the Declaration of Independence.

STANDARDS

- Reading
  - ☐ Compare ideas, texts, or authors
  - ☐ Extend ideas
  - ☐ Generate relevant questions
  - ☐ Identify and analyze recurring themes
  - ☐ Prepare to read
- Writing
  - ☐ Integrate quotations and examples in written response
  - ☐ Prepare to write
  - ☐ Use writing for a variety of purposes
- Speaking
  - ☐ Compare events or ideas
  - ☐ Prepare to speak
- Language Study
  - ☐ Distinguish between denotative and connotative meaning
- Viewing
  - ☐ Assess different techniques or devices used
  - ☐ Gather details and examples for subsequent analysis of text
  - ☐ Identify organization of information
- Test Preparation
  - ☐ Comprehend information
  - ☐ Organize ideas

SUBJECT AREAS

- English language arts
- Health
- Humanities
- Mathematics
- Science
- Social studies

USES

- Ask useful questions
- Assess student performance
- Develop academic literacy
- Extend ideas beyond obvious
- Facilitate discussion
- Gather evidence to support claims
- Generate ideas
- Identify themes
- Make connections
- Prepare to read
- Prepare to write
- Respond to reading
- Support critical reading
- Synthesize ideas
- Take notes while reading

Science and other content area teachers could even adapt the prompts as needed to make it better suit their needs as a note-taking tool for a lab process.

Interactive Notes can be used in most classes. Here are some general examples:

- Give a group one Interactive Notes page to use as they discuss a text they read together (i.e., appoint a note taker).
- Have each student in a group take his or her own Interactive Notes for individual use later on as the group reads and discusses a text together.
- Copy the Interactive Notes form onto a transparency that you then give to a group. The group records its notes on the transparency and then presents its ideas to the class, using the Interactive Notes overhead to facilitate the class discussion and support its own claims.
- Put a transparency of the Interactive Notes tool on the overhead and use it to guide the class in discussion as they read and discuss a particular text in class.
- Send kids home with their own copy to use as the students read; be sure they have learned how to use the tool before doing this.

NOTES AND EXAMPLES

Example One: *Of Mice and Men*

Early on I often have students use the Interactive Notes to get them to pay attention to the important details of the book they are reading. What they write in the Before column depends on whether they are first beginning to read the text or have been reading it already. In the example in Figure 6.1, the student was already reading Steinbeck's *Of Mice and Men*. Thus he wrote down what had been going on before he continued to read the book; this backward glance to previous chapters oriented him and prepared him to read. Michael used the prompts more effectively in the During phase; again, the purpose here is to make the reading more interactive by asking that he stop and respond to what he is reading. Finally, Michael used the After prompts to further comprehend this portion of the story. The prompts helped him connect what he read to what he knew; they also helped him assess the extent to which he understood what he had read.

Example Two: Nonfiction

The example in Figure 6.2 follows the same process outlined above for Example One. I include this one to show the different ways of using the tool with notification, in this case, a newspaper article.

Interactive Notes

Name Michael Dacluk	Date
Topic	Class/Subject

Directions: Use Interactive Notes to help you read informational or literary texts. Interactive Notes guide you through a reading process to help you develop your ideas and express them in academic language. You may put questions, comments, connections, or favorite lines in any column; then use the prompts (or create your own) to help you write.

BEFORE **Prepare to Read**	**DURING** **Question & Comment**	**AFTER** **Summarize and Synthesize**
• List: √ title(s) √ headers √ subheaders √ captions √ objectives √ themes √ words to know • Ask questions • Make predictions • Set a purpose • Decide what matters most	• I wonder why.... • What caused... • I think... • This is similar to... • This is important because... • What do they mean by... • What I find confusing is... • What will happen next is... • I can relate to this because... • This reminds me of... • As I read, I keep wanting to ask...	• Three important points/ideas are... • These are important because... • What comes next... • The author wants us to think... • At this point the article/story is about... • I still don't understand... • What interested me most was... • The author's purpose here is to... • A good word to describe <u>this character/this story's tone</u> is...because... • This idea/story is similar to...
• Lennie go into a fight • Lennie and George were thinking about a dream. • Lennie was taking care of a puppy. • Slim killed Candy's dog • Candy is in depression	• I wonder why Lennie likes a puppy so much because it can't talk to him like George can. • I think that Slim did the right thing of killing Candy's dog because it was old and can't eat it • I think that Candy should get over his dog getting killed because one of the guys told him he could have one of his pups to raze and kept it. • I like Lennie because he is never mad at anyone and he is a hard worker. • I think that Lennie is going to get in a fight with Croobs because he is making him mad and he is know worried that George might be injured.	• I don't understand why Lennie wants to hold that puppy so much. • The author wants us to think that George and Lennie have been together for a long time and have got in lots of trouble with each other also. • The thing that I think that is going to come next in the story is that George and Lennie get fired and it was all Lennie's fault of them getting fired.

FIGURE 6.1 Sample Interactive Notes for Steinbeck's *Of Mice and Men*

Interactive Notes

Name Aliye Teregui	Date
Topic	Class/Subject

Directions: Use Interactive Notes to help you read informational or literary texts. Interactive Notes guide you through a reading process to help you develop your ideas and express them in academic language. You may put questions, comments, connections, or favorite lines in any column; then use the prompts (or create your own) to help you write.

BEFORE Prepare to Read	DURING Question & Comment	AFTER Summarize and Synthesize
• List: √ title(s) √ headers √ subheaders √ captions √ objectives √ themes √ words to know • Ask questions • Make predictions • Set a purpose • Decide what matters most	• I wonder why.... • What caused... • I think... • This is similar to... • This is important because... • What do they mean by... • What I find confusing is... • What will happen next is... • I can relate to this because... • This reminds me of... • As I read, I keep wanting to ask...	• Three important points/ideas are... • These are important because... • What comes next... • The author wants us to think... • At this point the article/story is about... • I still don't understand... • What interested me most was... • The author's purpose here is to... • A good word to describe <u>this character/this story's tone</u> is...because... • This idea/story is similar to...
• some graduates postpone college for well paid jobs. • Part-time job at Excite at home. • Hightech detour • Some delay college for hightech jobs • People who hold off college to get hightech jobs. • They want their dreamcar and a house on the hills. • Cisco systems networking academy.	• This is about students who put off college to get a job at an internet company • Most people can't really get ahead in life with only a highschool diploma. • Students get offered $25.00 an hour as contract employees. • People who don't go to college might miss out on a valuable experience.	• This job might be good to go to part-time and also go to college part time but you might be to busy and not get really any free time. • Highschool graduates go to the internet jobs and miss out on college or put it off. • People with highschool diplomas make $33,779 while people who are a bachelor's degree make $59,048. • But not every student is reach for a four year college experience after highschool.

FIGURE 6.2 Aliye's Interactive Notes on a newspaper article

Linear Array

7

DESCRIPTION

Students need tools to help them compare, to help them see and sense differences—in quality, importance, performance, or understanding. The very concept of importance is elusive for many students, especially those who struggle in school. When we say, as English teachers often do, "Find the most important line in the text," we make many assumptions. Do we mean most important to the story, the author, or ourselves? How do you determine importance? A Linear Array, also referred to as a continuum here, allows students to visually represent the spectrum from not important to essential. They understand the notion of "On a scale of one to ten, how did you do?" so they have a certain familiarity with the way this tool works.

This tool provides a useful structure for discussing a variety of subjects. A linear array allows us to place characters or events alongside each other and, using a continuum, decide which one is more important and why. It also allows students to better understand the subtle differences between one word (e.g., *courageous*) and another (e.g., *daring*). When put up on the board, preferably through full-class collaborative development, the Linear Array helps support dynamic, precise conversations about often very abstract subjects like heroism, ethics, importance, or love, many of which students encounter in the literature they read.

NOTES AND EXAMPLES

Example One: Continuum of Importance

Working with struggling readers, I quickly realized that *importance* is an elusive, very abstract concept that we must talk about often. The sample Linear Array in Figure 7.1, while visually different from the computer-designed tool shown in Figure 7.2, was done collaboratively to help students figure out what is important enough to include in their notes when reading a textbook. We pushed it a bit further so they could use it to answer the question "Will this be on the test?" The array stretches from not important to essential. I then drew the continuum on the whiteboard and said, "Okay, how can you tell if something is important?" Kids came up with a variety of ways to determine if something is important enough to include; specific examples were font size, typeface,

STANDARDS

- Reading
  - ☐ Evaluate the arguments presented in a text
  - ☐ Generate relevant questions
  - ☐ Prepare to read
- Writing
  - ☐ Organize information and ideas in logical, appropriate format
  - ☐ Prepare to write
  - ☐ Use sensory, concrete, or illustrative details to support claims
- Speaking
  - ☐ Compare events or ideas
- Language Study
  - ☐ Distinguish between denotative and connotative meaning
  - ☐ Expand vocabulary
- Viewing
  - ☐ Assess different techniques or devices used
  - ☐ Gather details and examples for subsequent analysis of text
- Test Preparation
  - ☐ Comprehend information
  - ☐ Organize ideas
  - ☐ Prioritize information
  - ☐ Remember information

SUBJECT AREAS

- English language arts
- Health
- Humanities
- Mathematics
- Science
- Social studies

USES

- Ask useful questions
- Compare two or more items, aspects, or people
- Determine importance of ideas and information
- Develop academic literacy
- Evaluate ideas
- Extend ideas beyond obvious
- Facilitate discussion
- Gather evidence to support claims
- Generate ideas
- Identify themes
- Make connections
- Prepare to read
- Prepare to write
- Respond to reading
- Support critical reading
- Synthesize ideas
- Visualize what is read

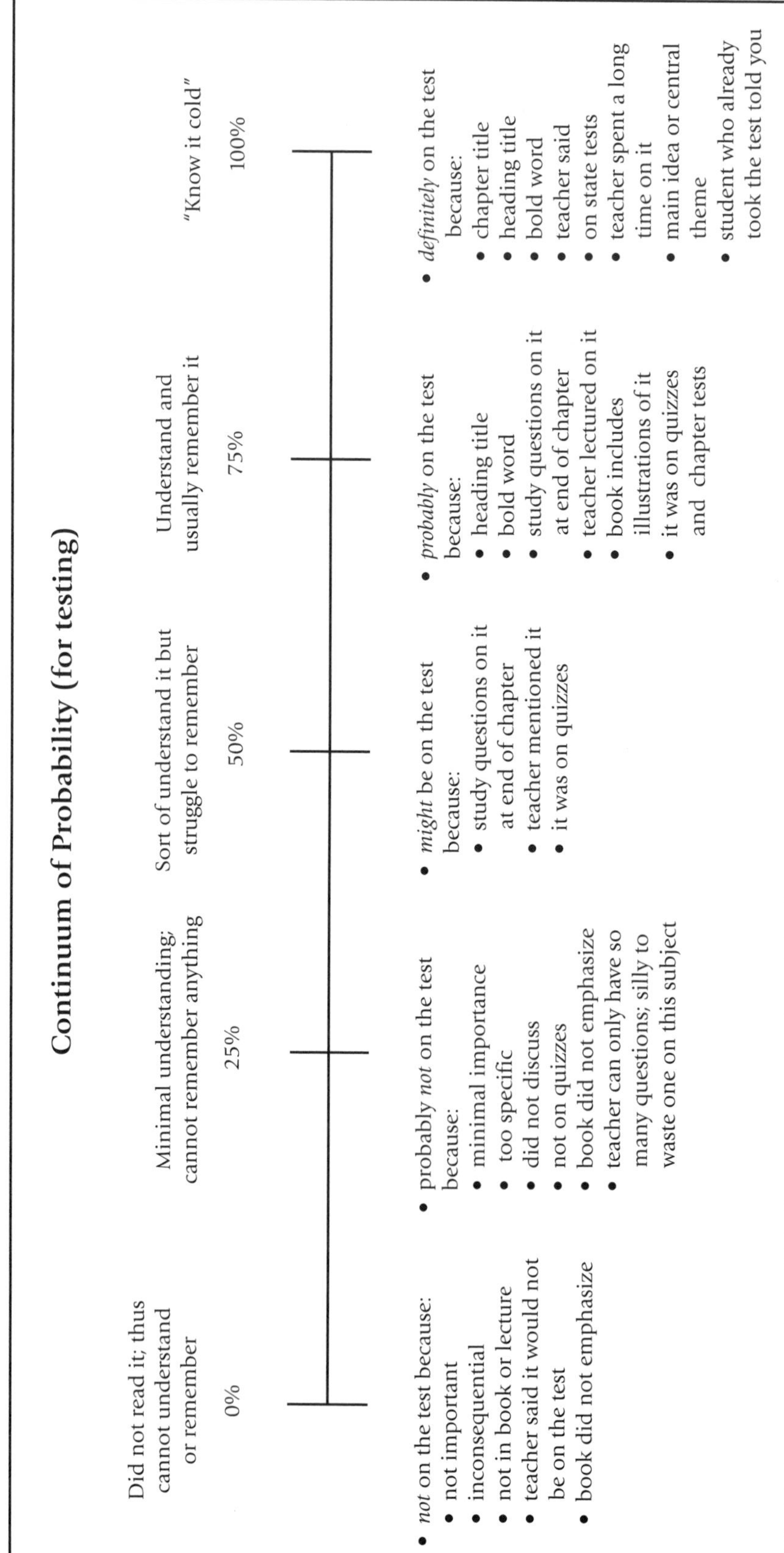

FIGURE 7.1 We developed this continuum of importance as a class on the board.

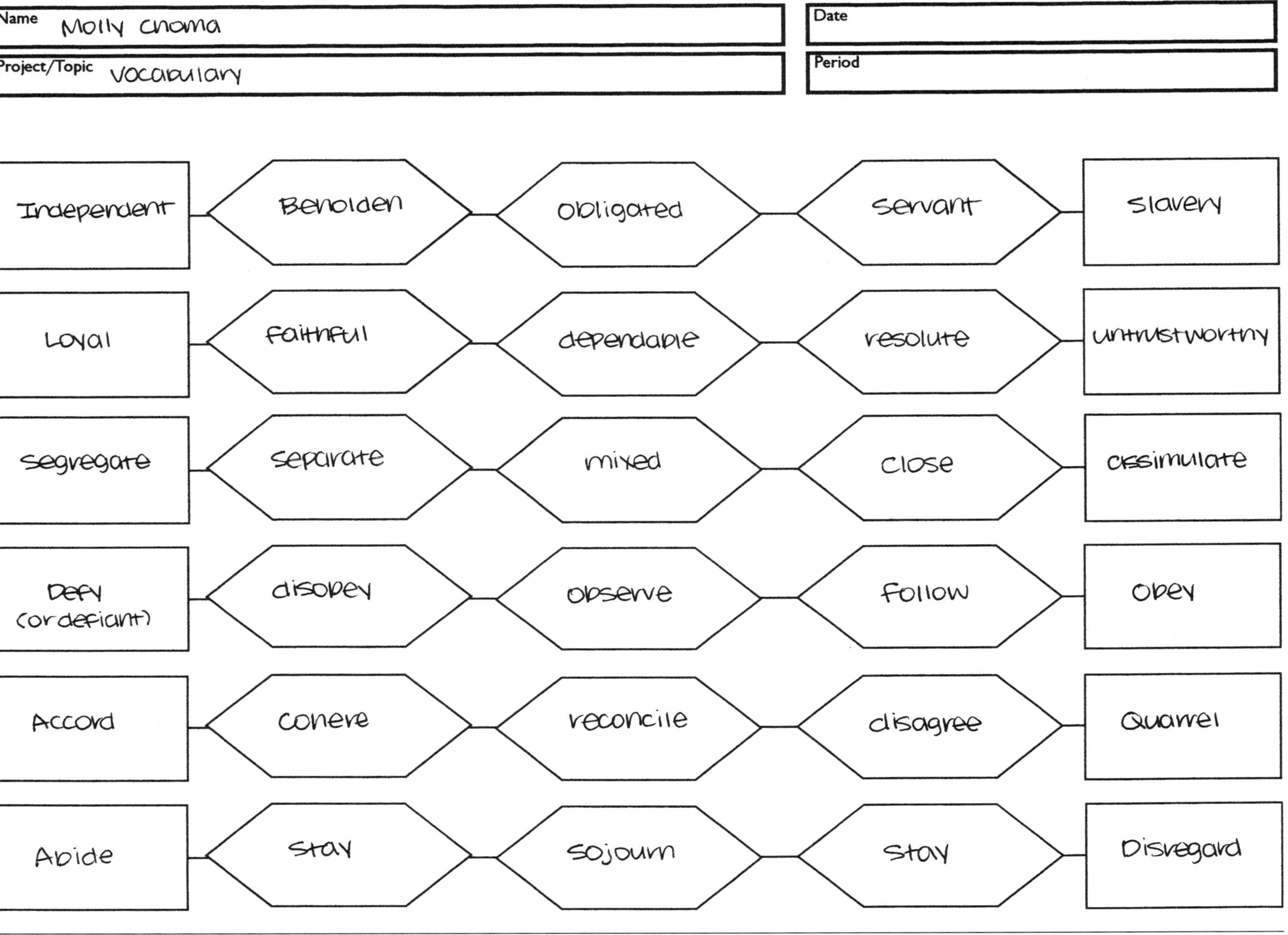

FIGURE 7.2 Molly Choma used this Linear Array to study a continuum of meaning among words.

placement (e.g., at the beginning of a paragraph), and teacher's continued reference to the subject (which implies the teacher thinks it is really important). This array created a visual means of evaluating information as the students read. Moreover, it established a common tool we could all refer to when discussing an idea. "Where would you place that on the continuum of importance?" we might ask, and it not only helped people visualize the importance (or irrelevance) of the item but also helped them comprehend it in the larger context of the other items arranged along the continuum. Along the top we described how ready they were creating by a continuum of understanding.

Example Two: Vocabulary Development

When studying *Lord of the Flies*, my students examined the different connotative meanings of words related to the story. (See Figure 7.2.) The Linear Array tool helped them develop their language sense, to see that *loyal* is different from *faithful*—related, yes, but not the same. So it is with *dependable* and *loyal*. I chose this method for *Lord of the Flies* because the book's central ideas invite careful discussion so students can better understand the subtle differences between words and ideas. It also provides a useful opportunity to learn to use the thesaurus, another tool—along with the dictionary—we need to learn to use.

Example Three: Concept Development

This example stems from the same unit with *Lord of the Flies*, except that instead of vocabulary, we examined how the boys move back and forth along the continuum of, for example, behavior or needs. (See Figure 7.3.) I give the students the tool and have them huddle up to complete it as a group. I first model how to do it so they have a solid grasp of the method and outcome. Then they collaborate to fill it in, developing multiple words to extend their vocabulary as they think about the idea at hand. We then use their arrays as the foundations for a discussion. I will typically ask them to defend or explain their inclusion or placement of a word or idea on the continuum, saying, "I'm not sure how that word is different from the one before it. Please explain and give us an example that illustrates your point." I then use writing, as Cameron Duncan's subsequent paragraphs show, to help them synthesize their thinking into the latest version of their understanding. Here is Cameron's response:

> *Ralph*: Civilization will hit Ralph hard. Reflecting back on the events of the island will shock and hurt him. The island situation will seem surreal to Ralph because he is a down-to-earth guy; when he gets reacquainted with civilization the island will seem like a whole other world.
>
> *Jack*: The shock of the events on the island will hit Jack too, but not as hard as they hit Ralph. If Jack has been changed so much by the island into a savage he might find it hard to get back into society and go to school. He might even look back on the island with regret for things he never did or for his island days.
>
> *Simon*: Simon had somewhat set himself apart from the other boys and events on the island. He never took part in hunting, destruction, or killing. He will have had his view of people changed. He went into the island believing human nature was good, but by the end he realized that people were essentially bad at heart. He will maintain his faith in God, but he probably won't trust people and he will question their intentions.

Linear Array

Name

Date

Project/Topic

Period

	· Before / Beginning · unimportant · Innocent · For / Proponent				· After / End · Essential · corrupted · Against / opponent
MORALS	· respect · obey · fairness · family morals · schools morals	· morals first kept · tried to live by them	began to abide by diff because they could not survive by old ones.	New way of life New morals	all morals basically corrupted because of need for survival.
BEHAVIOR	· Proper · polite – shy · respectful · rational	· organized, sat each other down & shared names, chose leader	· disobeyed did not want to do jobs.	· agression because of survival of the fittest · went by own opinion	· terrorists · violent · rude · killers
NEEDS	· order / understanding · nourishment · civilization	· order choose a / divide jobs leader	· control · cooperation · survival	· need to survive · 2 tribes	· nothing besides themselves.
ADAPTATIONS	adjustments to survive	to environment choose a leader · divide jobs	· searched island · became more agressive · changed clothes	· comfortable · enough to be on their own	· adapted to island · comfortable · new culture · new way of life
RELATIONSHIPS / BONDS	· uncomfortable · didn't know each other	· learned eachother's names · started bonding to cooperate	· comfortable with each other but still some tension at times jealosy	· fighting · competition · overpowering others	· fights no agreement · survival on their own

FIGURE 7.3 Cameron Duncan used this Linear Array to describe how the boys change as *Lord of the Flies* unfolds. On the left side you see "Before" to indicate how the boys were before they arrived; the far right says "After" to indicate what they were like after they left the island.

Then the students use these notes to write a paragraph that tries to synthesize their thinking about the text and its characters. Here's Cameron's example:

> Teenagers today, according to Schneider and Sterenam, are usually much too ambitious. Realistic goals aren't set, and adolescents are surprised that it is hard to get into college to become a doctor or a lawyer. Parents also add to the problem because they feel it's the school's responsibility to prepare their students for college. Compared to the teens of the 1950's, teenagers today are much more ambitious, more costly, and more unrealistic. Adolescents should learn to be more hardworking and keep their ambition, but to set realistic goals.

Literature Circle Notes

8

DESCRIPTION

Literature Circles (Daniels 2001) put kids in the driver's seat, giving them control, in most cases, of what they read and what they discuss. It is a very organized, though not scripted, activity that can be used for one period or an extended period of time. It is more than a strategy or technique: it is a way of working, an approach to learning. The tools in this chapter are also designed to develop students' capacity to read critically but independently; thus ultimately the students would not need these tools because they would have internalized the different questions and ways of reading. The tools provided here, while helpful, will ultimately get in their way once students become competent participants in the Literature Circle. The nature of the Lit Circles, owing their similarity to book groups, is a familiar one: a community of readers who contribute to intelligent and engaged conversations about the books they read. Finally, it is important to provide models when you are either introducing the technique or trying to raise the level of your students' performance.

The original approach called for students in groups to choose their own books. In some classes this might mean that students huddle up and decide which book they want to read. If they need to buy their own copies of a book their teacher does not have, they can do so, as long as it falls within the teacher's guidelines. Other teachers provide more focus, requiring groups to choose which of the available books about South Africa their group wants to read, for example. Other configurations are possible. You could have students use the same configuration and have them choose from different primary source documents, for example, or choose a range of poems to read among themselves.

Students can begin immediately in their groups, learning the roles as they rotate them. Another approach is to stagger the introduction of the roles over a period of time, having everyone, for instance, take Discussion Director Notes so they learn that role together. Then, when you want them to form actual Literature Circles, they have all learned the roles and can move ahead with the book they are going to read.

Lit Circles themselves are a powerful tool in the hands of a teacher; however, they are not a fix-all for everything, nor appropriate to all situations. Harvey Daniels' latest edition of *Literature Circles* (2001) tells you how

STANDARDS

- Reading
  - ☐ Analyze organizational patterns of information
  - ☐ Compare ideas, texts, or authors
  - ☐ Evaluate the arguments presented in a text
  - ☐ Extend ideas
  - ☐ Generate relevant questions
  - ☐ Identify and analyze recurring themes
  - ☐ Prepare to read
  - ☐ Synthesize information from multiple sources
- Writing
  - ☐ Establish a main or controlling idea
  - ☐ Integrate quotations and examples in written response
  - ☐ Prepare to write
  - ☐ Use sensory, concrete, or illustrative details to support claims
  - ☐ Use writing for a variety of purposes
- Language Study
  - ☐ Distinguish between denotative and connotative meaning
  - ☐ Examine and use different Greek and Latin roots of words
  - ☐ Know and use different parts of speech
- Listening
  - ☐ Improve note-taking skills
  - ☐ Organize information
  - ☐ Record information
- Viewing
  - ☐ Assess different techniques or devices used
  - ☐ Gather details and examples for subsequent analysis of text
  - ☐ Identify organization of information
- Test Preparation
  - ☐ Comprehend information
  - ☐ Organize ideas
  - ☐ Prioritize information
  - ☐ Remember information

SUBJECT AREAS

- English language arts
- Humanities
- Science
- Social studies

USES

- Ask useful questions
- Assess student performance
- Compare two or more items, aspects, or people
- Develop academic literacy
- Evaluate ideas
- Extend ideas beyond obvious
- Facilitate discussion
- Gather evidence to support claims
- Generate ideas
- Identify themes
- Make connections
- Prepare to read
- Prepare to write
- Respond to reading
- Support critical reading
- Synthesize ideas
- Take notes while reading
- Visualize what is read

to use them in your class. My purpose in this book is to share with you the tools I have made—and teachers have found effective—for introducing and supporting the use of this wonderful technique.

NOTES AND EXAMPLES

Example One: South African Literature Unit

In our integrated Modern World History and English class, students study South Africa. This is a country, like our own, whose study (and story) cannot be trusted to any one person or group. We use a group of South African books, most of which are fiction and several of which are autobiographical. Lit Circles offer students the chance to choose the genre and subject, and the results have been much improved over the days when they all had to read Alan Paton's novel *Cry, the Beloved Country*. To prepare them to use the notes, we began with a short but perfect poem by Mbuyiseni Oswald Mtshali called "Walls" so they could learn to use the tools and how to play the different roles. Each person accepts responsibility for a different role and, in addition to helping others read the poem, teaches them how to do her or his role. The primary difference in my tools is the inclusion of prompts and other features that develop the novice's ability to read and work in this way. I now have the students in each class learn the different roles over the course of the year. I will, for example, say, "I want everyone to go home and take Illustrator's Notes on this segment of the story." I will then take the best examples from that batch and, to teach the others, put them on an overhead and make them the focus of our lesson about how to read this way and respond using the Literature Circles Notes tools. Figure 8.1, for example, shows Jacqui de Borja's work as Illustrator in a group reading Mark Mathabane's *Kaffir Boy*. I always have kids explain what they draw; about this illustration, Jacqui wrote:

> I drew this picture to show that even thought Apartheid still exists, whites and blacks are friends through tennis. Blacks are allowed to beat whites in tennis matches. Johannes was able to express his opinion openly to whites at a tennis club. The whites there treated him as an equal and accepted the real news of the Soweto riots and the black view of Apartheid. The friends Johannes made through tennis help him whenever he is in need and will break the law of Apartheid if they feel it is wrong.
>
> *Reflections*:
>
> - Johannes's eyes became infected and swollen and were cured either by a witch doctor or western medicine.
> - A teacher told Johannes that it will be kids like him that will end Apartheid.
> - The Soweto riots started and the schools were either burned down or closed.
> - Johannes made friends with a German man who told Johannes he would risk his life for him.
> - Arthur Ashe won Wimbledon.
> - Johannes freely spoke his mind in front of whites at a tennis club.

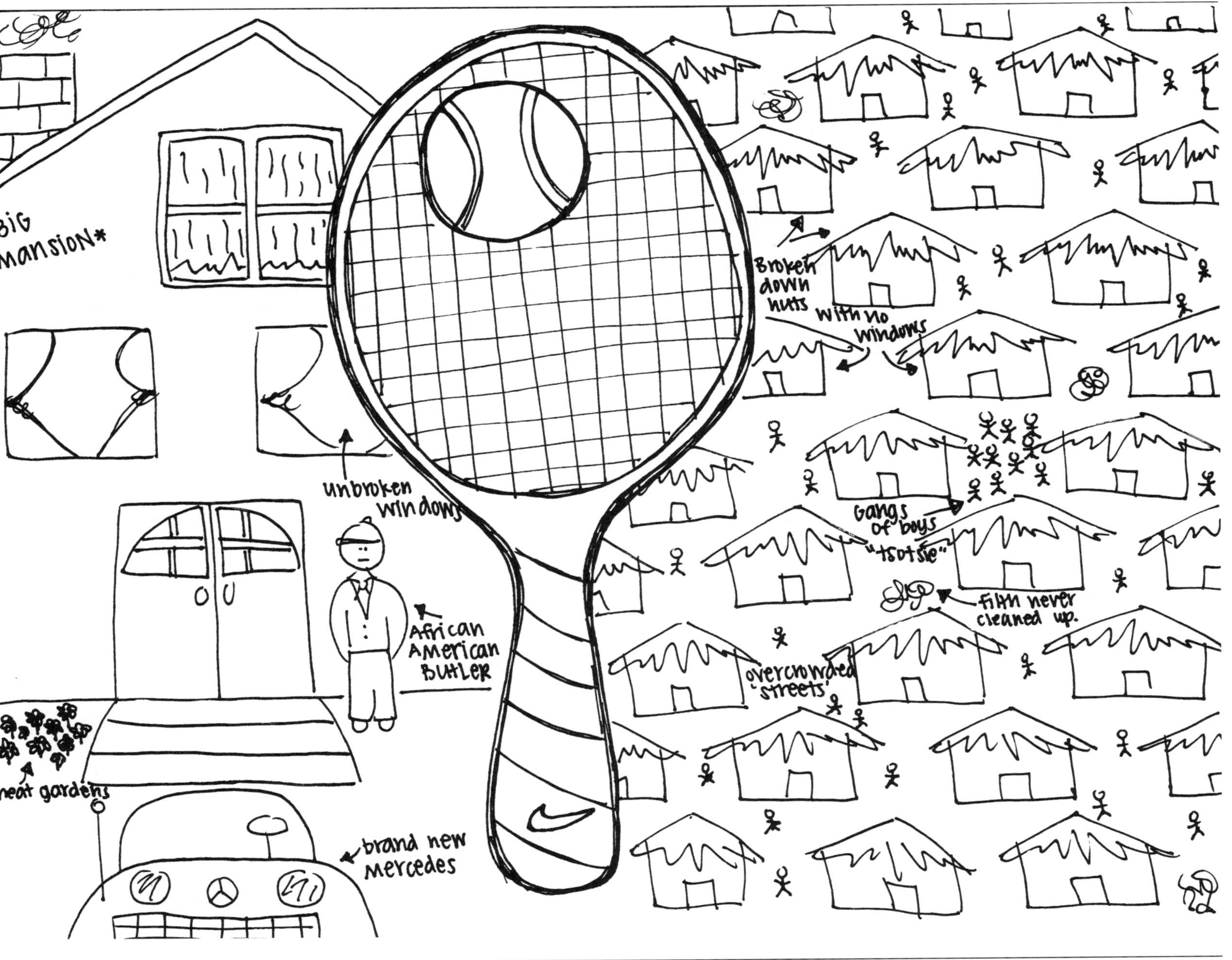

FIGURE 8.1 Jacqui de Borja's drawing for her Literature Circle role as Illustrator

Lit Circle Notes: Examplars

ILLUMINATOR	RESPONSE
"I was told by my father that I had no free will, no control whatsoever over my destiny, that each minute detail about my life, my existence—before now and to come—were all contained in a big scroll made of my life, over which my ancestors pondered day and night as they alternately tossed random situations into my life . . ." (p. 126, ¶4, from Kaffir Boy*)*	*This quote is important because it makes you think about your future. When I was reading this, I stopped and thought about my destiny. There is no way you can avoid the future. Every second counts. In a few seconds you can make a wrong decision. Sooner or later those seconds turn into minutes, which turn into hours that turn into days . . . Your destiny is something you come up with by making those decisions. What if someone just scrambled a few obstacles together and then put them in our destiny book? We must learn to make correct choices. They might just change some obstacles in the destiny book. We might be able to overcome those challenges that were put in the future. (Jessica Perez about* Kaffir Boy*)*

CONNECTOR	RESPONSE
What other places can you compare this to?	*This passage reminds me of Germany during the Holocaust. The police in South Africa are just like the Nazis banging on the Jewish doors and looking for the Jewish star or other required identification papers; this is how they use the blacks' passbooks in South Africa. (Jen Lescher about* Kaffir Boy*)*

SUMMARIZER	RESPONSE
What are the most important events?	*He was being rude to the "shit men" and they made him get in a bucket of night soil. Also they had to move out of their shack and into another one and Alexandra will soon be torn down. He almost died from the brazier being inside.*
Why is this important?	*It taught him not to make fun of people, especially for their jobs because they don't want to do what they are doing. Moving into another shack is important because it shows how poor they are and how they do whatever the whites say, including picking up their lives and leaving. They do what they say because they fear being arrested. (Jen Lescher about* Kaffir Boy*)*

DISCUSSION DIRECTOR	RESPONSE
Did they depend on witchcraft and voodoo so they wouldn't have to take ownership of bad things that happened?	*Yes, they depended very much on voodoo and witchcraft. They seemed to blame everything bad on the witches and evil ancestral spirits. They blamed no money, not being able to find a job, the police. They were all some sort of evil spirit. It was never the fault of the living person, but always the doing of a nonliving spirit.* [They believed this because . . . I also noticed that when *x* would happen, they believed . . .] *(Jennifer Edl about* Kaffir Boy*)*

DOWN HERE YOU SHOULD REVIEW, RETELL, OR REFLECT ON WHAT YOU READ SO FAR. (USE THE BACK IF NECESSARY.)
Johannes goes to the tribal land at this point in the book. He goes with his father and finds his witchdoctor. His family leaves to another part of the city because Alexandra got bulldozed. They move to another place where they are in poverty. Johannes turns to begging. Mother gets upset and talks with Johannes. He is now paranoid about police raids and witches. (Jessica Perez about Kaffir Boy*)*

FIGURE 8.2 These exemplars come from the students themselves; this activity is part of the feedback loop designed to continually improve their performance.

Example Two: Additional Instruction

When I am ready, I gather up examples from the different roles and create a single page like the one in Figure 8.2. I bring such a sheet in, give kids a copy to refer to, and put another on the overhead. I then proceed to think out loud, explaining what they did and how it worked (or did not). I continue this cycle of culling out the useful samples until students demonstrate a level of competence. Each time, they get their own copy to refer to; I then put mine on the overhead and explain what these examples do or do not do well. In this way, the cycle of improvement continues throughout the year, for the examples always represent the next level of difficulty.

9 Outlines Notes

STANDARDS

- Reading
  - ☐ Analyze organizational patterns of information
  - ☐ Compare ideas, texts, or authors
  - ☐ Extend ideas
  - ☐ Generate relevant questions
  - ☐ Identify and analyze recurring themes
  - ☐ Prepare to read
  - ☐ Synthesize information from multiple sources
- Writing
  - ☐ Establish a main or controlling idea
  - ☐ Integrate quotations and examples in written response
  - ☐ Organize information and ideas in logical, appropriate format
  - ☐ Prepare to write
  - ☐ Use sensory, concrete, or illustrative details to support claims
  - ☐ Use writing for a variety of purposes
- Speaking
  - ☐ Compare events or ideas
  - ☐ Organize information in a logical sequence
  - ☐ Prepare and deliver multimedia presentations
  - ☐ Prepare to speak
- Listening
  - ☐ Improve note-taking skills
  - ☐ Organize information
  - ☐ Record information
- Viewing
  - ☐ Assess different techniques or devices used
  - ☐ Gather details and examples for subsequent analysis of text
  - ☐ Identify organization of information
- Test Preparation
  - ☐ Comprehend information
  - ☐ Organize ideas
  - ☐ Prioritize information
  - ☐ Remember information

SUBJECT AREAS

- English language arts
- Health
- Humanities
- Mathematics
- Science
- Social studies

USES

- Ask useful questions
- Assess student performance
- Compare two or more items, aspects, or people
- Develop academic literacy
- Evaluate ideas
- Extend ideas beyond obvious
- Facilitate discussion
- Gather evidence to support claims
- Generate ideas
- Identify themes
- Make connections
- Narrow or refine subject
- Organize information
- Prepare to read
- Prepare to write
- Respond to reading
- Support critical reading
- Synthesize ideas
- Take notes while reading

DESCRIPTION

I often tell my students they must learn to "think in buckets," or "grow a tree in their head," by which I mean organize the information into natural or appropriate categories. Forming the right buckets allows them to sort the ideas in useful ways that they can then arrange to suit their purposes.

The outline is an old, familiar tool, but it has many uses. Computers have made it much easier to "think in outlines," as they effortlessly format themselves, leaving us to concentrate only on putting in the information. As tools, outlines help us organize and generate ideas, forcing us to establish the categories and then generate examples or other content to fill them. They can be used to prepare a writer or support a reader who is trying to organize information into categories. Speakers find them equally useful, as they create a logical flow into the main categories of their talk. Many texts, such as textbooks, are created using outlines; thus taking Outline Notes allows the reader to mirror and better understand the organization of information in the text. Students may add to their Outline Notes any annotations or other strategies (e.g., Q Notes) they think are appropriate for a given task.

NOTES AND EXAMPLES

Example One: Newspaper Article

Students in my reading classes read a feature article in the newspaper each week. (The local newspaper provides a class set of that day's newspaper free to any class that requests it.) After modeling how to use Outline Notes, I circulate around the room to be sure they properly identify and organize the important ideas. Outline Notes require that students determine the main idea of the article before reading so they can evaluate the information in subsequent paragraphs to determine its importance. In Figure 9.1, for example, Rex breaks the article into clearly defined categories that most, even without reading the article, can tell are appropriate. He then knows whether he picked the right categories by the ease with which he can find examples and details to fill in the subcategories. He brings it all together at the bottom. This synthesis at the bottom develops, even as it tests, the reader's understanding of the text he read. Though

Name R. Vaughn Ludwig	Date 2-2
Project/Topic	Period 1°

Main Idea/Subject I. Arafat makes last-minute trip to U.S.

Support/Idea A. Why a last-minute trip

Details/Examples
1. Before Clinton is out of office
2. Might to hard to work with Bush
3. Choices and options about Clinton's proposal
4. Wants to settle something before
5. another terrible thing happens

Support/Idea B. Hopeing to achieve

Details/Examples
1. Mideast peace proposals
2. Peace among the Islamis.
3. hoping to unite and come together
4. hoping find an agreement
5. find a new prime minister

Support/Idea C. Clinton's proposal

Details/Examples
1. Could lead to direct high-level talks
2. between Israel and the Palestians
3. has Arafat asking questions?
4. Clinton is determined to get along with the Proposa
5. Clinton wants to do it right away before he leaves.

Support/Idea D. Past history between Clinton and Arafat

Details/Examples
1. Burak accepted Clinton's proposals as basis.
2. Arafat advisors condemned Clinton's proposals
3. met together before about proposals.
4. Clinton was unwilling to indulge the
5. Palestinians / Clinton has changed his mind on the score.

Summary/Observations

I notice that Clinton and Arafat wants to make these sudden decisions before Clinton will be gone from office. I read they are hoping to achieve Mideast peace proposals, and hope to unite together.
I also notice that Clinton's proposal could lead to chaos because Arafat now has questions about the proposals. I also have read that Clinton and Arafat have contacted each other before about this.

FIGURE 9.1 Sample Outline Notes taken while reading a newspaper article

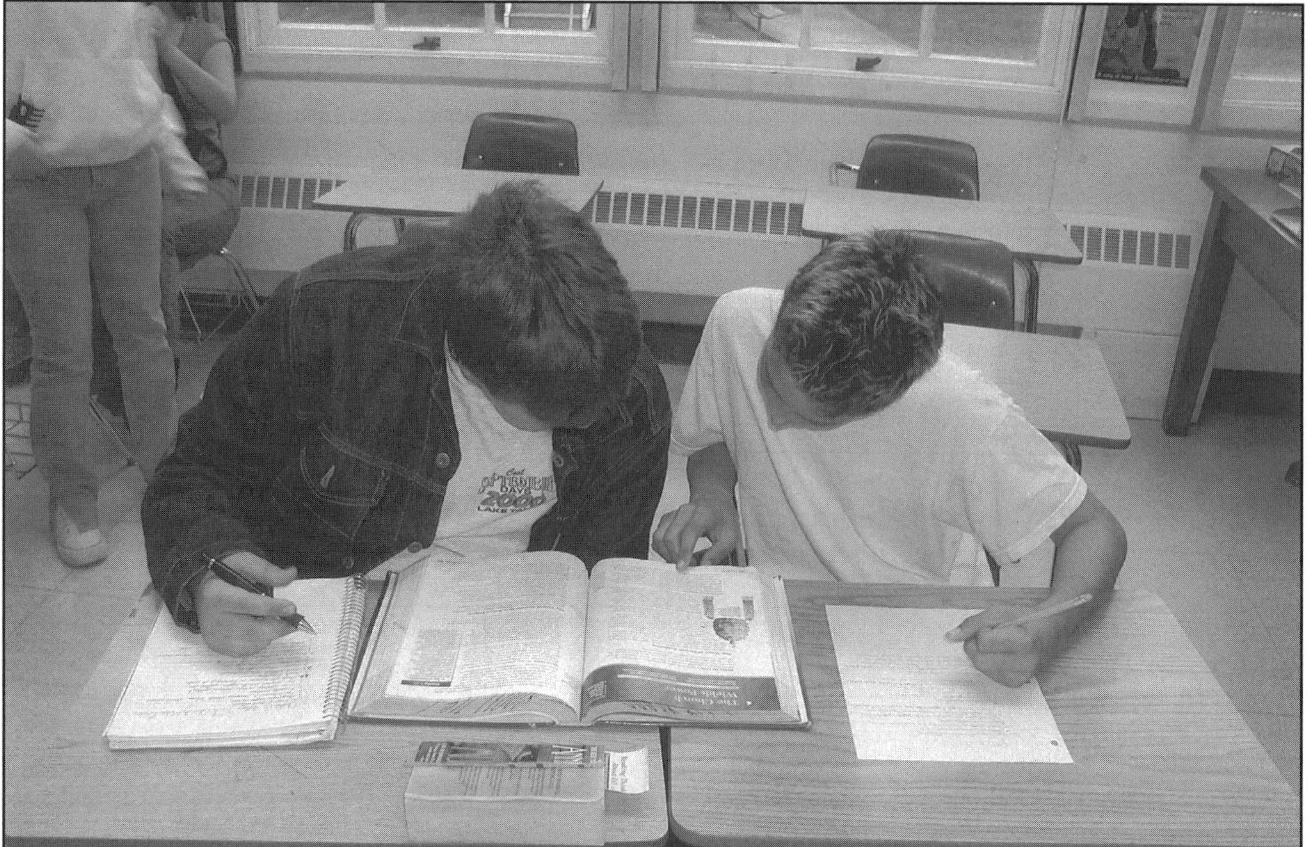

FIGURE 9.2 Jon and Jeff take Outline Notes while reading their history textbook. Collaborating allows them to discuss what, for example, the main ideas or categories are while taking notes.

Rex did not do it here, some readers use the left margin to post sample quiz questions that the corresponding category answers.

Example Two: Outline Notes Plus Q Notes

Students in my ACCESS classes are concurrently enrolled in the college prep Modern World History class, which uses a textbook written at the ninth-grade level. (See Figure 9.2.) Teachers require the students to take Outline Notes. What's more, students can use their Outline Notes on the quiz the next day. However, these notes are only helpful when they are well organized so the students can find the information they need quickly. Q Notes, combined with Outline Notes, create a powerful tool in such a situation, for the students must then go through and anticipate what the quiz questions will be, thereby creating their own practice quiz (and eventual test). Note the integration of Visual Explanations in the notes in Figure 9.3; this further integration of other note-taking techniques reinforces the idea that this is a set of skills, a canon of methods (Scholes 1998) we must be able to choose from based on the requirements of the assignment.

Outline Notes + Q Notes = Improved Reading and Test Performance

Overview I created the following example (thanks to Jessica Johnson for lending me her excellent notes!) to help you see how you can turn your Outline Notes for any class into Q Notes to help you prepare for the quizzes and tests.

- *Step One*: Take Outline Notes as you read the assigned chapter. Leave an extra wide margin (about 2 inches) on the left side of the page.
- *Step Two*: Identify the information you will be expected to know on the quiz or test; create a test question in the margin next to the area where you will find the answer.
- *Step Three*: Fold the paper so that only the questions are visible; use this to quiz yourself.
- *Step Four*: After the quiz, update your notes by adding the questions you did not think of; this will help you on the larger test or final exam.
- *Step Five*: Use your Q Notes to create your Summary Sheet (one page study sheet for test).
- *Step Six*: Turn your Q Notes into a practice test.
- *Step Seven*: Turn your Q Notes into Q Cards (question on one side; answer(s) on the other).

What is feudalism?	**Chapter 13.2: "Feudalism in Europe" (pgs. 322–336)**
	I. New Invasions Trouble Western Europe
	• Invasion destroyed Carol. Empire b/w 800–1000
	• Muslims seized Sicily; sacked Rome 846
When did the Muslims sack Rome?	A. Vikings: Raiders, Traders, and Explorers
	1. from Scandinavia
	2. aka "Northern" or "Norsemen"
What was another name for the Vikings?	3. great shipbuilders: up to 300 warriors
	4. accepted Christianity and stopped raiding monasteries
	B. Magyars and Muslims
Who were the Magyars?	1. Magyars
	a. nomadic people
	b. attacked and sold people as slaves
	2. Muslims
	a. controlled Mediterranean Sea
	b. settled Europe
	c. attacked settlements on Atlantic and Med.
What is a knight?	C. Feudalism Structures Society
What is a serf?	1. Knight: mounted warrior pledged to defend lord's land in exchange for a fiefdom
How is the 'Feudal Pyramid' organized?	2. Serf: people who could not lawfully leave place where born
	3. The Feudal Pyramid

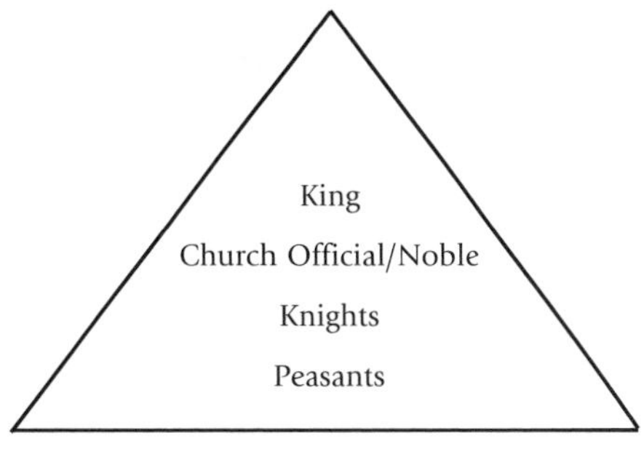

FIGURE 9.3 Students combine Outline Notes and Q Notes to help them better understand what they read and to prepare for their tests in history.

10 Pyramid Notes

STANDARDS

- Reading
  - ☐ Analyze organizational patterns of information
  - ☐ Evaluate the arguments presented in a text
  - ☐ Extend ideas
  - ☐ Generate relevant questions
  - ☐ Identify and analyze recurring themes
  - ☐ Prepare to read
- Writing
  - ☐ Establish a main or controlling idea
  - ☐ Integrate quotations and examples in written response
  - ☐ Organize information and ideas in logical, appropriate format
  - ☐ Prepare to write
  - ☐ Use sensory, concrete, or illustrative details to support claims
- Speaking
  - ☐ Organize information for desired effect on audience
  - ☐ Prepare to speak
- Listening
  - ☐ Organize information
- Test Preparation
  - ☐ Comprehend information
  - ☐ Organize ideas
  - ☐ Prioritize information
  - ☐ Remember information

SUBJECT AREAS

- English language arts
- Health
- Humanities
- Science
- Social studies

USES

- Ask useful questions
- Assess student performance
- Compare two or more items, aspects, or people
- Evaluate ideas
- Extend ideas beyond obvious
- Facilitate discussion
- Gather evidence to support claims
- Generate ideas
- Identify themes
- Make connections
- Narrow or refine subject
- Observe patterns
- Organize information
- Prepare to read
- Prepare to write
- Respond to reading
- Support critical reading
- Synthesize ideas
- Visualize what is read

DESCRIPTION

The triangle is a familiar but useful shape: it implies a broad-based foundation or, if inverted, an effort to narrow or refine to a single point, a main idea. It offers the note taker a visual shorthand to explain a phenomenon such as social ranking or a hierarchy that describes the relation of one class to another. Because it is a familiar shape, the student can adapt it to suit innovative purposes as well as capture the basic ideas in a text.

NOTES AND EXAMPLES

One obvious example would be Maslow's hierarchy of human needs (see Figure 10.1), which arranges itself into a nice pyramid to suggest that the "basic" needs provide the foundation on which all others are built. When using it as a note-taking tool while reading, you can put at the top the main idea of the whole article (or the most important event, character, or aspect) and then arrange the subordinate ideas in order of importance beneath that. If students are taking notes on their reading or a lecture, it is useful to integrate a pyramid into their notes to help them visualize the information (e.g., the social hierarchy during the Middle Ages).

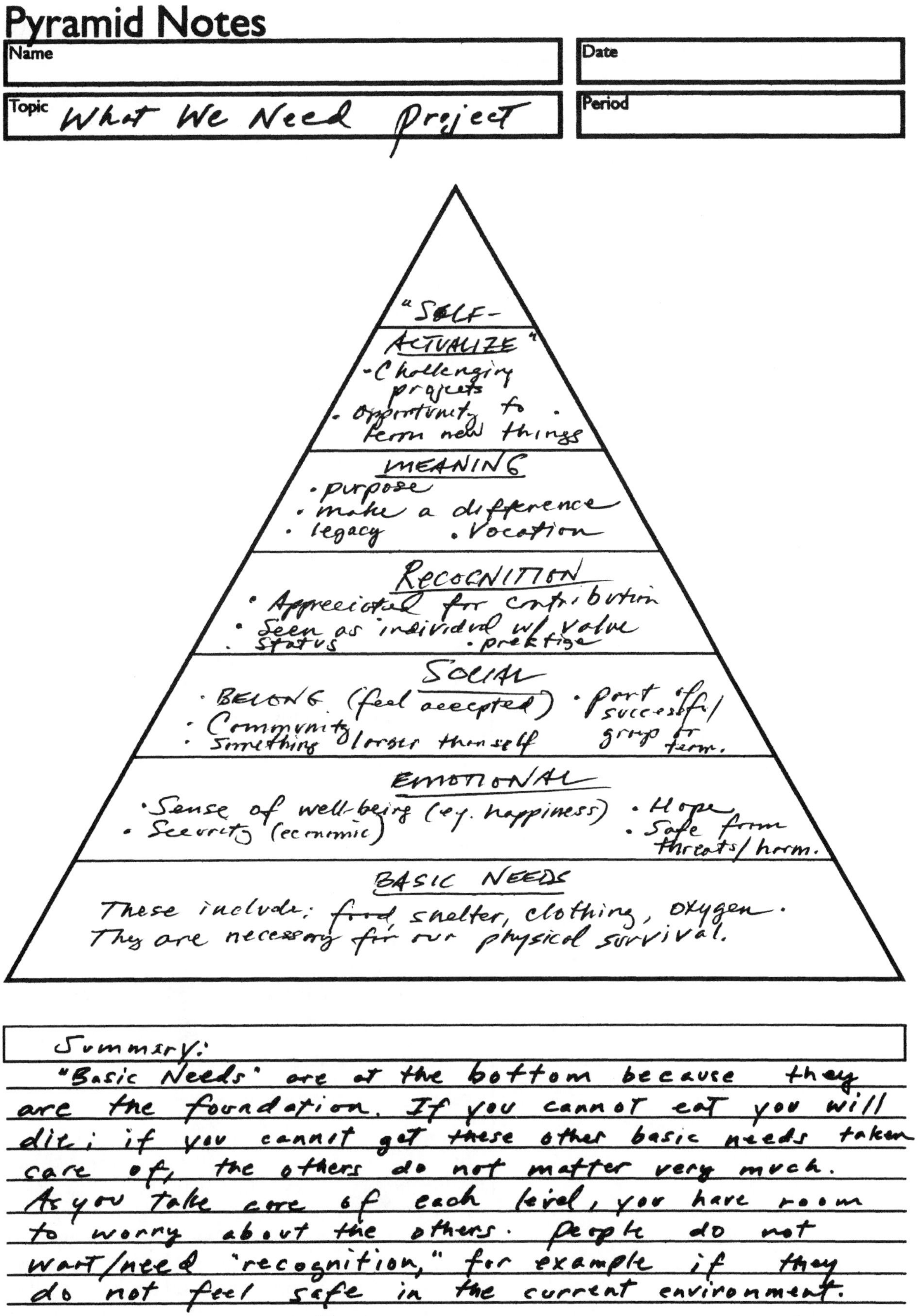

Pyramid Notes

Name | Date

Topic What We Need Project | Period

"SELF-ACTUALIZE"
- Challenging projects
- Opportunity to learn new things

MEANING
- purpose
- make a difference
- legacy
- Vocation

RECOGNITION
- Appreciated for contribution
- Seen as individual w/ value
- Status
- prestige

SOCIAL
- BELONG (feel accepted)
- Community
- Something larger than self
- part of successful group or team.

EMOTIONAL
- Sense of well-being (e.g. happiness)
- Security (economic)
- Hope
- Safe from threats/harm.

BASIC NEEDS
These include: ~~food~~ shelter, clothing, oxygen. They are necessary for our physical survival.

Summary:
"Basic Needs" are at the bottom because they are the foundation. If you cannot eat you will die; if you cannot get these other basic needs taken care of, the others do not matter very much. As you take care of each level, you have room to worry about the others. People do not want/need "recognition," for example if they do not feel safe in the current environment.

FIGURE 10.1 Students in Frank Firpo's Social Studies class examine and rank the different human needs, then apply them to subsequent readings in both his class and their English class.

11

Q Notes

STANDARDS

- Reading
  - ☐ Evaluate the arguments presented in a text
  - ☐ Extend ideas
  - ☐ Generate relevant questions
  - ☐ Identify and analyze recurring themes
  - ☐ Prepare to read
- Writing
  - ☐ Establish a main or controlling idea
  - ☐ Integrate quotations and examples in written response
  - ☐ Organize information and ideas in logical, appropriate format
  - ☐ Prepare to write
  - ☐ Use sensory, concrete, or illustrative details to support claims
- Speaking
  - ☐ Analyze devices used in others' speeches
  - ☐ Prepare and deliver multimedia presentations
  - ☐ Prepare to speak
- Listening
  - ☐ Improve note-taking skills
  - ☐ Organize information
  - ☐ Record information
- Viewing
  - ☐ Assess different techniques or devices used
  - ☐ Gather details and examples for subsequent analysis of text
- Test Preparation
  - ☐ Comprehend information
  - ☐ Organize ideas
  - ☐ Prioritize information
  - ☐ Remember information

SUBJECT AREAS

- English language arts
- Health
- Humanities
- Mathematics
- Science
- Social studies

USES

- Ask useful questions
- Assess student performance
- Compare two or more items, aspects, or people
- Develop academic literacy
- Evaluate ideas
- Extend ideas beyond obvious
- Facilitate discussion
- Gather evidence to support claims
- Make connections
- Narrow or refine subject
- Prepare to read
- Prepare to write
- Respond to reading
- Support critical reading
- Synthesize ideas
- Take notes while reading

DESCRIPTION

Questions accomplish so much. They focus our attention. They establish a purpose when we are reading and writing; we figure out what question we are trying to answer when we read. They are, in short, the engine that drives much of our best thinking. If we do not know what question we are trying to answer, we are like a boat setting out with no rudder. Q Notes prompt you, as you read, to continually ask yourself, "What question am I trying to answer?" or "What question does this sentence/paragraph answer?" When introducing Q Notes you should take time to discuss the qualities of a good question, providing students examples of both good and poor questions.

The Q Notes tool combines two well-known and powerful methods: Survey Question Read-Recite-Review (SQ3R) and Cornell Notes. I call it Q Notes because students can only write Q-uestions in the left-hand margin; when they prepare for a Q-uiz, the Q-uestions serve as *cues* to remind them what they must know. When using these notes to study, students can fold the right edge of the paper over so that it lines up with the dotted line. They should then be able to see only their questions in the left column. They can use these to quiz themselves.

Q Notes are a powerful tool for readers in all the content areas; they get readers focused when working with textbooks or other informational texts. The formation of a question establishes the students' purpose. Moreover, you can move around the room and assess their performance by asking what question(s) they are reading to answer. If they offer the "wrong" question, you can stop and help them clarify or revise their purpose.

NOTES AND EXAMPLES

Example One: *To Kill a Mockingbird*

In order to teach students to ask questions when reading and which questions to ask, I use Q Notes in my academic literacy classes. Students in my reading classes read different books for various English teachers, so Q Notes allow me to use one tool to meet the needs of many students reading a variety of texts. We need tools and techniques that develop critical thinking and close reading capacities, but which are not text specific (i.e., designed only for *To Kill a Mockingbird*, for example). I model for them how to use the tool, then circulate

Q Notes

Name Emily Wagstaffe	Date 4-23
Topic cornell notes	Class

Overview: Q Notes combines two well-known and powerful methods: SQ3R and Cornell Notes. I call it "Q Notes" because you can only write Q-uestions in the left-hand margin; when you prepare for a **Q**-uiz, the **Q**-uestions serve as CUES to remind you what you must know. When using these notes to study, fold the **right-edge** of the paper over so that it lines up with the dotted line. You should then only be able to see your questions in the Q-column. Use these to **Q**-uiz yourself.

Directions: Turn the titles, subheadings, and topic sentences into questions in this column.	**Directions: In this area, you write the answers to the questions. Use bullets and dashes to help organize your ideas. Also, use symbols and abbreviations to help you take notes more effeciently.**
What is the setting of the novel? where is Maycomb? What is it like? Why is this relevent?	- Alabama, small southern town, where everybody knows everybody else, 1940's
Why does aunt Alex come & stay with Jem, Scout, and Atticus?	- Because (especially Scout) the kids need a mothertype figure, Atticus will not be home to care for the children so they need someone to watch Scot & Jem
What does Harper Lee think of the schools?	- Grammar school is from K-6 grade. Then highschool goes from 7-12 grade. She also thinks that teachers don't teach at all. Because Scot's teacher told Scot to stop reading.
What do you think happened between Mayella & Tom? What is your evidence?	- I think that Bob Ewell raped his daughter, Mayella. She was severely beaten on the right side of her face. So the person who beat & raped her used the left hand. And Tom can't use his left hand.
Are all peope created = in a court of law	- Yes & No what people are created = But in this case everyone is not 100% towards Tom even if he is innocent. But in the end he pleads guilty. A big %. because he's black.
How do various people react to the trial & the verdict?	- This Trial was a big event in Maycomb county. Almost all adult citizens went to watch it & most were fine with the verdict except Atticus & the kids because the whole town is very racist.

Down here you should review, retell, or reflect on what you read so far.

FIGURE 11.1 Emily Wagstaffe used Q Notes to help her focus on the important details of *To Kill a Mockingbird.*

around the room to help them ask good questions. If I am introducing the technique for the first time, or using it in a new way, we take time to discuss what makes a good question. We might look at different sample questions, examining what they are asking and predicting what kind of answer such questions might yield. On this particular day (see Figure 11.1) we did not use the box at the bottom of the page, but in other situations I have students synthesize their ideas to bring the current reading to a close.

Example Two: Combining Q Notes and Outline Notes

If you look back at Figure 9.3 you will see a variation on Q Notes that combines the function of Q Notes with the format of Outline Notes. This example shows the value of the technique for taking notes when reading textbooks or other infotexts.

Questions

12

DESCRIPTION

Questions are the jackhammers, the crowbars, the blasting caps of thinking. They are also the engine behind our best work; they send us on a *quest* to discover, to solve some problem that will not leave us alone. It is not enough, however, to just ask questions; we must learn which questions to ask and when to ask them if we are to get the end we seek. If asked at the right time, a good question is the skeleton key that opens all doors to the house we are trying to enter.

How many types of questions can there possibly be, you might be thinking. The types of questions—and how and when you ask those questions—depend on the answer to that first important question: *Why* am I doing this? Once you establish a purpose for yourself, you can then ask which questions will help you achieve your goal. The questions at the end of this chapter are arranged in five categories; these different types of questions will help you or your students:

- Design
- Clarify
- Plan
- Evaluate
- Reflect

Good readers begin asking questions before they even start reading and keep asking questions while and after they read. Here are some examples:

BEFORE

- What do I need to know about this subject to read this text?
- What do I know about this author that might help me?
- Why I am I reading this?
- How should I read it (e.g., carefully, quickly, leisurely)?

STANDARDS

- Reading
  - ☐ Compare ideas, texts, or authors
  - ☐ Extend ideas
  - ☐ Generate relevant questions
  - ☐ Identify and analyze recurring themes
  - ☐ Prepare to read
- Writing
  - ☐ Integrate quotations and examples in written response
  - ☐ Prepare to write
  - ☐ Use writing for a variety of purposes
- Speaking
  - ☐ Compare events or ideas
  - ☐ Prepare to speak
- Language Study
  - ☐ Distinguish between denotative and connotative meaning
- Viewing
  - ☐ Assess different techniques or devices used
  - ☐ Gather details and examples for subsequent analysis of text
  - ☐ Identify organization of information
- Test Preparation
  - ☐ Comprehend information
  - ☐ Organize ideas

SUBJECT AREAS

- English language arts
- Health
- Humanities
- Mathematics
- Science
- Social studies

USES

- Ask useful questions
- Assess student performance
- Develop academic literacy
- Extend ideas beyond obvious
- Facilitate discussion
- Gather evidence to support claims
- Generate ideas
- Identify themes
- Make connections
- Prepare to read
- Prepare to write
- Respond to reading
- Support critical reading
- Synthesize ideas
- Take notes while reading

DURING

- What does this character want?
- What will happen next?
- How does this relate to my own experience, knowledge, or previous reading?

AFTER

- How did the character change by the end of the story?
- What was the big idea in this article?
- What continues to confuse me?
- To what extent have I achieved my stated purpose—and what evidence can I provide?

Generating good questions takes time and practice. The clarity of your answer depends entirely on the clarity of your question. When I first introduce questions, I give students questions of varying types and qualities, then ask them to evaluate them. Here is an excerpt from a sample list. Using a score of 1–5 (1 = weak, 5 = excellent), students must evaluate the quality of these questions and be able to justify their scores.

- Why can't we all just get along?
- Will the young become like their elders?
- Why did the author choose this (e.g., word, symbol, image)?
- Do you think that Jasmine compares to Ender from *Ender's Game?*
- How is Wen Fu related to Pearl?
- What characteristics do you share with Wen Fu?
- Do you believe in divorce? Does divorce affect you as it did the characters in *Kitchen God's Wife?*
- Are teens (and their lives) in other countries the same or different?
- What point of view is the narrator speaking from?
- Are all teenagers like the younger stones in the story "The Stones"?
- Who was the antagonist?
- Have you ever kept secrets from your family or friends?
- Why do Winnie and Jasmine (and other characters from books we've read) grow wise? Relate this to yourself also.
- Have you ever felt stuck in one spot, unable to move?
- How is Jasmine a lot like Pearl?

When they finish evaluating these questions, most of which relate to books we have been reading, students create the traits of a good question. Here is one student's scoring rubric:

1 not clear; a yes or no question; obvious

2 confusing; irrelevant; some thought involved

3 can read in only one direction; average question; simple but not necessarily obvious; not thought-provoking

4 good question: solid, gets you thinking beyond the obvious

5 well written; requires serious thought; inspirational; the question itself reveals a whole new side of the subject you had not considered

Students then had to complete the following prompt: "A good question. . . ." The same student above wrote:

A good question:

- Requires you to think
- Must be original
- May help you out
- Must be specific
- Makes sense

Another student in the class wrote that a good question "scares you because there are so many new concepts that you haven't even thought about most of the ideas. You have to sit and concentrate for a while just about how you will begin to ATTEMPT to answer the question."

Here is a sample set (i.e., my lesson plan) of questions from my sophomore English class, which at the time was reading Remarque's novel *All Quiet on the Western Front:*

- Write down three characteristics of a good question.
- Compile these on the board; ask people to explain and clarify as needed.
- Pick the three most useful questions and explain why they are such good questions. Discuss.
- Ask: If you could ask the author one question, what would that be?
- Ask: Why is that a good question, according to our traits of good questions?
- If you could ask one of the characters a question, who would you ask and what would you ask him or her? (Why would you want to know that?)
- Ask: Why is that a good question, according to our traits of good questions?
- Formulate one question about an event, idea, or experience in the book.
- Ask: Why is that a good question, according to our traits of good questions?

- Create a "bridging question" (i.e., a question that builds a bridge between you and what you are reading).
    - Part One Example: Why don't the men respect Himmelstoss?
    - Part Two Example: Who is someone that you respect—and why do you respect him or her?

Target Notes, discussed later in this book, offer a useful tool for generating questions. I will often put a blank Target on the overhead and write the subject in the middle—poetry, war, a character's name, a book's title—and ask the kids what things we should consider when discussing it. I then ask them to identify questions we should ask to guide our examination of each category.

Teachers have different names for the questions they use. My colleague Marilyn Nelson uses "thin" and "thick" questions; others call these thin and thick questions "above the surface" and "below the surface," which refers to the reciprocal teaching strategy. Marilyn uses a different set of questions to guide her Socratic Seminar: literal, interpretive, and applied. She describes them as follows:

- *Literal Questions* are "fact questions" whose answers can be found right in the text (e.g., What is Lennie thinking about when he dies?").
- *Interpretive Questions* are "meaning" questions whose answers you must figure out from evidence in the text. Interpretive questions can:
    - Uncover hidden conflicts, motivations, and attitudes (e.g., How does Crooks feel about Lennie, Candy, and Curley's wife visiting him?)
    - Lead to meaningful comparisons (e.g., What are some differences between Crooks' loneliness and Curley's wife's loneliness?)
    - Point to meaningful connections between events (e.g., How does Lennie's fatal mistake in the barn affect George's and Candy's lives?)
    - Track character development (e.g., How does Crooks' attitude change as the conversation between Lennie, Candy, Curley's wife, and him develops?)
    - Spark evaluative analysis (e.g., How do Crooks' handicap and age affect him?)
    - Explore themes (e.g., How does the novel support the idea that dreams often grow from a specific void in a person's life?)
- *Applied Questions* are "real-life" questions that make you think about the novel in relation to your own life and the real world. (They make you apply something in the novel to real life.) Applied questions often involve your own opinion, and their answers can't be found in the novel (e.g., How does Candy's fear of being discarded compare to our society's treatment of the elderly?).

These three types of questions are similar to, though not the same as, the set of questions Christenbury and Kelley (1983) describe in their Dense Question Strategy (see Figure 24.3).

The Coalition of Essential Schools (1989) organizes its entire curriculum around "essential questions," seeing the asking of such questions as one of the crucial habits of mind of an independent, thoughtful learner. Here is a sample of some of their questions (you can learn more about their work at <www.essentialschools.org>).

A Collection of Essential Questions

Notice that many questions lend themselves to multiple disciplines and can be used with different age groups.

COMMUNITY

- What is a "community of learners"?

MATH

- What is a function?
- Why is learning math important?
- What are good problem-solving strategies?
- How is geometry used in the real world?
- What is the role of geometry in advertising, fabric design, agriculture, architecture, etc.?
- What are rules that govern the transformation of a curve in a coordinate plane?

SCIENCE

- Is light a particle or a wave?
- Do chemicals benefit society or us?
- Is evolution fact or theory?
- Is altruism biological in nature?
- What can the Turtle do?
- Are animals essential for man's survival?
- Can science provide the answers to all questions?

ENGLISH

- What is a great book?
- How do we learn about life through fiction?

WRITING AND READING

- What is good writing?
- What do you want to get out of reading?
- Why read?
- Why do people write?
- Do reading and writing mean anything?

HISTORY

- How does perceived style influence the perception and creation of history?
- How have Ancient Greeks/Romans influenced our society today?

TECHNOLOGY

- How do you use the computer as a tool?
- How can you use tools together?
- How can you use a computer to solve a problem?
- How do people who use computers communicate with each other?

THE ARTS

- Why is art necessary?
- How do people express themselves through the arts today?
- How is culture reflected in the urban arts?
- What is urban or grassroots art?
- What is the difference between Art and art?
- What values are expressed in the arts of diverse cultures?

The list of questions that follows, divided up into five sections, is the result of every grant I've written, meeting I've planned, Web page I've designed, book I've conceived, and lesson I've taught. Any categories are inevitably whimsical, but these made sense based on my experience.

PLANNING

- Am I part of the problem or the solution?
- Can this be done? Should it be done?
- Does this matter to others?
- How does this connect to what comes next?
- How much time do I have?
- How will X perceive this event, object, idea, feature, statement?
- Is this action consistent with my beliefs?
- Is this X sustainable?
- Is X consistent with what I have thought and/or done in the past?
- To whom is this important?
- What are my options?
- What are the guiding principles, values, assumptions?
- What are the necessary or ideal conditions?
- What biases, concerns, or questions will my audience have?
- What can I do to help people most effectively see, believe, or understand this?
- What do I already know?

- What do I think will happen?
- What do I want to walk out of this situation having accomplished, knowing, feeling, or believing?
- What do the people involved need?
- What do I want to have accomplished by X date?
- What do I expect to happen as a result of doing this?
- What do I need (resources) to do that?
- What does X want more than anything else?
- What effect do I want to create at first? By the end?
- What groups or individuals might acquire special (e.g., economic or political) power as a consequence of X (e.g., technological change)?
- What is the best tool for the job?
- What is the most effective way to communicate this idea/info?
- What is the question I am trying to answer?
- What is my purpose?
- What questions do I need to ask myself when I read X? Why?
- What questions must I ask to arrive at a given answer?
- What should I do after?
- What should I do before?
- What should I do during?
- What's first?
- What's last?
- What's next?
- Who asks the questions?
- Who can help me with this?
- Who is in charge?
- Who is my audience?
- Who is responsible for X?
- Who should be invited?

EVALUATING

- At what cost will this improvement come?
- Based on what evidence?
- Compared to what?
- For what purpose was it constructed/created/intended?
- How and why does this change?
- How did X happen?
- How did I arrive at X?
- How does it work?

- How does or will the environment/setting affect what happens?
- How is this organized?
- How much is enough?
- How would X be improved if I changed/added Y?
- Is this a difference (between A and B) that makes a difference?
- Of all the different information in this text, what is important to pay attention to?
- Of the different events, which are most important?
- So what?
- What are my strengths and weaknesses?
- What are the categories?
- What are the implications of this change?
- What are the qualities of an X?
- What changed?
- What do I need to know and be able to do?
- What does the user/reader/audience need to know and be able to do?
- What does X have to do with Y?
- What happened?
- What are the causes?
- What are the questions I am not asking?
- What is the source of my confusion/frustration?
- What started this? Why? How?
- What worked and what did not—and why?
- What would happen if I changed A to B?
- What would happen if I changed the sequence?
- What would happen if I took X out of the equation/story?
- Where am I now and how did I get here?
- Which factor(s) make the biggest difference?
- Who will benefit from it?
- Why did X change?
- Why do I need it?
- Why has it endured?
- Why is this important?
- Why is X behaving this way?

DESIGNING

- How can I adapt X to meet the needs of Y?
- How can I make this easier to use?

- How will this improve what I currently do?
- How would it change things if I . . . ?
- What are the criteria on which my work will be judged?
- What are the rules?
- What are the variables?
- What do I want this to do?
- What is the context?

REFLECTING

- How did I come up with that?
- How is this similar/different from the past or what was expected?
- How would this look to X?
- What are the origins of X?
- What do they want more than anything else?
- What do they want the most?
- What evidence can I provide?
- What if it were otherwise?
- What is "good enough"?
- What is being emphasized?
- What is my role?
- What is the end I am trying to achieve?
- What is the problem for which I think X is the solution?
- What matters most?
- What will create the most significant, lasting, or useful change?
- What will that accomplish?
- What will this cost me?
- What will this look like after X amount of time?
- What's related?
- Why am I doing this?
- Why do I/they think that?
- Why do I/they want to know this?
- Why do you think that?
- Why do I want to (be able to) do that?
- Why is this a good X (e.g., question)?

CLARIFYING

- How do I define that?
- How do I know?

- What are the questions I should ask after?
- What are the questions I should ask before I begin?
- What are the questions I should ask during?
- What does it look like?
- What does that mean?
- What does this remind me of?
- What is the source of this information?
- What would this sound like if it were translated into music or transformed into a pattern?

I end this chapter with a passage from Neil Postman's *Building a Bridge to the Eighteenth Century: How the Past Can Improve Our Future* (1999). In this book Postman offers five suggestions for developing "critical minds" in students, the first of which is to teach them "the art and science of asking questions":

> No one, I assume, would deny that all knowledge we have is a result of our asking questions; indeed, that question-asking is the most significant intellectual tool human beings have. Is it not curious, then, that the most significant intellectual skill available to human beings is not taught in school? (161)

Reporter's Notes

13

DESCRIPTION

Sometimes called "the five Ws"—who, what, where, when, why—these questions are the engines of both reading and writing. Each one is a powerful tool that identifies and establishes the essential information in any article, film, chapter, or story. Often students can clarify what they are reading by asking simply, "Which of the five Ws does this statement answer?" If you think of a history book, for example, you can quickly imagine that each sentence deals with a who (a historical figure), a when (dates and times), a where (place, region, location), a why (causes of an event), or the what (what occurred).

Reporter's Notes as presented here includes a few other questions that sometimes add useful information. The question "How?" ensures we learn, for example, about the method someone used to achieve some end (e.g., How did Hamlet's father die?). And the question "So what?" forces us to think deeper about a subject to determine its importance (The United States broke from England to become its own country—so what?). It is a blunt question, but one that cuts to the heart of the subject in a way no other can. The other important feature of the Reporter's Notes tool is the Most Important column on the right side. There are often many answers to the question "Who?" when we read or write. One character generally stands above the others, however, or one of the many places or objects is more important in the context of the text than any other. This far-right column challenges the reader to evaluate the text in order to determine which element is most important. Students can then write a brief note or discuss why they think this is the most important.

NOTES AND EXAMPLES

Example: *Kitchen God's Wife*

Students need help gathering the essential information when reading complex novels, especially those that incorporate historical information. Reporter's Notes help gather the essential information needed to understand what is going on in any text. Reporter's Notes get my students oriented as they begin a novel, giving them crucial questions to answer; they are, for example, reading to answer the question "Where is this taking place?" In

STANDARDS

- Reading
  - ☐ Analyze organizational patterns of information
  - ☐ Compare ideas, texts, or authors
  - ☐ Extend ideas
  - ☐ Generate relevant questions
  - ☐ Identify and analyze recurring themes
  - ☐ Prepare to read
- Writing
  - ☐ Establish a main or controlling idea
  - ☐ Integrate quotations and examples in written response
  - ☐ Prepare to write
  - ☐ Use sensory, concrete, or illustrative details to support claims
  - ☐ Use writing for a variety of purposes
- Speaking
  - ☐ Analyze devices used in others' speeches
  - ☐ Compare events or ideas
  - ☐ Organize information for desired effect on audience
  - ☐ Prepare and deliver multimedia presentations
  - ☐ Prepare to speak
- Listening
  - ☐ Improve note-taking skills
  - ☐ Organize information
  - ☐ Record information
- Viewing
  - ☐ Gather details and examples for subsequent analysis of text
  - ☐ Identify organization of information
- Test Preparation
  - ☐ Comprehend information
  - ☐ Organize ideas
  - ☐ Prioritize information
  - ☐ Remember information

SUBJECT AREAS

- English language arts
- Health
- Humanities
- Science
- Social studies

USES

- Ask useful questions
- Assess student performance
- Compare two or more items, aspects, or people
- Develop academic literacy
- Extend ideas beyond obvious
- Facilitate discussion
- Gather evidence to support claims
- Generate ideas
- Make connections
- Narrow or refine subject
- Observe patterns
- Organize information
- Prepare to read
- Prepare to write
- Respond to reading
- Support critical reading
- Synthesize ideas
- Take notes while reading

Reporter's Notes

Name Drew Shiller	Date
Topic	Period

Reporter's Notes helps you get the crucial information, not "just the facts, Ma'am," but the meaning of the facts, too. These are the questions any reporter asks when they write their article. These are the questions that good readers ask. Not all questions are always appropriate; you decide if it's okay to leave one or more blank, but be sure you can explain why that information is absent.

WHO (is involved or affected)	Most Important WHO
Pearl, Auntie Helen, Bao-bao (Roger), Phil (Pearl's husband), Cleo, Tessa, mother	Pearl—narrator – main character – her aunt that has died – has to deal with her mom
WHAT (happened)	**Most Important WHAT**
Phil and Pearl and their family had to travel to San Francisco from San Jose to attend Bao-bao's engagement party – attend Auntie Du's funeral.	Phil, Pearl, and family had to come up on the weekend to the funeral.
WHERE (did it or will it happen)	**Most Important WHERE**
· mother's store in Chinatown (San Francisco) · banquet room – funeral · her old room – saw her teenage years again	Chinatown – funeral takes place, her old home is, mother's shop is.
WHEN (did it or will it happen)	**Most Important WHEN**
. early to mid 90's after '89 earthquake	· when she goes to her mother's flower shop in Chinatown – sees all of the old store owner she used to know.
HOW (did they do it or did others respond)	**Most Important HOW**
· How grand auntie Du died – affected mother greatly, all relatives came into Chinatown for the funeral.	· How Phil isn't very sympathetic because it's the for him to relate to the Chinese culture – didn't understand.
WHY (did they do this, react this way)	**Most Important WHY**
· Pearl has a disease – never tells mother · all care about mother – need to be there for her · came to attend engagement party – funeral just happened to happen there for her.	Pearl didn't want to have extra stress on mother to have to worry about her.
SO WHAT? (Why is this event/info/idea important?)	**Most Important SO WHAT?**
· important that auntie Du died – sympathy to mother · important that Pearl saw her old heritage – experienced past	that Pearl and family came to S.F. for family that they care.

FIGURE 13.1 Drew Shiller's Reporter's Notes helped him establish the important details early on in Amy Tan's novel *The Kitchen God's Wife.*

order to teach students to use this tool, I had them help me fill in an example on the overhead, discussing the answers together. (See Figure 13.1.) In this way, the tool supports collaborative reading and whole-class use. When we discuss what the most important Who is, for example, we do so as a class, using the tool to focus and extend our discussion.

Later on, when they use this tool with infotexts and textbooks, the kids will know how it works and be able to use it independently to gather "Just the facts, Ma'am"—and then explain the meaning of them.

14 Sensory Notes

STANDARDS

- Reading
  - ☐ Compare ideas, texts, or authors
  - ☐ Extend ideas
  - ☐ Generate relevant questions
  - ☐ Identify and analyze recurring themes
  - ☐ Prepare to read
- Writing
  - ☐ Integrate quotations and examples in written response
  - ☐ Prepare to write
  - ☐ Use sensory, concrete, or illustrative details to support claims
- Language Study
  - ☐ Distinguish between denotative and connotative meaning
  - ☐ Examine and use different Greek and Latin roots of words
  - ☐ Know and use different parts of speech
  - ☐ Study the author's use of language
- Viewing
  - ☐ Assess different techniques or devices used
  - ☐ Gather details and examples for subsequent analysis of text
- Test Preparation
  - ☐ Comprehend information
  - ☐ Prioritize information

SUBJECT AREAS

- English language arts
- Health
- Humanities
- Science
- Social studies

USES

- Ask useful questions
- Assess student performance
- Compare two or more items, aspects, or people
- Extend ideas beyond obvious
- Facilitate discussion
- Gather evidence to support claims
- Generate ideas
- Make connections
- Narrow or refine subject
- Observe patterns
- Organize information
- Prepare to read
- Prepare to write
- Respond to reading
- Support critical reading
- Synthesize ideas
- Take notes while reading
- Visualize what is read

DESCRIPTION

Not all texts contain the rich sensory detail of literature or nonfiction. Such details allow readers to visualize what they read, to create a movie in their heads as they read. Yet not all readers are so naturally attentive to these details; as a consequence, they often cannot see and thus understand what they read. Sensory Notes guide the readers' attention, telling them what to look for as they read. Sensory Notes train their eyes to see, their ears to hear, their nose to smell. Whether it is imagining the scent of old London streets during Dickens' time, or the sound of bullets whisking through the air in World War One, this technique helps students read more carefully. As with Reporter's Notes, this technique asks readers to evaluate the different sensory information and determine which of all the sounds, for example, is most important. Then they must, in writing or through discussion, explain why they think it is so important. This provides one final benefit to the technique: it allows you to assess students' understanding of the text since you can see not only what they "hear" or "feel," but which element they think is most important. If they offer some unusual response to the question of "Which one is most important?" you can ask them how they arrived at their reading and, if necessary, help them revise their interpretation.

NOTES AND EXAMPLES

Example: "Pain for a Daughter"

While reading Amy Tan's novel *The Kitchen God's Wife*, my students read a variety of poems that complement the novel's themes. Our focus was on reading the novel, but it's not adequate to turn the kids loose with a poem if they are not able to read it successfully. Literary language is heavy with imagery and sensory details that authors use to help readers visualize what they read. Still, many students, especially those with reading difficulties, struggle to pick up such sensory details, as they often lack the skill of visualizing what they read. I asked kids to use Sensory Notes with Anne Sexton's poem "Pain for a Daughter" because the poem is rich in such details; it is also a difficult though accessible poem for kids. (See Figure 14.1.) Sensory Notes helped them get into the poem. (They also used Episodic Notes to help

Sensory Notes

Name cassie zakatchenko	Date 12/5
Topic "PAIN FOR A DAUGHTER"	Period 6°

Directions

Sensory Notes is a tool and technique designed to help you pay closer attention to details while you read. Effective readers use all their senses while they read. Use this sheet to take notes on what you see, hear, smell, feel—and think—as you read. Be specific and, if possible, write down the page numbers for future reference.

I SEE... 1. long-necked marchers and churners 2. a pony and a foal 3. the underside of the jaw swelling like an enormous grape 4. pus like milk on the barn floor 5. the horse stepping on the girl's foot 6. the girl's as she sits in the bathroom	**Most Important Image** (explain) ③ It's the first image put in my mind.
I HEAR... 1. pus as it hits the barn floor 2. horses neighing 3. the muffled cries of the girl 4. bubbling hydrogen peroxide	**Most Important Sound** (explain) ③ It helps to better express the pain the girl is experiencing, and triggers the emotional pain the mom feels
I FEEL... 1. blind with love 2. blind with loss 3. blind with pain ⇒ pain of the horses foot on my foot 4. angry 5. afraid 6. sympathy for the girl's mother 7. pus running down my hand 8. excruciating pain & sloshing blood 9. texture of towel in my mouth	**Most Important Sensation** (explain) ③ Most unbearable pain, author spends lots of time explaining it in detail
I SMELL... 1. pus 2. the hay filled barn 3. scent of horses 4. hydrogen peroxide	**Most Important Scent** (explain) ① This smell is probably the strongest and hardest to deal with, can't be ignored
I THINK... 1. of how hard it would be for her to overcome her fear 2. about what kind of emotions the mother might be going through 3. about the different types of pain as I read the poem	**Most Important Thought** (explain) ③ This helped me to understand the poem more clearly and helped me see the changes

FIGURE 14.1 This is the follow-up to Cassie's Episodic Notes for Anne Sexton's "Pain for a Daughter."

them determine the important moments in the poem and its organization.) They then had to identify what they felt was the most important aspect in each category. Then they explained why they thought that "the muffled cries of the girl," for example, is the most important detail. Students were then prepared to discuss or write about the poem, as Cassie's following paragraph shows. Cassie compared the mothers and daughters in both the poem and Tan's novel. I was able to quickly assess the quality of students' reading performance by surveying the room as they worked on their Sensory Notes. When you read something like the following response, you know the technique is working.

> Many parents find it difficult to accept that their children will grow up someday. They want that little girl who always cried for mom when she got hurt to stay the same forever. They wish that the little boy who ran to the door when dad came home would never change. But eventually kids have to get older and they do grow up. The poem "Pain for a Daughter" describes the struggles that both a mother and daughter go through in life. The daughter has to overcome her fear to help her horse get better. This girl who is "too squeamish to pull a thorn from the dog's paw," loved her horse so much that she was willing to do anything for it. In the same way, her mother wants the best for her and will do whatever she can to make it possible. In Amy Tan's *Kitchen God's Wife,* similar feelings are also felt by Winnie and her daughter Pearl. Winnie wanted to make the best life possible for Pearl, and she thought she accomplished a part of this by hiding her past from her daughter. She still treated Pearl like her little, young daughter. It was only when she looked in Pearl's "secret box" that Winnie realized her girl was really grown up. The same thing happens in the poem when the girl cries, "O my God, help me!" instead of running to her mother. Both moms "stand at the door" watching their daughters grow up.

Spreadsheet Notes

15

DESCRIPTION

Computers have given us many powerful new ways to think. These become more familiar all the time: the bullet, the database, and the spreadsheet. The Spreadsheet Notes tool is a loosely defined arrangement of rows and columns of any number, all of which are used to compare and organize information. In the examples that follow, you'll see spreadsheets designed to gather useful information about characters in a novel; key information and its importance in a history textbook; a comparison of three books as they relate to a given theme; and a comparison of a film and the novel from which it was made.

The tool is helpful as a means of visually organizing information with which a student must work. This visual organization gives students with special needs or those still learning English a helpful way to arrange their ideas and a useful way to check how they are doing. Moreover, teachers can move around the room, quickly assessing what (and how) students are doing; the visual content of the spreadsheet enables the teacher to see from some distance whether the student does or does not have the necessary information. Creating the categories (of rows and columns) also reinforces students' ability to evaluate the information and identify the proper categories into which things should be arranged. Students can use their notes to write a reflection on or participate in a class discussion during which they can explain what they did and why, and what they learned about the text they read.

NOTES AND EXAMPLES

Example One: The Need for Hope

Students in my sophomore English class had to read a book they chose on their own. In this case the student chose John Howard Griffin's *Black Like Me*. Meanwhile, we were reading Remarque's *All Quiet on the Western Front*. At semester's end, I wanted them to connect the novel we read, their own book, and their own lives. To do this I first had them generate the different needs common to all humans (see Figure 10.1). Then they needed to apply these different needs to the different books they read and the one we studied together. In Figure 15.1, the student makes remarkable connections across the three

STANDARDS

- Reading
  - ☐ Analyze organizational patterns of information
  - ☐ Compare ideas, texts, or authors
  - ☐ Extend ideas
  - ☐ Generate relevant questions
  - ☐ Identify and analyze recurring themes
  - ☐ Prepare to read
  - ☐ Synthesize information from multiple sources
- Writing
  - ☐ Integrate quotations and examples in written response
  - ☐ Organize information and ideas in logical, appropriate format
  - ☐ Prepare to write
  - ☐ Use sensory, concrete, or illustrative details to support claims
  - ☐ Use writing for a variety of purposes
- Speaking
  - ☐ Compare events or ideas
  - ☐ Organize information for desired effect on audience
- Language Study
  - ☐ Distinguish between denotative and connotative meaning
  - ☐ Examine and use different Greek and Latin roots of words
  - ☐ Know and use different parts of speech
- Listening
  - ☐ Improve note-taking skills
  - ☐ Organize information
  - ☐ Record information
- Viewing
  - ☐ Gather details and examples for subsequent analysis of text
- Test Preparation
  - ☐ Comprehend information
  - ☐ Organize ideas
  - ☐ Prioritize information
  - ☐ Remember information

SUBJECT AREAS

- English language arts
- Health
- Humanities
- Science
- Social studies

USES

- Ask useful questions
- Assess student performance
- Compare two or more items, aspects, or people
- Develop academic literacy
- Evaluate ideas
- Extend ideas beyond obvious
- Facilitate discussion
- Gather evidence to support claims
- Generate ideas
- Identify themes
- Make connections
- Narrow or refine subject
- Observe patterns
- Organize information
- Prepare to read
- Prepare to write
- Respond to reading
- Support critical reading
- Synthesize ideas
- Take notes while reading

The Need for Hope

PAUL BAUMER (*ALL QUIET*)	JOHN HOWARD GRIFFIN (FROM *BLACK LIKE ME*)	MYSELF
EXAMPLES/DETAILS • Paul needed to keep alive the hope that the war would end. • He needed to have hope that his friends would survive. • He needed to have hope that there was more food coming. • He needed to have hope that the man he stabbed would live. • He needed to have hope that Kat was still alive as he carried him to the infirmary.	EXAMPLES/DETAILS • John needed to have hope that the attitudes of white people would change. • He needed to have hope that the situation for black people would change. • He needed to have hope that someday all of the hate would go away. • He needed to have hope that one day blacks and whites would live peacefully.	EXAMPLES/DETAILS • I hope that I will do well on my final exams. • I hope that I get good grades. • I hope that I will go to college. • I hope that I will be successful when I grow up. • I hope that one day I will have kids.
RESPECT • Paul wanted Col. Himmel-stoss to respect him. • Paul wanted to be respected as a soldier. • Paul wanted his peers to respect him.	RESPECT • John wanted white people to respect black people. • John wanted white people to respect him.	RESPECT • I want everyone to respect me (e.g., my peers, adults, family, and teachers).
ACCEPTANCE • Paul wanted the acceptance of his peers. • Paul wanted to be accepted by the French girls.	ACCEPTANCE • John wanted to be accepted as a respectable person. • He wanted whites to accept black people as equals.	ACCEPTANCE • I want to be accepted by my peers. • I want to be accepted by my family.
SECURITY • Paul wanted to feel safe and secure whenever he fought. • Paul wanted to know his family was safe.	SECURITY • John wanted to feel secure "in his own skin." • He wanted to feel secure doing everyday things.	SECURITY • I want to feel secure going to school. • I want to feel secure doing everyday things.
FRIENDSHIP • Paul wanted all his friends to live so they could be friends forever.	FRIENDSHIP • He wanted to be friends with other blacks and for whites to be friends w/ blacks.	FRIENDSHIP • I want to keep the friends I have. • I want to make more friends.

FIGURE 15.1 Spreadsheet Notes helped this student organize and generate ideas across domains.

domains. Spreadsheet Notes are perfect for such thinking because they challenge students to think in categories and across domains, yet in parallel terms (i.e., unless you can get an example of respect for each of the three categories, forget it). When students finish, they are prepared to write a very well-organized, balanced essay exploring the concept of need as it applies to a range of characters as well as their own life.

Example Two: *Lord of the Flies* Film Comparison

A different spreadsheet formation allowed Ashley Arabian to compare two different film adaptations of William Golding's novel *Lord of the Flies*. (See Figure 15.2.) Her decision to put the point of comparison—mood, characters, music—in the middle helped her focus on what she needed to compare when she watched and, eventually, when she wrote. As Ashley's example shows, she was prepared to write a coherent comparison that made effective use of her notes to compare the two versions:

> There are more differences between the two adaptations of *Lord of the Flies* than just character differences. I found differences between settings, attitudes, dialogues, and physical appearance. The 1961 version seemed to be more general in terms of the characters' feelings. They didn't seem to elaborate on what was going through the boys' minds. The other version expressed their emotions better with music, expressions, and their dialogue. The way they spoke was more formal than the 1961 version. I suppose it was because they came from a military school instead of boarding school. This somewhat affected the mood of the movies. I like how the later version set it better with music and shots with the camera. Then again, the older version set a better view on the choirboys. When they entered the beach, they looked like a cult. I believe both movies portray the book very well, yet they are quite different from each other.

Example Three: Character Directory

Many novels have more characters than students can keep track of. Bharati Mukherjee's novel *Jasmine*, for example, has many characters, all of whom are distributed between three different countries and points in time; moreover, the main character adopts a total of six different names by the end of the book. Keeping track of these names and her relationship to the different people is a serious challenge. (See Figure 15.3.) I use the Character Directory whenever a novel has more characters than the student can safely remember. A novel like *Of Mice and Men* would not need this; Homer's *Odyssey* certainly does.

Example Four: Study for Tests

Students in my academic literacy class do not arrive in September with good organizational capacity. They do not have the categories other, more successful students have created in their minds, categories that help them read better and prepare for tests more effectively. This tool, in conjunction with the Summary Sheet, teaches them to sort the information they are studying into relevant categories they can more easily remember and better understand. In

Spreadsheet Notes (3-Column)

Name Ashley Arabian	Date
Topic Lord of the Flies	Period 5°

1961	AREA/POINT OF COMPARISON	1989
• Tribal drums, beating intense	• music	• Militaristic - violent whistle, sets a better mood.
• The choir boys had a grand entrance: book. not a very large intro.	• mood	• set better with scenery and music • much power given to Jack - called "Sir"
• Didn't give much power to Ralph		• Choirs singing sets a mood of living on nothing • Fire is set → choas breaks
• Shows pictures of crash, but mood isn't set as well of a chaotic crash.	• setting	• Shows children in choas after crash
• Showed like the book told found each other on island.	• arrival	• Boys arrived on island book; found eachother on island
• Accents seperated the boys	• Dialogue	• Students called "Sir" & kernal from military.
• No adults - like in book	• characters	• There was an adult on the island
• Jack was more jealous in the beginning	• attitudes	• Jack somewhat kinder • Alot of intensity between Piggy and Jack.
• No injuries on boys, just like the book. Jack was tall and strong	• appearance	• Ralph had a broken arm. Jack was skwirmy.

FIGURE 15.2 Spreadsheet Notes helped Ashley analyze the films and prepare to write a comparison of the different versions as they relate to Golding's novel *Lord of the Flies*.

Who's Who? The Character Directory

Title____________________ **Name** Kristin Landucci **Period** 4

Directions: When deciding which characters to include in the directory below, you must distinguish between major and minor characters. If you organize all the characters along a continuum of importance, some would be at one end (e.g., a zero: not important) while others would be at the other end (e.g., a ten: essential, or most important). Before adding a character's name to the directory, ask yourself whether they are important enough, and if so, why they are so important.

Character's Name	Relationship/Role	Location	Description/Notes
Jyoti (from *Jasmine*)	Main character; one of several names she has.	Hasnapur, India	Original name given to her by her grandmother; means "Light"
Jasmine	name given to her from Prakash	India	given by Prakash
Jane	another name for her	Iowa, USA	everyone in Iowa calles her Jane
Jazzy	name given by Lillian	Florida	called by Lillian Gorden
Jassy	name Wylie gave her	New York	called by Wylie Hayes.
Jase	name Taylor gave her	New York	called by Taylor
Dida	grandma	India	gave her name, told her to stay with mom.
Masterji	teacher	Hansbur India	beloved teacher; killed by K Lions.
Paterji	Father	Hansbur India	was widowed.
Pitaji	mother	India	killed by bull.
Prakash	husband	India	wants to move to USA
Sukkni Sukhwinder	husband killer	India	set music box - bomb
Lillian Gorden	women took her in	New York	took her in when homeless
Professorji	man fell in love w/	Hansbur India	loved Prakash: took Jasmine when in NY.
Bud	soon to be husband	Elsa county	old man wheelchair, own 1st bank of
Du	son	Elsa county	The son of Jasmine
Karin	Bud's divorced wife	Elsa county	jealous ex wife
Mother Ripplemeyer	Bud's mom	Elsa county	Bud's mom introduces Jane & Bud
Gene Lutz	Dead Friend	Elsa county	54 years 300 lbs - died from chocking
Darrel Lutz	Friend	Iowa - Elsa county	really religious - generous
Taylor Hayes	almost married	New York	married Wylie
Duff Hayes	girl took care of	New York	Jase is care giver of Duff.

FIGURE 15.3 Sample Character Directory

Spreadsheet Notes Name Spencer Parker Date December 12 Period 2

Topic/Chapter: Chapter 20-21			
Subject (Who or What)	**Where**	**When**	**Why (Important)**
Cosimo de Medici	Italy (Florence)	1389-1464	Major patron of the arts during the Renaissance
Christopher Columbus	Italian; went to Spain	1492	First landed in W. Indies, Dominican Republic; opened door for European exploration.
Hernando Cortés	Spain/Mexico	Early 1500s	Conquered Aztecs in Mexico
Montezuma II	Aztec King	Early 1500s	King of the Aztecs
Mestizo	Mexico		Person of mixed euro/Indian heritage; considered lowest in the social pyramid.
Encemienda	Americas	1500s	System of labor, where Spanish landlords use local people as laborers.
New France	N. America	Early 1600s	French colony in New World
Jamestown	Virginia	1607	First British colony in America

FIGURE 15.4 Tools like this one, created by Spencer, benefit everyone, but especially those with learning difficulties, by helping them focus on what they need to find and understand.

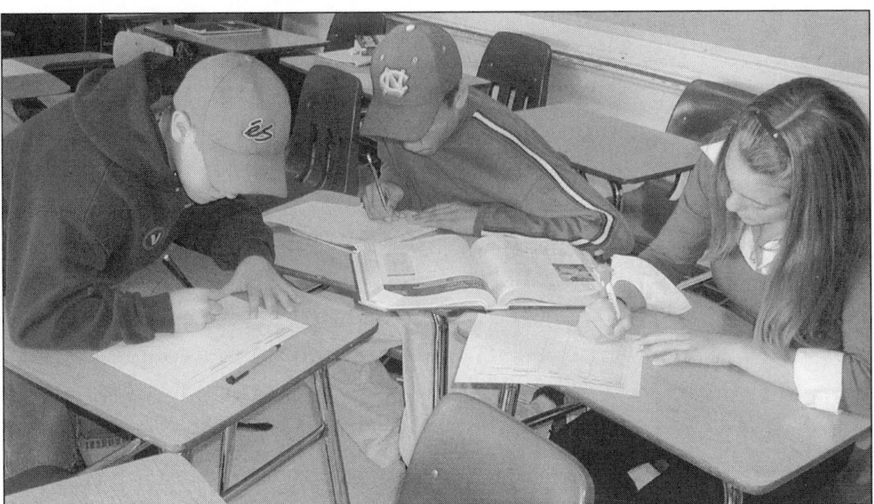

FIGURE 15.5 Omar, Jesse, and Jessica work to complete their Spreadsheet Notes as they prepare for an upcoming exam in their history class.

my academic literacy class, we take time on Monday to preread their history books and fill in the Subject column with the bold words, title words, and other details that seem likely to be included on the quizzes and exams to come. (See Figures 15.4 and 15.5.) The sheet also forces them to make connections and process the information differently than if they are just taking regular notes. It is important to note that this Spreadsheet Notes technique should never replace more complete note-taking using tools such as Q Notes. Spreadsheet Notes as described in this example are designed to prepare students for tests.

16 Story Notes

STANDARDS

- Reading
  - ☐ Analyze organizational patterns of information
  - ☐ Extend ideas
  - ☐ Generate relevant questions
  - ☐ Identify and analyze recurring themes
  - ☐ Prepare to read
- Writing
  - ☐ Organize information and ideas in logical, appropriate format
  - ☐ Prepare to write
  - ☐ Use sensory, concrete, or illustrative details to support claims
- Speaking
  - ☐ Analyze devices used in others' speeches
  - ☐ Compare events or ideas
  - ☐ Organize information for desired effect on audience
  - ☐ Prepare and deliver multimedia presentations
  - ☐ Prepare to speak
- Language Study
  - ☐ Distinguish between denotative and connotative meaning
  - ☐ Study author's style and use of language
- Listening
  - ☐ Improve note-taking skills
  - ☐ Organize information
  - ☐ Record information
- Viewing
  - ☐ Assess different techniques or devices used
  - ☐ Gather details and examples for subsequent analysis of text
  - ☐ Identify organization of information
- Test Preparation
  - ☐ Comprehend information
  - ☐ Organize ideas
  - ☐ Prioritize information
  - ☐ Remember information

SUBJECT AREAS

- English language arts
- Health
- Humanities
- Social studies

USES

- Ask useful questions
- Assess student performance
- Compare two or more items, aspects, or people
- Develop academic literacy
- Extend ideas beyond obvious
- Facilitate discussion
- Gather evidence to support claims
- Generate ideas
- Identify themes
- Make connections
- Observe patterns
- Organize information
- Prepare to read
- Prepare to write
- Respond to reading
- Support critical reading
- Synthesize ideas
- Take notes while reading
- Visualize what is read

DESCRIPTION

Narratives follow patterns (Bell 1997); they have only a few design structures, but one is most commonly used. The Story Notes tool directs students' attention to these different elements by giving them spaces to fill in and places to synthesize their understanding of the text. There are three versions of the tool; which one you choose depends on the needs of the reader. The third option, which is really a Visual Explanation, offers a more visual description of a story. (See Figures 16.2 and 16.3.) The Story Notes tool that resembles a house (see Figure 16.1) introduces or reinforces the standard literary terms while giving students a visual organization of a story's shape. Questions near the bottom ask students to evaluate and explain the importance of different phases in the narrative. Readers can make final observations about the text in the space at the very bottom.

These tools can also be used for writing or prereading. Giving students the list of names for a book and asking them to make up a story using the names prepares them to read a story by drawing them in through their imagination. Using the same technique to help them think through a story they themselves are writing allows them to check whether they have the necessary elements of a good story. The Visual Explanation offers a variation on these, one that invites the readers to explain what they are describing in their Story Notes. Teachers should look for opportunities to study different directions in students' narrative designs, asking, for example, what would happen if the event at the climax did not occur or were different. Would it change the course of the story, and if so, how? And what if we used the tool to describe the events in a phase of our own life? What would such a diagram look like?

Finally, Story Notes remind us that stories are built (Bell 1997), that a text is something you make, something that abides by a certain design in order to reach a specific end.

NOTES AND EXAMPLES

Example One: *Othello*

Teaching *Othello* was a new experience for me, one I wanted to succeed at with my freshmen, many of whom had never read Shakespeare. We used Story Notes to describe the action but also to study the narrative design

Cameron Duncan
4/16 5°

Story Notes

1. **Exposition:** Background information that establishes the setting and describes the situation in which the main character finds themselves.
2. **Rising action:** Characters face or try to solve a problem. This results in conflicts within themselves or with others; these conflicts grow more intense and complicated as the story unfolds.
3. **Climax:** Eventually the story reaches a crucial moment when the character must act.
4. **Falling action:** Sometimes called the denouement, this part of the story explores the consequences of the climactic decision. The reader feels the tension in the story begin to ease up.
5. **Resolution:** The story's central problem is finally solved, leaving the reader with a sense of completion, though the main character may not feel the same way.

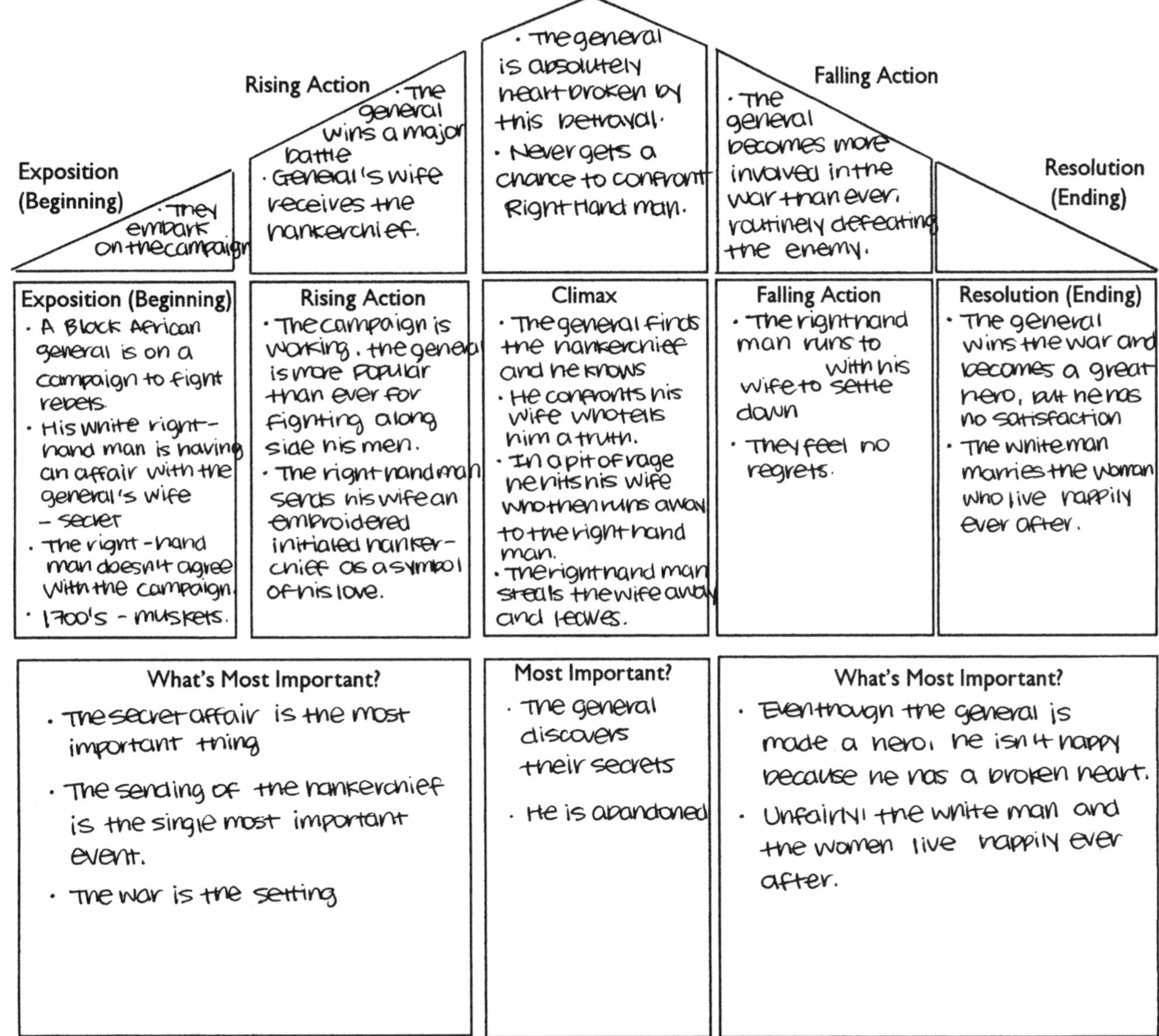

Climax
- The general is absolutely heart-broken by this betrayal.
- Never gets a chance to confront Right Hand man.

Rising Action
- The general wins a major battle
- General's wife receives the hankerchief.

Exposition (Beginning)
- They embark on the campaign

Falling Action
- The general becomes more involved in the war than ever, routinely defeating the enemy.

Resolution (Ending)

Exposition (Beginning)	Rising Action	Climax	Falling Action	Resolution (Ending)
• A Black African general is on a campaign to fight rebels. • His white right-hand man is having an affair with the general's wife – secret • The right-hand man doesn't agree with the campaign. • 1700's – muskets.	• The campaign is working. the general is more popular than ever for fighting along side his men. • The right hand man sends his wife an embroidered initialed hanker-chief as a symbol of his love.	• The general finds the hankerchief and he knows • He confronts his wife who tells him a truth. • In a pit of rage he hits his wife who then runs away to the right hand man. • The right hand man steals the wife away and leaves.	• The right hand man runs to with his wife to settle down • They feel no regrets.	• The general wins the war and becomes a great hero, but he has no satisfaction • The white man marries the woman who live happily ever after.

What's Most Important?	Most Important?	What's Most Important?
• The secret affair is the most important thing • The sending of the hankerchief is the single most important event. • The war is the setting	• The general discovers their secrets • He is abandoned	• Even though the general is made a hero, he isn't happy because he has a broken heart. • Unfairly, the white man and the women live happily ever after.

Observations: Possible themes, important characters, notes on the author's style
- Deceit
- What's important

FIGURE 16.1 Sample Story Notes

of the story. Shakespeare's plays are ideal for this method, as they perfectly conform to the five parts of a story (i.e., each of his five acts correspond to the five story parts—exposition, rising action, climax, falling action, and resolution). The visual format reinforces what is happening in the play at a given time. I was not, however, content with simply describing what happened; thus I asked students to evaluate the importance of different phases of the story. Requiring them also to bullet their ideas adds a level of clarity and further organization. The space at the bottom supports a range of uses. In this case we used it only to identify themes the kids wanted to explore for a possible essay. Cameron was particularly interested in deceit, clearly a relevant idea throughout the play. (See Figure 16.1.) Story Notes worked just as well to support close reading as it did to support collaborative discussions or whole-class conversations about what, for example, the climax of the story was and why we thought that.

Example Two: *Romeo and Juliet*

While the example in Figure 16.2 is better described as a Visual Explanation, it fits well in this area and shows how you could adapt the Story Notes idea to suit other purposes. Students reading *Romeo and Juliet* had to examine the crucial decisions throughout the play. To prepare them for this, I had them do something similar based on events in their own lives. (See Figures 25.7 and 25.8.) Beginning with the more familiar, concrete details of their own lives prepared them for working with the more elusive, abstract aspects of Shakespeare.

Example Three: *Othello*

This is another Visual Explanation, but one, like the previous example, that shows a different way to chart the progress of a story's plot. My directions were simple and open-ended (intentionally so): "Find a way to visually explain what happens in the first three acts of *Othello*." This group of advanced freshmen came up with the idea of representing the play's action as a stock exchange in which market forces drive the value of one stock (read: character) up or down depending on certain variables. They came up with the innovative way of representing certain events, such as depicting a marriage as a corporate merger and death as the equivalent of bankruptcy. Their approach still achieved the same objective—that is, to explain how the story is designed—as the other variations, yet it showed a different way to describe a story. (See Figure 16.3.)

Example Four: *The Odyssey*

Students preparing to read Homer's *Odyssey* got warmed up by creating their own version of the story before they knew anything about it. I gave them a list of character names and told them to use the Story Notes page to guide their creation of the story and its elements. (See Figure 16.4.) They then used this tool to help them retell their version of Homer's epic. Such playful yet productive prereading enables readers to enter the real story with greater confidence and more comfort; their own predictions help them read more effectively as they can compare what they thought the story was about to what it really is about, or who they thought this guy named Odysseus was versus who he really is.

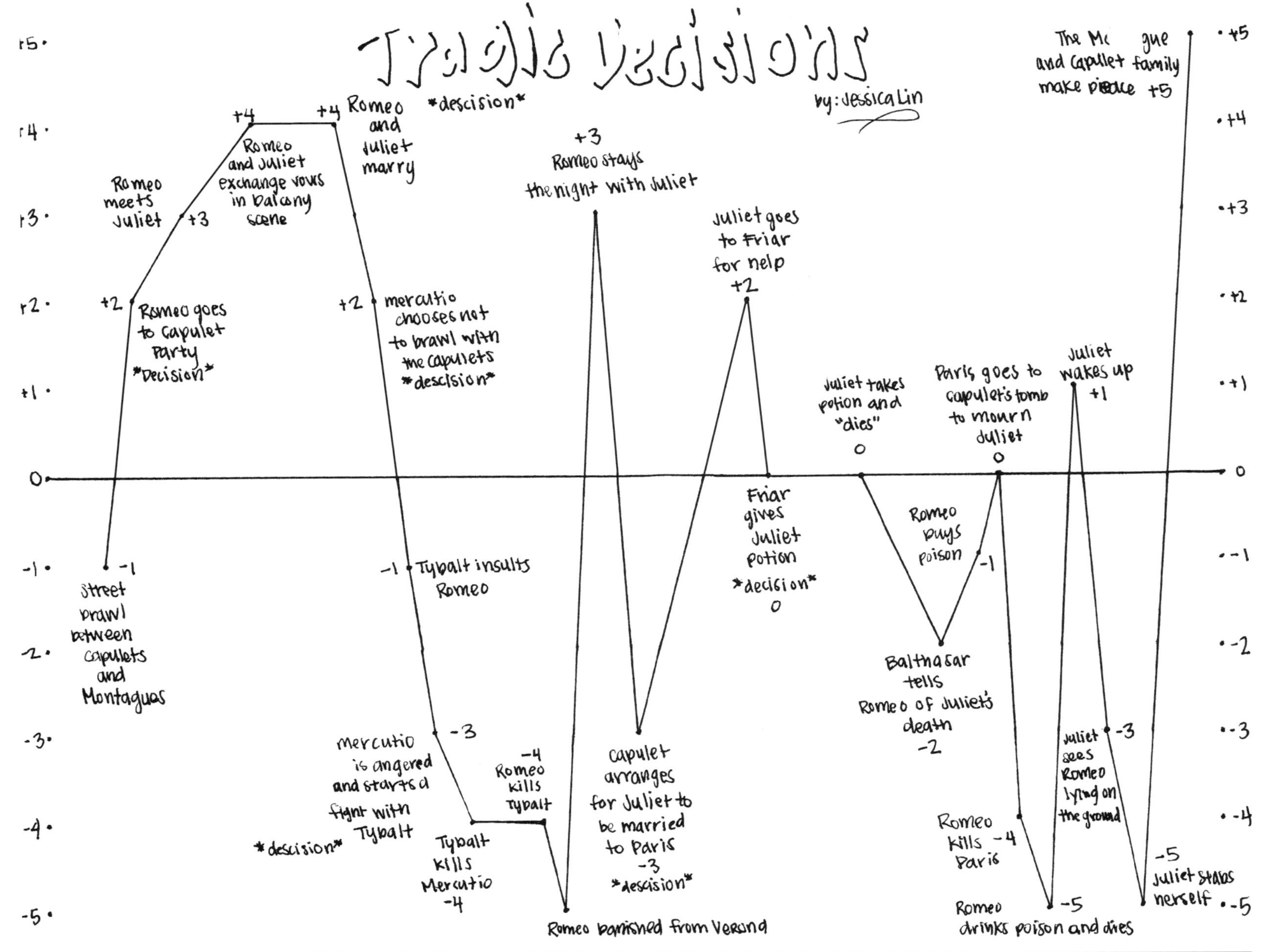

FIGURE 16.2 Jessica Gee's diagram charts the ups and downs of *Romeo and Juliet.*

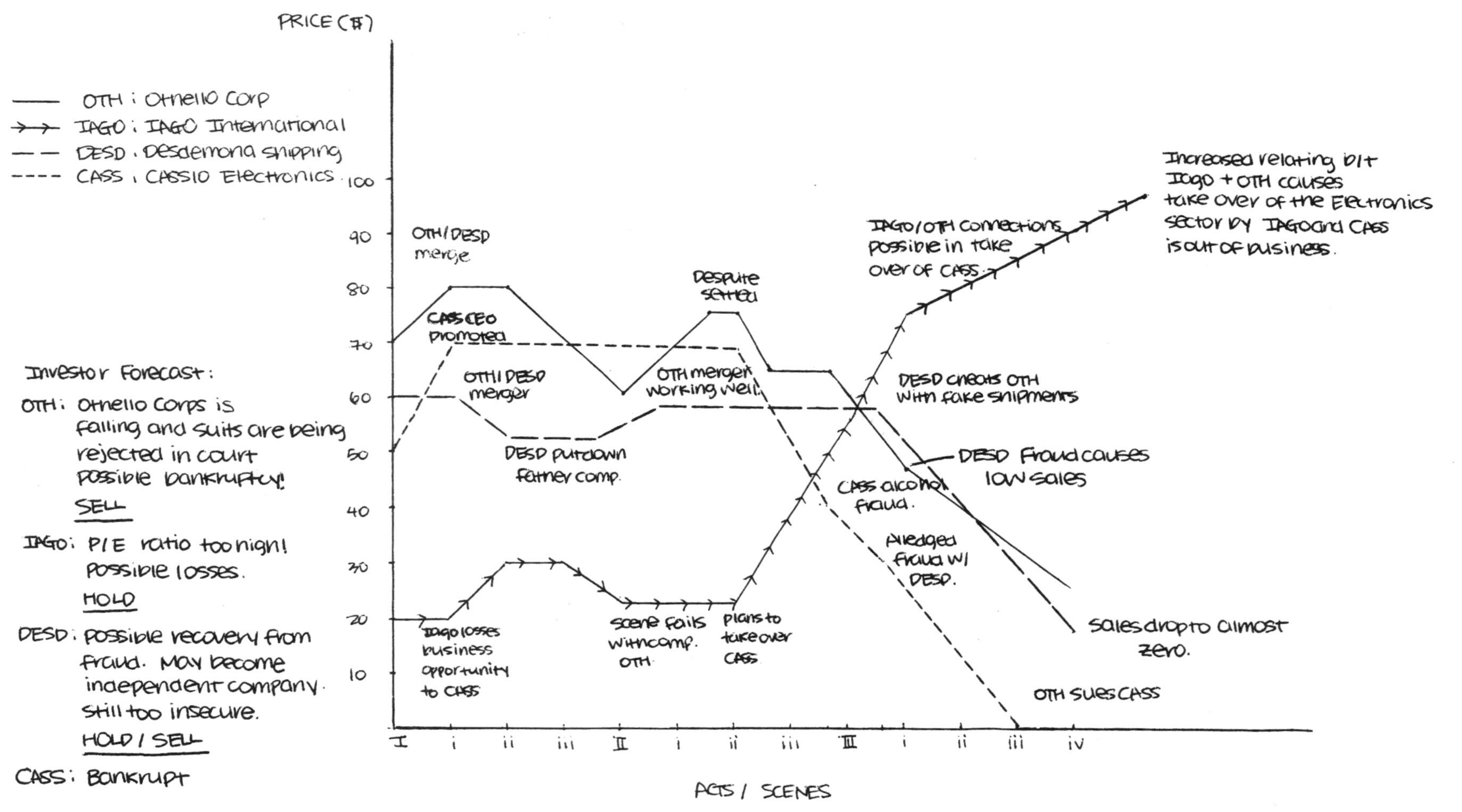

FIGURE 16.3 Sample visual Story Notes of a story's action using the metaphor of the New York Stock Exchange

Story Notes

Name

Date

Topic

Period

Main Characters (Tip: Before listing them, determine what makes someone a "main character."

Setting (Tip: Setting includes not just time, but place and atmosphere)

Bootcamp – modern time
– california desert, in middle of nowhere
– tense & extremely hot!, summer

Primary Conflicts/Central Problems

Odysseus is sent off to bootcamp by stepfather, Zeus, and his mentor (his counsler). Leaving behind his best friend, girl friend, and dog, Odysseus longs for home.

List the main events in the story (Tip: Before listing them, determine the criteria for a "main event.")

- Odysseus heads to bootcamp
- Fight between Odysseus' soldiers & The Laestrygonians & The Lotus Eaters.
- Penelope gets hit on by suitor.
- Odysseus & buds get tempted by nurses (sirens)
- Penelope is pregnant & no one knows but Odysseus
- Tries to escape with Poseidon
- Circe tries to attack Penelope.

Climax

Odysseus and Poseidon escape Bootcamp and almost captured by "Cyclopes"

Resolution

escapes, goes to real father's home & marries Penelope & have son.

Observations/Conclusions (Tip: Consider important themes, surprises, and connections to your life, other books, or classes.)

FIGURE 16.4 Students used this blank Story Notes sheet to create a story using the names from the *Odyssey*. They were preparing to read the epic; this helped them get ready and have some fun while they thought about how stories worked.

17 Summary Notes

STANDARDS

- Reading
  - ☐ Compare ideas, texts, or authors
  - ☐ Evaluate the arguments presented in a text
  - ☐ Generate relevant questions
  - ☐ Identify and analyze recurring themes
  - ☐ Prepare to read
  - ☐ Synthesize information from multiple sources
- Writing
  - ☐ Establish a main or controlling idea
  - ☐ Integrate quotations and examples in written response
  - ☐ Prepare to write
  - ☐ Use sensory, concrete, or illustrative details to support claims
  - ☐ Use writing for a variety of purposes
- Listening
  - ☐ Improve note-taking skills
- Viewing
  - ☐ Assess different techniques or devices used
  - ☐ Gather details and examples for subsequent analysis of text
  - ☐ Identify organization of information
- Test Preparation
  - ☐ Comprehend information
  - ☐ Organize ideas
  - ☐ Prioritize information
  - ☐ Remember information

SUBJECT AREAS

- English language arts
- Health
- Humanities
- Mathematics
- Science
- Social studies

USES

- Ask useful questions
- Assess student performance
- Develop academic literacy
- Evaluate ideas
- Gather evidence to support claims
- Identify themes
- Make connections
- Narrow or refine subject
- Organize information
- Prepare to write
- Respond to reading
- Support critical reading
- Synthesize ideas
- Take notes while reading

DESCRIPTION

Being able to summarize information, whether from a lecture or a printed text, is an important but sometimes difficult skill. Summaries have their own governing conventions, most of which dictate what they should include. Summarizing information, especially if done from multiple sources, requires students to evaluate all contents for their importance, measuring what they read against the criteria for importance or their stated purpose. This tool is designed to develop readers' capacities to read in this way. It is not a tool students need to use repeatedly; instead they should use it as long as they are learning to summarize. Once they have learned, they can graduate to binder paper from that point on. The tool develops their ability to summarize as well as the academic language they need to write their summaries. The use of certain prompts moves students toward independent practice.

The tool follows the reading process, breaking the tasks down into three phases: before, during, and after. The tool also develops students' academic vocabulary by suggesting appropriate verbs and modeling effective sentence structures that they need to master. As students write their notes down, they should provide an additional level of ranking and organization by using bullets and an informal outline format to visually distinguish between different ideas.

NOTES AND EXAMPLES

Example One: Gestures Article

Students in my academic literacy classes read a short article about gestures as they relate to public speaking. I gave them a sample by Jackie Ardon, a former student (see the Summary Notes form in the Appendix); this helped them see what theirs should look like. However, some were initially confused by the assignment, thinking that it was Jackie's example they were supposed to read and summarize. While they worked on this, I circulated and checked for comprehension of the article and proper use of the Summary Notes tool and techniques. (See Figure 17.1 for an example.)

Summary Notes

Name	Date
Topic	Class/Period

BEFORE
1. Determine your purpose.
2. Preview the document.
3. Prepare to take notes.

DURING

4. Take notes to help you answer these questions:
   - Who is involved?
   - What events, ideas, or people does the author emphasize?
   - What are the causes?
   - What are the consequences or implications?
5. Establish criteria to determine what is important enough to include in the summary.
6. Evaluate information as you read to determine if it meets your criteria for importance.

AFTER

7. Write your summary, which should:
   - identify the title, author, and topic in the first sentence
   - state the main idea in the second sentence
   - be shorter than the original article
   - begin with a sentence that states the topic (see sample)
   - include a second sentence that states the author's main idea
   - include 3-5 sentences in which you explain---*in your own words*---the author's point of view
   - include one or two interesting quotations or details
   - not alter the author's meaning
   - organize the ideas in the order in which they appear in the article
   - use transitions such as "According to" + the author's name to show that you are summarizing someone else's ideas
   - include enough information so that someone who has not read the article will understand the ideas

Sample verbs: The author :
- argues
- asserts
- concludes
- considers
- discusses
- emphasize
- examines
- explores
- focuses on
- implies
- mentions
- notes
- points out
- says
- states
- suggests

Use of Gestures:
- Body language, use of hands and arms
- Size, weight, shape, direction, location.
- Show audience how important your point is.
  - Comparison + contrast
    - both hands at same time show similarities
      move opposite to show differences
    - Helps audience understand message

The Importance of Rehearsal
- Deliberate and precise, look natural
- Rehearse in front of mirror

Presenting the talk
- while speaking, relax
  - Nervous
    - controlled body movement
    - showing object, center your audience attention on it.
    - But maintaine eye on audience

By Learning how to use gestures & facial expressions you emphasize parts of your speech, you are showing the audience what you mean as well as telling them. Each gesture should be large enough to be seen by everyone. But you shouldn't exaggerate. Eventhough you are familiar with using gestures, you should practice using them before an audience. When you are talking, you should be relaxed and calm. Your gestures should come natural!

FIGURE 17.1 Sample Summary Notes about an article on public speaking

18 Summary Sheet

STANDARDS

- Reading
  - ☐ Compare ideas, texts, or authors
  - ☐ Generate relevant questions
  - ☐ Identify and analyze recurring themes
  - ☐ Prepare to read
  - ☐ Synthesize information from multiple sources
- Writing
  - ☐ Integrate quotations and examples in written response
  - ☐ Organize information and ideas in logical, appropriate format
  - ☐ Prepare to write
  - ☐ Use sensory, concrete, or illustrative details to support claims
  - ☐ Use writing for a variety of purposes
- Language Study
  - ☐ Examine and use different Greek and Latin roots of words
  - ☐ Know and use different parts of speech
- Listening
  - ☐ Improve note-taking skills
  - ☐ Organize information
- Viewing
  - ☐ Assess different techniques or devices used
  - ☐ Gather details and examples for subsequent analysis of text
  - ☐ Identify organization of information
- Test Preparation
  - ☐ Comprehend information
  - ☐ Organize ideas
  - ☐ Prioritize information
  - ☐ Remember information

SUBJECT AREAS

- English language arts
- Health
- Humanities
- Mathematics
- Science
- Social studies

USES

- Ask useful questions
- Assess student performance
- Compare two or more items, aspects, or people
- Develop academic literacy
- Evaluate ideas
- Extend ideas beyond obvious
- Facilitate discussion
- Gather evidence to support claims
- Generate ideas
- Identify themes
- Make connections
- Narrow or refine subject
- Observe patterns
- Organize information
- Prepare to read
- Prepare to write
- Respond to reading
- Support critical reading
- Synthesize ideas
- Take notes while reading
- Visualize what is read

DESCRIPTION

This tool helps students identify essential categories and provides a space into which they can organize that information. It develops students' ability to arrange information into a useful format so they can prepare for tests. The tool will no doubt support other uses. In its original use, however, students might go through a history chapter, for example, and organize the main ideas into nine different categories (e.g., religion, economy/trade, art, military, and so on). The Quick Picks column allows students to make a list of, for example, essential vocabulary words or names of people and places they would be expected to know. The space at the top asks students to write a sentence that ties it all together: what, in a sentence, was the Renaissance all about? Of course it's silly to pretend you can do this, but the act of trying begins a process of synthesizing information and provides an opportunity for productive discussion in class. If the students create one Summary Sheet for each unit, they will have by semester's end a perfect set of study tools to prepare them for their final exam. In college one professor allowed us to bring in a 4-by-6-inch index card with as many notes as we could pack on it. By the time I took the final I never looked at the index card I had spent so long creating. I didn't need to: I'd learned the information already in the process of making the card.

NOTES AND EXAMPLES

Example One: Modern World History

Many of my students find tests difficult. They struggle to organize what they read into useful notes that can help them prepare for the quizzes and exams. To help them, I adapted the Summary Sheet tool introduced in Adam Robinson's *What Smart Students Know* (1993). (See Figures 18.1 and 18.2.) We did this together for a period of time until students demonstrated initial mastery; then it was up to them to create one or not. I put a blank version of the same page on the overhead so I could model how I used it as we went. I made a point of insisting that they organize their page into the same nine categories arranged in the same sequence so they could more easily visualize the page. Thus we would begin by asking, "What category is in the upper right-hand corner?" I also insisted that they bullet their information for further visual organization of separate ideas.

Summary Sheet

Name ______________________ Unit/Subject ______________________

Period ______________ Date ______________ Class ______________

QUICK PICKS names • dates • words	OVERVIEW: Summarize the topic or chapter in one sentence.		
	Religions	**Political Systems**	**Leaders (Political/Religious)**
Islam	• ISLAM (submission) Allah/Mohammed. *Text:* Koran; Type: monotheistic. Arabia. *5 Pillars:* Faith, prayer (×5), fasting, alms (charity) to poor, and hajj (Mecca). • CHRISTIANITY God/Jesus. *Text:* Bible (New Testament) Type: monotheistic. Sects: Anglican, Catholic, Protestant, Lutheran, Calvinist. • BUDDHISM Buddha. 4 Noble Truths. India. • JUDAISM God/Moses. *Book:* Old Testament (Torah/Talmud); Type: monotheistic. 10 Commandments. • HINDUISM Polytheistic: Vishnu and Krishna. *Book:* Vedas. Caste System: 1. Brahmin (preists/scholars); 2. Kshatrias (warriors/rulers); 3. Vaisyas (merchants/farmers); 4. Sudras (laborers); 5. Pariah/Harijans (outcasts, aka Untouchables). • ATHEISM: Belief that there is no god.	• ANARCHY Definition: Example: • MONARCHY (Autocracy) Definition: Example: • OLIGARCHY (Aristocracy) Definition: Example: • PLUTOCRACY Definition: Example: • MERITOCRACY Definition: Example: • DEMOCRACY Definition: Example:	
Buddhism			
Hinduism			
Judaism			
Confucianism			
Atheism			
Christianity			
• Calvinism			
• Catholicism			
• Anglicanism			
• Protestantism			
• Lutheranism			

FIGURE 18.1 I gave students in my ACCESS classes this sample and provided three categories. They got only the suggested *religions* for their first category and had to fill in the rest.

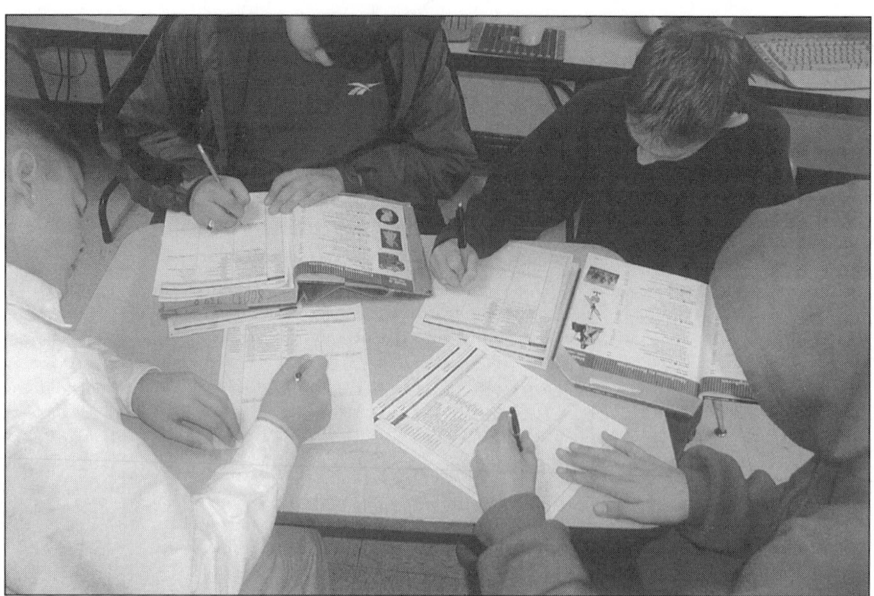

FIGURE 18.2 Here a group of freshman boys huddles up for a cram session prior to a history exam; they use the Summary Sheet to evaluate and organize what is most important in each chapter.

This unit was on Mayan civilization. In the left column, called "Quick Picks," students can list names of people or places that do not fit into the categories but which they must remember. This sheet should be revised over time so that by the final exam, students can crunch everything onto one page. They then use this, once it is complete, to quiz themselves for the upcoming test.

Synthesis Notes 19

DESCRIPTION

Synthesis Notes ask the reader to bring together all the different pieces of information about a narrative text and evaluate the importance of these details. This tool directs students' attention to those aspects of a narrative that matter most. Additional prompts are provided in parentheses to help the novice better understand what she is supposed to say. Encourage students to use bullets to organize their entries so they can better distinguish between them. Finally, of the many different aspects of each category, readers must learn to weed through the different pieces and determine what is most important. While students learn to use Synthesis Notes, you should take time to help them create a continuum of importance they can use to determine which character, for example, is most important and why. Part of that process might include questions they could ask to determine importance. The tool could then be used for writing or subsequent group or class discussion about the text. During such a discussion, students should be asked to compare their "Most Important Aspects" to see if they agree; either way, they should discuss with their groups or the class why they thought something or someone was so important.

NOTES AND EXAMPLES

Example One: *Othello*

Students reading *Othello* need help understanding the story and its many elements. I give them the Synthesis Notes tool and have them work together to complete it through collaborative discussion. (See Figure 19.1.) This allows them to piece together their understanding of *Othello* (or any other story they might be reading). I ask them to use bullets to help organize their ideas. I also ask them to evaluate the different pieces of information and determine their importance; thus they must decide who, for example, is the most important character and why. Such a tool provides me a means of assessing their comprehension of the story; it also supports them as writers and participants in a class discussion. In some instances there is nothing to discuss; style, for example, is not always present, or may not be something students are prepared to discuss. I use the tool to facilitate whatever we are ready to discuss or study in greater depth.

STANDARDS

- Reading
  - ☐ Analyze organizational patterns of information
  - ☐ Compare ideas, texts, or authors
  - ☐ Evaluate the arguments presented in a text
  - ☐ Extend ideas
  - ☐ Generate relevant questions
  - ☐ Identify and analyze recurring themes
  - ☐ Prepare to read
  - ☐ Synthesize information from multiple sources
- Writing
  - ☐ Integrate quotations and examples in written response
  - ☐ Organize information and ideas in logical, appropriate format
  - ☐ Prepare to write
  - ☐ Use sensory, concrete, or illustrative details to support claims
- Language Study
  - ☐ Distinguish between denotative and connotative meaning
  - ☐ Study author's style and word choice
  - ☐ Know and use different parts of speech
- Viewing
  - ☐ Assess different techniques or devices used
  - ☐ Gather details and examples for subsequent analysis of text
  - ☐ Identify organization of information
- Test Preparation
  - ☐ Comprehend information
  - ☐ Organize ideas
  - ☐ Prioritize information
  - ☐ Remember information

SUBJECT AREAS

- English language arts
- Humanities
- Social studies

USES

- Ask useful questions
- Assess student performance
- Compare two or more items, aspects, or people
- Develop academic literacy
- Evaluate ideas
- Extend ideas beyond obvious
- Facilitate discussion
- Gather evidence to support claims
- Generate ideas
- Identify themes
- Make connections
- Narrow or refine subject
- Observe patterns
- Organize information
- Prepare to read
- Prepare to write
- Respond to reading
- Support critical reading
- Synthesize ideas
- Take notes while reading

Synthesis Notes

Directions: Use this page to gather and organize the crucial information about the story. Use the right hand column to identify one aspect or character that seems vital to the story. You might determine what is most crucial by asking, "Which of all these (e.g., characters) makes the biggest difference in the story?" Some sections *might* be empty when you finish.

Story Title (and possible meanings) The Tragedy of Othello → sad (death, misfortune) The Moor of Venice → (different, dark, unaccepted) → (many passages, alleys, water)	**Most Important Aspect (Explain)** Tragedy – tells you what type of story it is & you can guess there will be deaths & misfortunes.
Characters (name, description, roles) Iago: plotting, jealous, angry, sneaky, sidekick, bad guy Othello: main character, self-confident, proud, respected Desdemona: Othello's wife, loves & respects him, wishes to go with Othello to Cyprus. Brabantio: Father of Desdemona, doesn't accept Othello, rich senator	**Most Important Aspect (Explain)** Iago: Puts the story together, introduces feelings of hate, deception, and secrecy.
Setting (where, when, atmosphere) • dark, murky, tense • takes place at night • medieval times • Venice – secret, shy, waterways, alleys.	**Most Important Aspect (Explain)** The setting is mainly dark & murky and gives a bad, tense vibe that creates fear.
Themes (idea(s) central to the story; include examples) • secrecy (Othello & Desdemona's marriage) (Iago's 2-faceness) (Cassio planning on stealing Desdemona) • power (Iago wants Cassio's position) (Othello has power over Desdemona) (Brabantio tries to control Desdemona's life)	**Most Important Aspect (Explain)** Secrecy is important because it helps run the story. If everyone told each other their secrets, the story would fall apart.
Plot (what happens) • Iago tells Roderigo he hates Othello. • Roderigo & Iago tell Brabantio of Desdemona's marriage. • Othello & Desdemona defend their marriage. • Iago tells Roderigo to steal Desdemona.	**Most Important Aspect (Explain)** Iago tells Brabantio about Desdemona's marriage. This sets the story and creates strong emotions.
Style (use of language, imagery, symbolism, dialogue) • language: accented, + raspy voices, exact words from book • imagery: dark, haunting, candlelit • symbolism: Iago with chessboard, Brabantio joins Othello & Desdemona hands, then steps away. • Dialouge: hushed, secretive, compelling	**Most Important Aspect (Explain)** Imagery plays a big role in Othello because everything is so dark and secretive. It sets a very mounting and chilling mood.
Point of View (tense, reliability, focus, narrator, in time) • sometimes misleading because can't be everywhere at once can skip some important parts & leave us to our imagination • captures all events but misses some less important, but significant moments.	**Most Important Aspect (Explain)** can be misleading – this sets the secretive mood and makes us wonder.
Design (linear, episodic; use of special form---e.g., letter, journal) • highlights special events • hops around catching strong emotions • Follows Iago more than Othello to see what trouble he is stirring up	**Most Important Aspect (Explain)** Because Iago is heard of more than Othello, we can see trouble being formed, and this keeps us in suspense.
Tone (what the story sounds like) • mystical (medieval, Shakespearian language) • creepy (dark, waterways) • secretive (tells you enough to get interested but no more)	**Most Important Aspect (Explain)** Because it is creepy, you focus on it and feel suspense because you have an idea of what's happening, but not completely.

FIGURE 19.1 Sample Synthesis Notes for *Othello*

T Notes

20

DESCRIPTION

The T Notes sheet is a very adaptable tool, one that can be used to compare or extend ideas. It provides students with a space at the bottom of the page to bring it all together, identifying patterns or important observations. While there are no prompts on this tool to develop students' comparative language, this tool provides an ideal context in which to teach students the language of comparison. If they organize their notes to this end, they can pair up contrasting examples for a parallel structure when they write. The tool is organizational but also generative: if you can identify one example on the left side, for instance, this helps you create its partner on the other side. These side-by-side notes then prepare students to write a very balanced, structured paragraph or paper in which their ideas line up nicely to create a coherent piece of writing.

NOTES AND EXAMPLES

Example One: The Reading Process

Students in my ACCESS class use *The Reader's Handbook* (Robb et al. 2001; Burke et al. 2002) to learn about the reading process. To help them generalize their learning, for use with other subject areas, I have them apply what we study to what they do and learn in other classes. In Figure 20.1, you see the notes Jessica Johnson took on the reading process. On the left side, she used an informal variation of Outline Notes to help her understand what she was reading; on the right side she provided examples of, for instance, "setting a purpose" to her other academic classes. Not all kids understand the assignment, as it asks them to do several things at one time. I thus begin by putting a blank T Notes page on the overhead and modeling what they should do. I read through the first couple of examples with them, telling them out loud what I am doing and why, then showing them what I want their notes to look like. I then leave mine on the overhead so they can refer to it if they get confused.

Example Two: Marriage in India Versus the United States

Students study India in their Modern World History class. One subject of particular interest to the kids is

STANDARDS

- Reading
  - ☐ Analyze organizational patterns of information
  - ☐ Compare ideas, texts, or authors
  - ☐ Evaluate the arguments presented in a text
  - ☐ Extend ideas
  - ☐ Generate relevant questions
  - ☐ Identify and analyze recurring themes
  - ☐ Prepare to read
  - ☐ Synthesize information from multiple sources
- Writing
  - ☐ Establish a main or controlling idea
  - ☐ Integrate quotations and examples in written response
  - ☐ Organize information and ideas in logical, appropriate format
  - ☐ Prepare to write
  - ☐ Use sensory, concrete, or illustrative details to support claims
  - ☐ Use writing for a variety of purposes
- Speaking
  - ☐ Analyze devices used in others' speeches
  - ☐ Compare events or ideas
  - ☐ Organize information for desired effect on the audience
  - ☐ Prepare to speak
- Listening
  - ☐ Improve note-taking skills
  - ☐ Organize information
- Viewing
  - ☐ Assess different techniques or devices used
  - ☐ Gather details and examples for subsequent analysis of text
  - ☐ Identify organization of information
- Test Preparation
  - ☐ Comprehend information
  - ☐ Organize ideas
  - ☐ Remember information

SUBJECT AREAS

- English language arts
- Health
- Humanities
- Science
- Social studies

USES

- Ask useful questions
- Assess student performance
- Compare two or more items, aspects, or people
- Develop academic literacy
- Evaluate ideas
- Extend ideas beyond obvious
- Facilitate discussion
- Gather evidence to support claims
- Generate ideas
- Identify themes
- Make connections
- Observe patterns
- Organize information
- Prepare to read
- Prepare to write
- Respond to reading
- Support critical reading
- Synthesize ideas
- Take notes while reading

T Notes

Name Jessica Johnson	Date 11/7
Subject The Reading Process	Period 1st

During the Reading process you should...	Apply to your classes
a. Set a purpose	ex) • eng – what took Odysseus so
– what is it?	long to return home?
– why	• MWH – what was the Renaissance?
b. Preview	ex) • MWH – chapter titles &
– what to expect and start	headers.
thinking about it.	• eng – Odyssey – background
– is to learn how you	information (back of book)
want to read.	
c. Plan	ex) • MWH – take organized, color
– decide best way to	coating notes.
reach it.	• math – solve easy problems
– decide on strategy	fast.
and tools.	
d. Read with a purpose	ex) • eng – how Odysseus used
– what are you looking	schemes to get home.
for?	• MWH – how slaves were
– what do I want (to learn)?	treated.
– why am I?	
e. Connect	ex) • MWH – I feel slave trade
– How does this touch you?	was wrong.
– Relate between questions.	• eng – I do similar things
– How do you feel	to reach my goal.
about it?	
f. Pause and Reflect.	ex) • eng – finished the Odyssey
– Did you meet what your	and learned about his
purpose was?	return home.
– Did you learn what you	• MWH – Renaissance life revolved
wanted to learn?	around church life.

Here (and on the back) you should write your obsevations, draw your conclusions, write your summary.

FIGURE 20.1 Jessica Johnson's T Notes helped her take good notes and then apply her reading to the other classes she was taking.

T Notes

Name	Date
Subject	Period

MARRIAGE : INDIA VS. U.S.

INDIA	UNITED STATES
• Arranged	• Free to choose
• Divorce is scarce	• Divorce is frequent
• Women respect men	• women do not respect men
• Men run household	• Both run household
• Usually only men work	• Usually both work
• Men & women grow to love each other as the marriage moves on	• The husband & wife love each other and decide to date other people.
• If women are not suitable, they are thrown out	• If women are not suitable, they just don't get married, but usually there are no non-suitable women in society.
• woman can not be in authority	• In most homes, the mother rules the family
• dowry payment → dowry death	• women are always outside & free
	• wife & husband's families both contribute to the wedding cost, and the families are often in debt of each other.
• look to astrology for marriage and make sure that Brahman is pleased with the match.	• Most couples do not look to horoscopes or ask others to see if their marriage is correct.
• If the wife does not give birth to a specific gender of baby they abort or the husband may divorce them.	• The Americans do not care a lot about the genders of the baby but abortions are still very frequent in the US.

Here (and on the back) you should write your obsevations, draw your conclusions, write your summary.

The United States has a lot more freedom than India, and probably other third world areas. India is a lot stricter towards a lot of things we consider really nothing.

FIGURE 20.2 Here Ashley Arata compares marriage in the United States and India as part of her study of India in social studies.

arranged marriage, something that seems so different from our own traditions. Like many subjects, however, the closer they look, the more similarities they find. Tools like T Notes help students see these similarities by giving more structure to their comparisons. I tell them to write down something on one side—"arranged," for example—and then, to reinforce their ability to think in pairs (i.e., parallelism), ask what the other culture does. (See Figure 20.2.) This way their ideas are aligned with each other; they are then prepared to write highly organized paragraphs about the differences. In fact, two of the main goals of this assignment for me is to improve their ability to compare and to write. As the following excerpt from Jennifer's paper shows, her T Notes helped her write well. During this assignment, we studied transition words the students could use to compare the two traditions and cultures. Jennifer's use of these transitions makes the following excerpt a very effective piece of writing:

> India is, in some respects, much different than the United States when marriage is concerned. One of the biggest factors that makes India so much different from the United States is that most U.S. citizens make their choice of whom to marry, but in India the marriage is arranged. Another difference is that when seeking a husband or a wife, most Americans look for their parents' consent, or occasionally, their own. The Indians seek matchmakers, astrology, or Brahmin to see to it that their child gets a spouse that is suitable for him or her and that the match is in agreement with Brahman. Although there may be differences between the two countries, not all differences are bad. For example, in India a person grows to love their spouse, but because Americans feel that there is always going to be a second chance, they jump right into the relationship and think that if there is a problem with the marriage, the quickest way out is through divorce. Indians' beliefs are, however, very different. Because they believe that you will slowly get attracted to your spouse, and that staying together is part of the dharma, divorce is scarce in India. Choosing your spouse is a big responsibility, and staying committed to that person means you are really serious about them, and you have no intention of changing your mind.

21 Target Notes

DESCRIPTION

Think in Threes asks students to consider a subject from three different perspectives, and the Conversational Roundtable invites four different perspectives; Target Notes, on the other hand, truly expands thinking. The Target Notes tool begins by asking the student to consider what is at the center of the inquiry. What is the student "aiming" at? The two strands of the target invite scaffolding of thought: the first strand calls for identifying categories or perspectives, which are then developed through examples, details, or quotations in the outer strand. At the bottom of the page, the students tie their thinking together through the paragraph (or more) they are asked to write. Because their ideas are well organized into sections, the writers are prepared to compose highly organized pieces of writing that incorporate details and supporting quotations into the paragraph. Extended further, they could take each section as the basis for a paragraph, which they now have the details to write. Thus a writer could take the completed Target as a sort of circular outline, using whatever is in the center as the basis for the introduction and thesis.

The Target is a versatile tool, one that can be used in any number of ways, as the examples that follow show.

NOTES AND EXAMPLES

Example One: Jen and Othello

To prepare students for the subsequent use of a Target for *Othello*, I had them do one about themselves. This makes it easier for them to learn to use any tool because they know the content and can focus on learning the tool and its techniques. In this case students put their name in the center and then identified six different people who saw them from different perspectives. They explained in the inner circle who each person was (i.e., the basis of their relationship with that person). (See Jen's example in Figure 21.1.) In the corresponding outer strand they wrote what they thought that person would say or think about them. This activity in multiple perspectives helped them see how subjective an opinion about a person can be. At the bottom they summed up the perspectives, drawing conclusions about how they and others see them. In the follow-up to Jen's Target, she put Othello at the center, then described six different characters' (one of whom was Othello himself)

STANDARDS

- Reading
  - ☐ Analyze organizational patterns of information
  - ☐ Compare ideas, texts, or authors
  - ☐ Extend ideas
  - ☐ Generate relevant questions
  - ☐ Identify and analyze recurring themes
  - ☐ Prepare to read
  - ☐ Synthesize information from multiple sources
- Writing
  - ☐ Establish a main or controlling idea
  - ☐ Integrate quotations and examples in written response
  - ☐ Organize information and ideas in logical, appropriate format
  - ☐ Prepare to write
  - ☐ Use sensory, concrete, or illustrative details to support claims
  - ☐ Use writing for a variety of purposes
- Speaking
  - ☐ Analyze devices used in others' speeches
  - ☐ Compare events or ideas
  - ☐ Organize information for desired effect on audience
  - ☐ Prepare to speak
- Language Study
  - ☐ Distinguish between denotative and connotative meaning
  - ☐ Examine and use different Greek and Latin roots of words
  - ☐ Know and use different parts of speech
- Viewing
  - ☐ Assess different techniques or devices used
  - ☐ Gather details and examples for subsequent analysis of text
  - ☐ Identify organization of information
- Test Preparation
  - ☐ Comprehend information
  - ☐ Organize ideas
  - ☐ Prioritize information
  - ☐ Remember information

SUBJECT AREAS

- English language arts
- Health
- Humanities
- Science
- Social studies

USES

- Ask useful questions
- Assess student performance
- Compare two or more items, aspects, or people
- Develop academic literacy
- Evaluate ideas
- Extend ideas beyond obvious
- Facilitate discussion
- Gather evidence to support claims
- Generate ideas
- Identify themes
- Make connections
- Narrow or refine subject
- Observe patterns
- Organize information
- Prepare to read
- Prepare to write
- Respond to reading
- Support critical reading
- Synthesize ideas
- Take notes while reading

Target Notes

Name	Date
Subject	**Period**

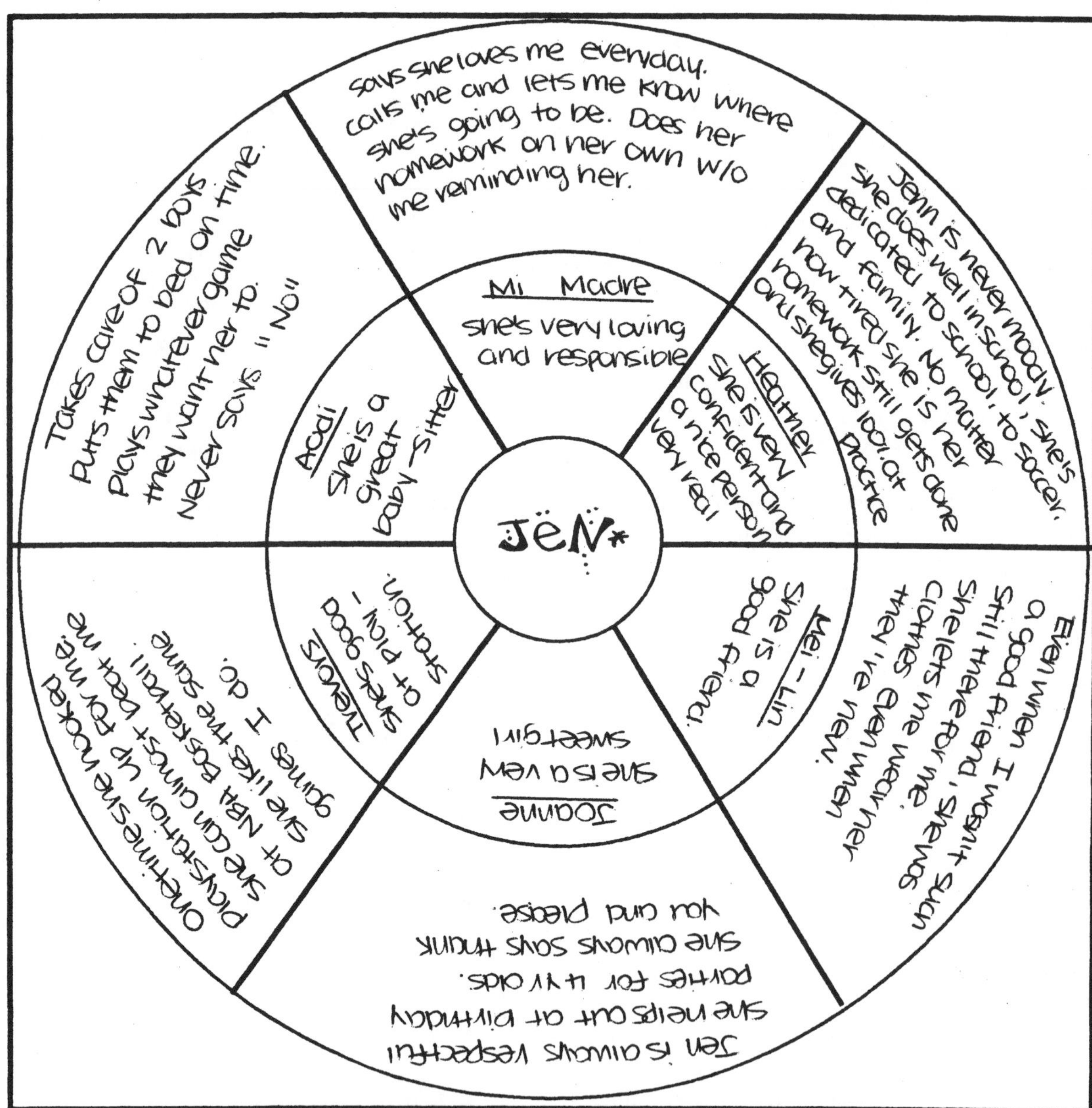

I am a very driven person. I have always strived to do my best. I set goals for myself and almost achieve them. Everything I do, I give a 110% of myself. I think of myself as a good friend and try to treat others the way I want to be treated. My personality traits are kind, smart, dedicated, and sweet. I'm also very shy and find it very difficult to say nice things about myself.

FIGURE 21.1 Jen Edl's Target Notes prepared her to read *Othello*.

perspectives on Othello. (See Figure 21.2.) Students had to find a quotation to support the character's opinion of Othello; in the outer strand they had to explain what the quotation meant and why that person would hold such an opinion of Othello. At the bottom, they synthesized their observations, incorporating quotations and examples to support their conclusions.

Example Two: What Matters Most: How to Tell What's Most Important

This Target Notes tool is useful in any class, but I find it most valuable in my academic literacy classes, where students often do not know how to determine what is important. (See Figure 21.3.) Here is a sample sequence describing one way to use it:

1. Put it up on the overhead (and give students a copy of their own)
2. Put the topic (e.g., "poetry" or "the Renaissance") in the center. This provides a focus and sets the purpose to your discussion: that is, you are trying to decide what is most important when talking about one of these subjects.
3. Brainstorm into the first level of spaces the categories appropriate to this subject. If discussing poetry, for example, students might identify such categories as imagery, language, sound themes, and so on.
4. Then have them read a poem (for which this activity was preparing them) straight through, taking no notes.
5. Next have them reread the poem, seeking examples of, for example, imagery, which they should then include in the appropriate space on the Target.
6. Share the Target contents in groups or as a class, having students use their notes to prepare them to write or participate in a class discussion.

The words in the outer four corners—*past, present, future,* and *always*—do not always apply but are helpful when they do. They remind you to ask if something is always important when discussing a certain subject, and if not, to examine why it will or will not be important in the future. I cross them out or use them selectively as seems appropriate. The Vocabulary of Importance section grew out of a continual need to clarify words I and others commonly use to identify something as important. The questions we develop depend on the nature of what we are studying or doing; one example, however, might be, "If you removed this (e.g., scene, character, event), would it change the text?"

Target Notes

Name	Date
Subject	Period

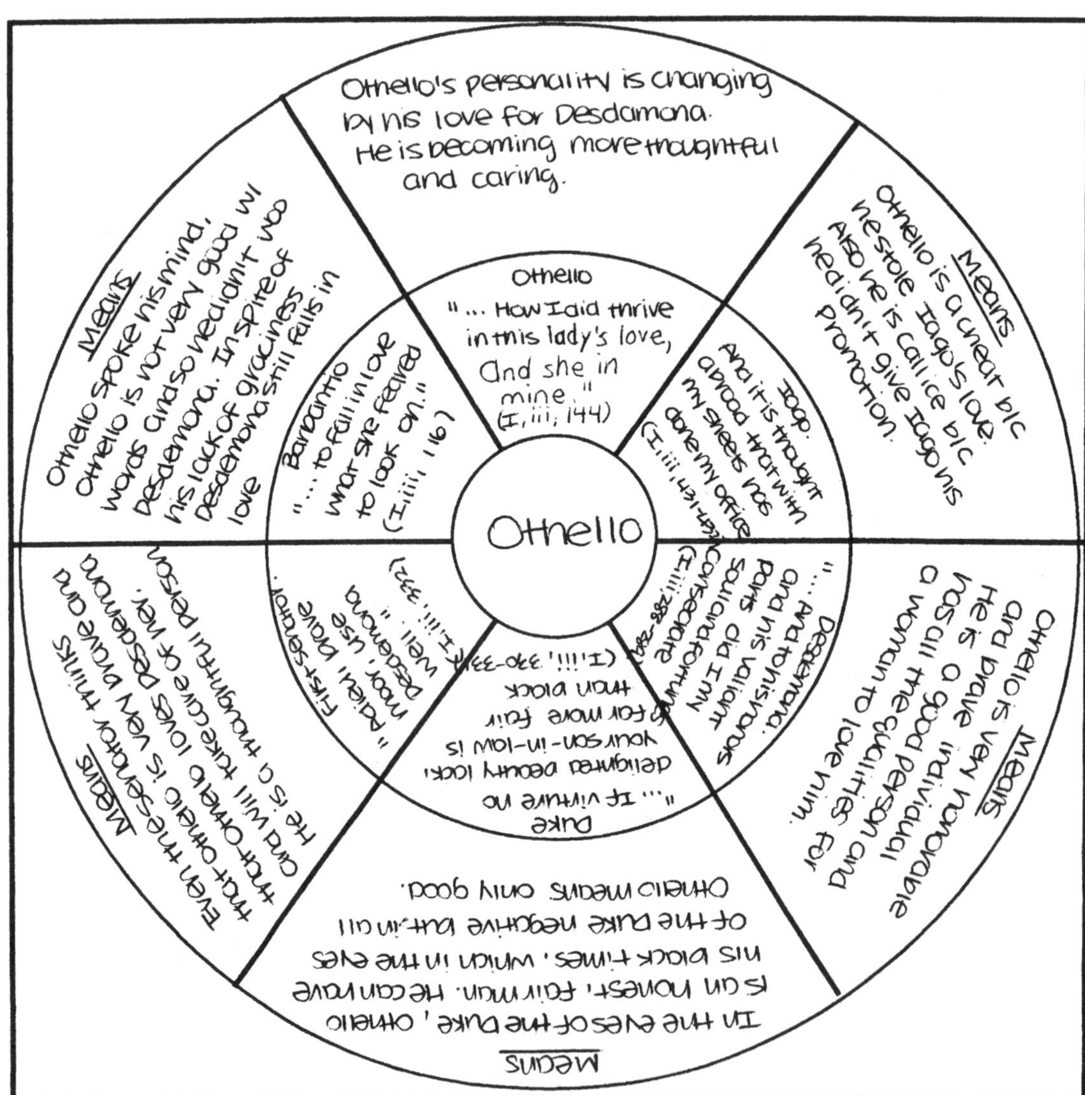
Othello's personality is changing by his love for Desdamona. He is becoming more thoughtful and caring.
Othello "... How I did thrive in this lady's love, And she in mine." (I, iii, 144)
Othello
Means
Othello is a cheat b/c he stole Iago's love. Also he is [illegible] b/c he didn't give Iago his promotion.
Iago: And it is thought abroad that twixt my sheets he's done my office
Means
Othello is very honorable and brave individual. He is a good person and has all the qualities for a woman to love him.
Desdemona: "... And to his honors and his valiant parts did I my soul and fortunes consecrate"
Means
In the eyes of the Duke, Othello is an honest, fair man. He can have his black times, which in the eyes of the Duke negative but in all Othello means only good.
Duke "... If virtue no delighted beauty lack, your son-in-law is far more fair than black." (I, iii, 330-331)
First Senator "Adieu, brave Moor, use Desdemona well." (I, iii, 322)
Means
Even the senator thinks that Othello is very brave and that Othello loves Desdemona and will take care of her. He is a thoughtful person.
Barbantio "... to fall in love what she feared to look on." (I, iii, 116)
Means
Othello spoke his mind, Othello is not very good w/ words and so he didn't woo Desdemona. In spite of his lack of graciness Desdemona still falls in love

Othello overall has the basic characteristics of a good man. He is very brave and the senators think the same thing about Othello. We see this when Duke says "valiant Othello, we must straight employ you." (I, iii, 57). Sometimes Othello speaks w/o thinking and even he knows this about himself when he states, "Rude am I in my speech." (I, iii, 96)
In some eyes Othello is seen as a cheat. Iago says this when he states "I hate the Moor, and it is thought abroad that "twixt my sheets..." (I, iii, 430)
B/C Othello is thought by most to be open and honest, others think this trait makes him a fool and easy to decieve. In I, iii, 442–445 Iago states this very well. The quote reads "the Moor is a free and open nature that thinks men honest but seem to be so, and will as tenderly be led.

FIGURE 21.2 Jen Edl's Target Notes on Othello helped her understand this character and how others in the play see him.

What Matters Most: How to Tell What's Important

Name ____________________ Date ____________

Subject ____________________ Period ____________

Suggestions for Use: Fill in the blanks with words like *Author, Teacher, Teenagers, Parents, Society,* a character's name, or some other person or agency appropriate to your inquiry. Think also about *when* it is important: always, the past, the present, or the future.

THE PAST

THE PRESENT

Why it's important

ALWAYS

THE FUTURE

0 ———————————— 12

Continuum of Importance/Performance

Questions to Help Determine Importance

1.

2.

3.

Vocabulary of Importance

1. important	7. urgent	13. necessary
2. significant	8. imperative	14. prominent
3. critical	9. main	15. remarkable
4. essential	10. substantial	16. key
5. crucial	11. eminent	17. major
6. vital	12. invaluable	18. primary

FIGURE 21.3 Target Notes: What Matters Most

22 Think in Threes

STANDARDS

- Reading
  - ☐ Analyze organizational patterns of information
  - ☐ Compare ideas, texts, or authors
  - ☐ Evaluate the arguments presented in a text
  - ☐ Extend ideas
  - ☐ Generate relevant questions
  - ☐ Identify and analyze recurring themes
  - ☐ Prepare to read
  - ☐ Synthesize information from multiple sources
- Writing
  - ☐ Establish a main or controlling idea
  - ☐ Integrate quotations and examples in written response
  - ☐ Organize information and ideas in logical, appropriate format
  - ☐ Prepare to write
  - ☐ Use sensory, concrete, or illustrative details to support claims
  - ☐ Use writing for a variety of purposes
- Speaking
  - ☐ Analyze devices used in others' speeches
  - ☐ Compare events or ideas
  - ☐ Organize information for desired effect on audience
  - ☐ Prepare and deliver multimedia presentations
  - ☐ Prepare to speak
- Language Study
  - ☐ Know and use different parts of speech
  - ☐ Examine author's use of language
- Viewing
  - ☐ Assess different techniques or devices used
  - ☐ Gather details and examples for subsequent analysis of text
- Test Preparation
  - ☐ Comprehend information
  - ☐ Organize ideas
  - ☐ Prioritize information
  - ☐ Remember information

SUBJECT AREAS

- English language arts
- Health
- Humanities
- Science
- Social studies

USES

- Ask useful questions
- Assess student performance
- Compare two or more items, aspects, or people
- Develop academic literacy
- Evaluate ideas
- Extend ideas beyond obvious
- Facilitate discussion
- Gather evidence to support claims
- Generate ideas
- Identify themes
- Make connections
- Narrow or refine subject
- Prepare to read
- Prepare to write
- Respond to reading
- Support critical reading
- Synthesize ideas
- Take notes while reading

DESCRIPTION

Think in Threes asks students to transcend either/or thinking (yes/no, right/wrong, good/bad) and consider a subject from one more side. It challenges students to think beyond the obvious, to generate additional possibilities. The idea owes its origins to the business world and anthropologist Mary Catherine Bateson (1990). Companies like Disney, for instance, use the model: when making a film, they think not only of the film but also about the product line and its corresponding attraction at the theme park. They think of not only the six-year-old but of the teenager and adult who might have to take the six-year-old to the movie, making sure there is something for everyone in the film. Bateson, a professor at Amherst College, found that students asked to compare two cultures inevitably ended up saying one was good and the other bad, a judgment reinforced by the two-country comparison. Adding a third culture for them to compare challenged them to think differently about the countries, noting differences and similarities but avoiding the reductionist thinking that one country is good and another bad.

Of course the tool can be used for other purposes, too. Students in my freshman English class read Bharati Mukherjee's novel *Jasmine* after reading Homer's *Odyssey*. When they finish these two books, they watch the film *City of Joy*, after which they do the Think in Threes on the different journeys of the three stories' main characters. The tool teaches them to think in parallel terms: if they write down examples of Odysseus' trials, they then learn to ask themselves if there are corresponding trials in *Jasmine* and *City of Joy*. When they finish viewing the film, they are left with well-organized notes that can serve as the basis for either a synthesizing paragraph or a larger paper on the theme of journeys. Whatever students do, the tool reinforces the notion of parallelism and organization in the students' minds, teaching them not only to think but write better than they might otherwise.

As the examples that follow illustrate, the tool allows for some measure of creativity, as students add symbols or images that relate to or extend the different sides being compared. In this and other respects, the tool helps students narrow or generate their thoughts on a subject.

NOTES AND EXAMPLES

Example One: Power

Students had to create their own final exam in my English class. The assignment demanded that they think about a subject we had studied—these included power, identity, moral codes, and needs—and compare or discuss it from three perspectives. They could look at it from three characters' points of view; from the viewpoint of three different authors through their books; from the perspective of the past, present, and future; or from some other interesting angle I could not dream up on my own. In this case, Omar looked at the concept and source of power in *Othello*, South Africa (which he had been studying in history), and his own world. (See Figure 22.1.) This three-way comparison allowed him to examine an abstract idea from different angles and make it more concrete in the process, all of which prepared him to write the fine paper he eventually wrote. Here is a sample of his thinking, on an assignment that asked the students to summarize what they were trying to say in their Think in Threes diagram:

> How does one's power affect others, the world, the universe, or even themselves? Power generates in infinite ways, it depends on the person to generate in the way his personality is. In *Othello*, power was apparent mainly in three different ways. The first way was generated by Desdemona. Her unique power was her beauty. The second power was generated by Othello. His power was his physical strength. The last and most important power was Iago's cunning and sly intelligence. All of these powers gave the play its fame and uniqueness. Iago, Othello, and Desdemona's power affected everyone in the play. South Africa has the most unique and odd power of all other countries. Their power is centered on Apartheid and conquering. South Africa generates its power in the social, racial, military, and governmental areas. These four powers led South Africa to what it is today. In my world I recognize power coming from the government, teachers, parents, and most of the peers. All these powers are the most significant in my world. My future is in the hands of all these kinds of people. Whether power comes from Othello, or South Africa or even the world, it is generated everywhere in a significant manner.

Example Two: *Midsummer Night's Dream*

Students put in the center an aspect they wanted to consider from three angles in Shakespeare's play. (See example in Figure 22.2.) In the next level they identified the three sides; in this case, love, hate, and jealousy, three feelings central to the play. In the next strand they wrote quotations from the play that related to the three feelings they were examining. Outside that, the student in this example added yet another series of insights to extend her study of, for example, love. At the bottom of her page, she provided the question that her whole page tries to answer: What's in the heart? She has used the tool to think about an abstract idea from three perspectives; read closely to support her assertions about the text; and extended her reading to make connections between characters, events, and themes in the story. Not bad for a freshman!

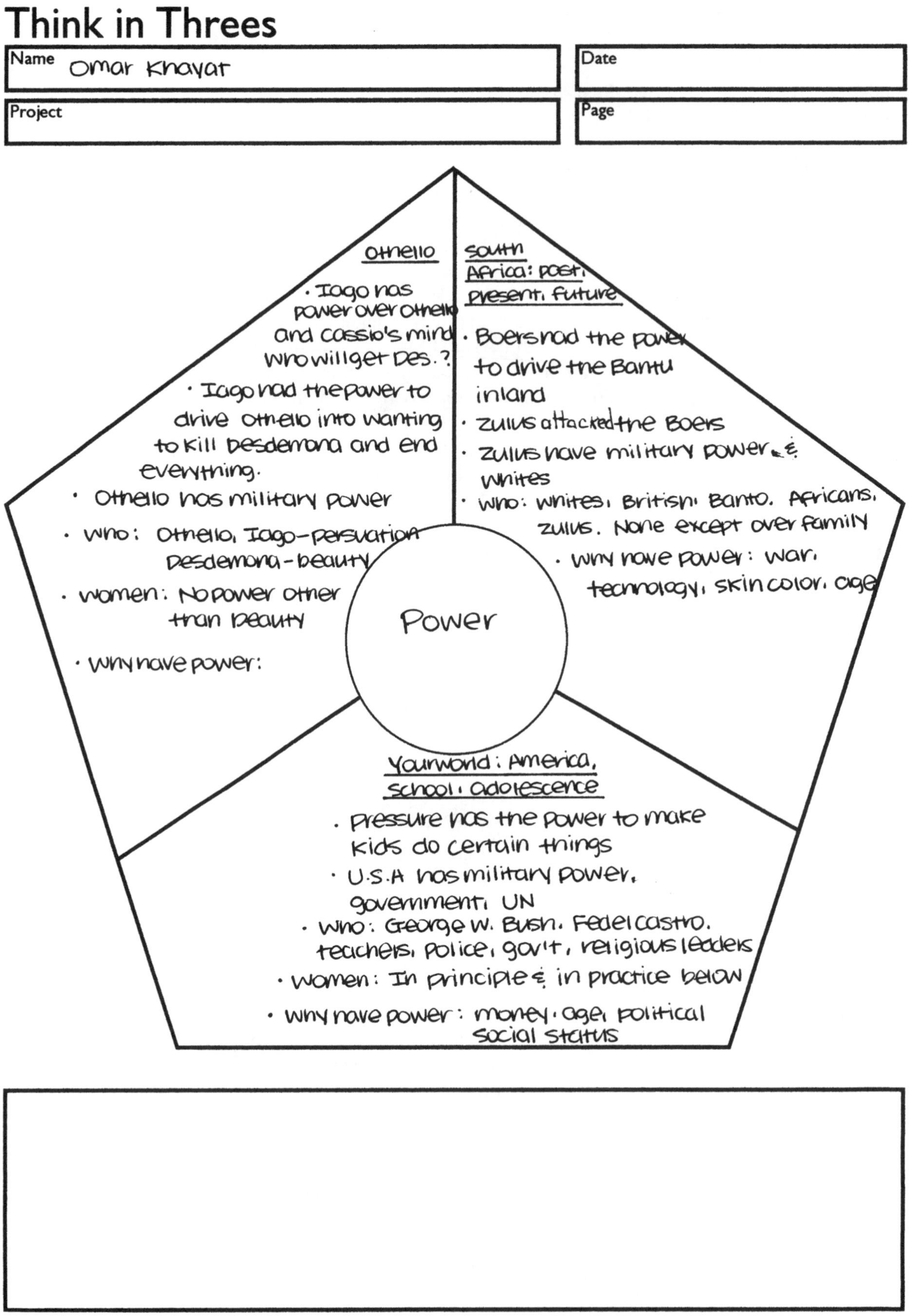

Think in Threes

Name Omar Khayat

Date

Project

Page

Othello
- Iago has power over Othello and Cassio's mind. Who will get Des.?
- Iago had the power to drive Othello into wanting to kill Desdemona and end everything.
- Othello has military power
- Who: Othello, Iago—persuation, Desdemona—beauty
- Women: No power other than beauty
- Why have power:

South Africa: past, present, future
- Boers had the power to drive the Bantu inland
- Zulus attacked the Boers
- Zulus have military power & whites
- Who: whites, British, Banto. Africans, Zulus. None except over family
- Why have power: war, technology, skin color, age

Power

Your world: America, school, adolescence
- Pressure has the power to make kids do certain things
- U.S.A has military power, government, UN
- Who: George W. Bush. Fedel Castro. teachers, police, gov't, religious leaders
- Women: In principle & in practice below
- Why have power: money, age, political social status

FIGURE 22.1 These Think in Three notes prepared Omar to write his essay at the end of the semester.

FIGURE 22.2 Sample Think in Threes: *Midsummer Night's Dream*

23 Time Line Notes

STANDARDS

- Reading
  - ☐ Analyze organizational patterns of information
  - ☐ Compare ideas, texts, or authors
  - ☐ Extend ideas
  - ☐ Generate relevant questions
  - ☐ Identify and analyze recurring themes
  - ☐ Prepare to read
- Writing
  - ☐ Establish a main or controlling idea
  - ☐ Organize information and ideas in logical, appropriate format
  - ☐ Prepare to write
  - ☐ Use sensory, concrete, or illustrative details to support claims
  - ☐ Use writing for a variety of purposes
- Listening
  - ☐ Improve note-taking skills
  - ☐ Organize information
- Viewing
  - ☐ Gather details and examples for subsequent analysis of text
  - ☐ Identify organization of information
- Test Preparation
  - ☐ Comprehend information
  - ☐ Organize ideas
  - ☐ Prioritize information
  - ☐ Remember information

SUBJECT AREAS

- English language arts
- Health
- Humanities
- Mathematics
- Science
- Social studies

USES

- Ask useful questions
- Assess student performance
- Compare two or more items, aspects, or people
- Develop academic literacy
- Evaluate ideas
- Extend ideas beyond obvious
- Facilitate discussion
- Identify themes
- Make connections
- Observe patterns
- Organize information
- Prepare to read
- Prepare to write
- Respond to reading
- Support critical reading
- Synthesize ideas
- Take notes while reading
- Visualize what is read

DESCRIPTION

Time Line Notes help students keep track of the order in which things happen. Whether reading Homer's *Odyssey* or their history textbook's chapter on the Civil War, this tool helps them chart the course of events. Such notes have several benefits for students. They see how one event leads to another. They also learn to examine why each event is important, and how one event leads to the next. This emphasis on sequence is also instructive to students who struggle with the organization of information in a narrative or chronological text. In addition, the visual aspect of the technique helps students with special needs and those learning English by providing a space they know they must fill. Such notes allow the teacher to quickly check the level of understanding or to notice that a student is struggling with an assignment. Another option would be to give the tool to those students who are having difficulty with a particular assignment with the hope that its more visual structure would benefit them.

NOTES AND EXAMPLES

Example One: *Odyssey*

Students need help keeping track of the events as they read books like Homer's *Odyssey*. The Time Line Notes sheet provides a useful organizational tool that helps students visually arrange events. It does more than that, however. Here the students must also provide a brief but insightful explanation of why something is the most important event. I usually ask them to identify what they think is the most crucial event in the chapter to include; this helps them read with purpose and explain why they chose the event they did. It also helps me assess their level of reading and the quality of their thinking. (See Figure 23.1.)

Example Two: *Lord of the Flies*

This Time Line (see Figure 23.2) does something very different than the first example: it charts the gradual changes in the boys over the course of the story. Each step, such as "Cooperation," names a behavioral phase, and includes a brief description of it. The tool helps students see how one phase leads to another and how all of them form a general trend as time passes.

Timeline: As you read look for those moments that indicate a new and crucial stage in a process or journey. On each bar of the timeline write the word(s) that will clearly delineate that stage from the others. Under the bar you should note the specific details such as date and what happened so you can use these notes later for writing or discussions. The important point is to identify the essential events and the order in which they occur.

1 Athena gives Telemachus hope

Telemachus wasn't sure who his father was, but Athena helped him realize who his father is. She also tells him he needs to grow up and take care of himself.

2 Telemachus leaves home.

This is the point in the book that Telemachus becomes a man. He learns how to be on his own and finally found the courage to leave his home and find his father he never met.

3 Telemachus visits King Nestor.

This part in the book is where Nestor remembers the day when he fought wi Odysseus in Troy. This helps Telemachus about his father more. This gives Telemachus a greater picture of who his father is.

4. Meaolus tells what he learned of Odysseus while stranded in Egypt.

This is where Menalus learns that Odysseus was stranded with Calypso. If he would have learned about Odysseus earlier, he might not have been stranded so long and return home earlier. This might have made Penelope's life and Laretr's a little easier.

5 Zeus sends Hermes to retrieve Odysseus

This point in the book is the turning point because this is where Odysseus leaves to go on to his journey home. Even though his ship got messed up, he still has hope of finally returning. It seems to me that Odysseus was starting to lose hope, but I think he will gain it back again.

6. Odysseus lands on the land of the Phaecians

This was important because this was the part of the book I think that Odysseus begins to regain hope. Even though the Phaecians took Odysseus into their army and gave him splendid gifts, he wanted to go home. He must have been afraid that the gods would plot against him because he did not leave for a while.

7. Odysseus goes to the King and promises him a safe journey home.

This helps Odysseus regain his hope. The King promises Odysseus a safe journey home after he has been entratianed I think this will help Odysseus to move on further so that he can move to his journey home.

8. The athleletic games are held and everyone thinks Odysseus lacks skill.

After Odysseus throws the discus, during the athletic games, his power is known to all. He proved everyone wrong. This gave him the strength mentally to leave this land because he finally realized that he was missed at home.

9. Cyclops encounters Odysseus.

When Odysseus made his men face the Cyclops, he was acting a little selfish. If he did not do that 2 of his men would have been alive. Also, this probably lowered his will to go on, since he lost two of his men.

10. Crew opens a bag of wind which was a mist

This act was a selfish act by the crew. It was also an act of greed. If the crew had not opened the bag of wind, they would have reached Itha much sooner. This showed that the crew was not very obedient and disrespected Odysseus' power.

11. Odysseus does as Circe says and reached the dead.

Odysseus takes her advice, while there Odysseus met many of the famous women and heros, including Achilles. A prophet warned him about his journey home.

12. Odysseus shows signs of selfishness.

Odysseus do need about not eating the cattle and by doing so the seal their own death. Odysseus now has lost all his men, and he alone is now on the island of Calypso

FIGURE 23.1 Sample Time Line for the *Odyssey*

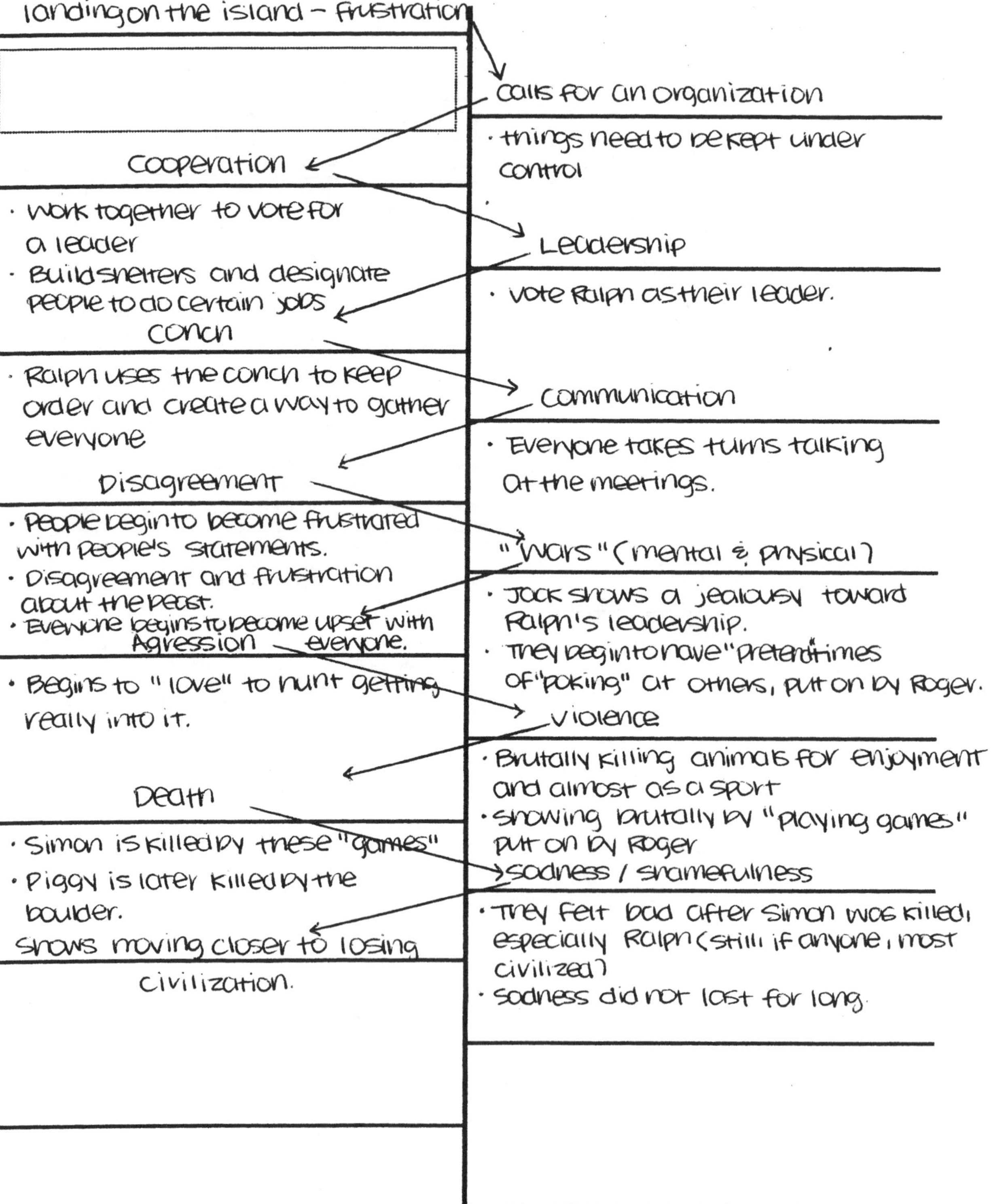

Timeline: As you read look for those moments that indicate a new and crucial stage in a process or journey. On each bar of the timeline write the word(s) that will clearly delineate that stage from the others. Under the bar you should note the specific details such as date and what happened so you can use these notes later for writing or discussions. The important point is to identify the essential events and the order in which they occur.
landing on the island – Frustration
calls for an organization
· things need to be kept under control
Cooperation
· work together to vote for a leader
· Build shelters and designate people to do certain jobs
Leadership
· vote Ralph as their leader.
Conch
· Ralph uses the conch to keep order and create a way to gather everyone
Communication
· Everyone takes turns talking at the meetings.
Disagreement
· People begin to become frustrated with people's statements.
· Disagreement and frustration about the beast.
· Everyone begins to become upset with everyone.
"Wars" (mental & physical)
· Jack shows a jealousy toward Ralph's leadership.
· They begin to have "pretend" times of "poking" at others, put on by Roger.
Agression
· Begins to "love" to hunt getting really into it.
Violence
· Brutally killing animals for enjoyment and almost as a sport
· showing brutally by "playing games" put on by Roger
Death
· Simon is killed by these "games"
· Piggy is later killed by the boulder.
Shows moving closer to losing civilization.
Sadness / Shamefulness
· They felt bad after Simon was killed, especially Ralph (still if anyone, most civilized)
· Sadness did not last for long.

FIGURE 23.2 Conceptual Time Line for *Lord of the Flies*

Venn Diagrams

24

DESCRIPTION

The Venn Diagram tool offers one more way to compare different subjects. This tool emphasizes the differences *and* the similarities inherent in most subjects. The tool is intuitive for most users because of its familiarity from other classes, especially math. It asks, in short, What are the distinctive traits of A and B? It also asks users to list those elements common to both A and B. It prepares the students to write once they have finished it; the information is already organized and ready to be shaped into thoughtful paragraphs in which students compare the different subjects.

The tool can be adapted in several useful ways. First of all, a Venn Diagram is not limited to two circles with one common area. You can, as the example of the dense question strategy in Figure 24.3 shows, use three. If it is appropriate to the task and subject, you can also use four, though this begins to get complicated. Another variation is to split a two-circle Venn Diagram lengthwise and create a two-level comparison, as shown in Figure 24.2.

Students should explain, in writing or class discussion, what they included in their diagram. Comparing how others organized the same information often leads to new insights about the subject they are studying. It is just as useful to fill in a diagram together as a class, thereby using it to give structure to the discussion, as it is to do it solo or through collaborative groups. Students at all levels find it useful; comparison is a complex task that this tool makes more comprehensible, thanks to its visual and intuitive design.

NOTES AND EXAMPLES

Example One: Comparing Eleanor Roosevelt and Barbara Bush

I used a paragraph in *Writer's Inc.* (Sebranek, Kemper, and Meyer 2001) about two former first ladies to introduce this tool and the technique for comparing two subjects. (See Figure 24.1.) Students read the paragraph and took notes as directed by the diagram. To be sure they understood how to do this, I modeled, putting a transparency on the overhead and reading the first few sentences to show them how I would take notes. I made a point of telling the students to clearly distinguish between one idea and the next. I generally urge them to

STANDARDS

- Reading
  - ☐ Analyze organizational patterns of information
  - ☐ Compare ideas, texts, or authors
  - ☐ Evaluate the arguments presented in a text
  - ☐ Extend ideas
  - ☐ Generate relevant questions
  - ☐ Identify and analyze recurring themes
  - ☐ Prepare to read
  - ☐ Synthesize information from multiple sources
- Writing
  - ☐ Establish a main or controlling idea
  - ☐ Integrate quotations and examples in written response
  - ☐ Organize information and ideas in logical, appropriate format
  - ☐ Prepare to write
  - ☐ Use sensory, concrete, or illustrative details to support claims
  - ☐ Use writing for a variety of purposes
- Speaking
  - ☐ Analyze devices used in others' speeches
  - ☐ Compare events or ideas
  - ☐ Organize information for desired effect on audience
  - ☐ Prepare and deliver multimedia presentations
  - ☐ Prepare to speak
- Listening
  - ☐ Improve note-taking skills
  - ☐ Organize information
- Viewing
  - ☐ Gather details and examples for subsequent analysis of text
  - ☐ Identify organization of information
- Test Preparation
  - ☐ Comprehend information
  - ☐ Organize ideas
  - ☐ Prioritize information
  - ☐ Remember information

SUBJECT AREAS

- English language arts
- Health
- Humanities
- Mathematics
- Science
- Social studies

USES

- Ask useful questions
- Assess student performance
- Compare two or more items, aspects, or people
- Develop academic literacy
- Evaluate ideas
- Extend ideas beyond obvious
- Facilitate discussion
- Gather evidence to support claims
- Generate ideas
- Identify themes
- Make connections
- Organize information
- Prepare to read
- Prepare to write
- Respond to reading
- Support critical reading
- Synthesize ideas
- Take notes while reading
- Visualize what is read

Venn Diagram

Name Jennifer Lee	Date 10/3
Topic comparing - From P103. Writer's Inc.	Period 6°

Eleanor Roosevelt

- wife of Democratic President Franklin D. Roosevelt
- lectured about youth unemployment
- supported the National Youth Administration.
- helped find jobs for young people
- promoted racial equality
- argued for desegregation
- chaired the commission that drafted the universal Declaration of Human Rights.

- shared a concern for social changes
- worked to improve the lives of the young
- championed their own special concerns
- used their positions to improve our society.

- wife of Republican president George Bush
- Helped young people by starting reading programs for children throughout the U.S.
- established the Barbara Bush Foundation for family literacy.
- promoted better health care
- raised money for cancer research
- assisted social agencies like soup kitchens and shelters for the homeless.

Barbara Bush

Observations/Conclusions:

FIGURE 24.1 Venn Diagram: Roosevelt/Bush comparison

use bullets to visually separate one idea from another.

Example Two: Women in Our World Versus Homer's *Odyssey*

The assignment in the previous example prepared students for this second step, which is more demanding. In the first example they had only to read and write down examples; in this instance, they had to generate the ideas and examples based on their overall reading and prior knowledge. To add an additional level of challenge and depth to the assignment, I divided the diagram lengthwise; this asked them to compare not only past and present but women and men. It demanded that they think in several directions at once. (See Figure 24.2.)

Example Three: The Dense Question

I learned about this technique from Christenbury and Kelly (1983). I use it often to help students create their own exam topics that meet my need to bring everything we've studied together in some challenging yet meaningful way. We walk through it step-by-step, first developing "text" questions, then "world," and so on, until they are ready to create their own dense question which I, of course, must approve prior to their final paper or exam. (See Figure 24.3.)

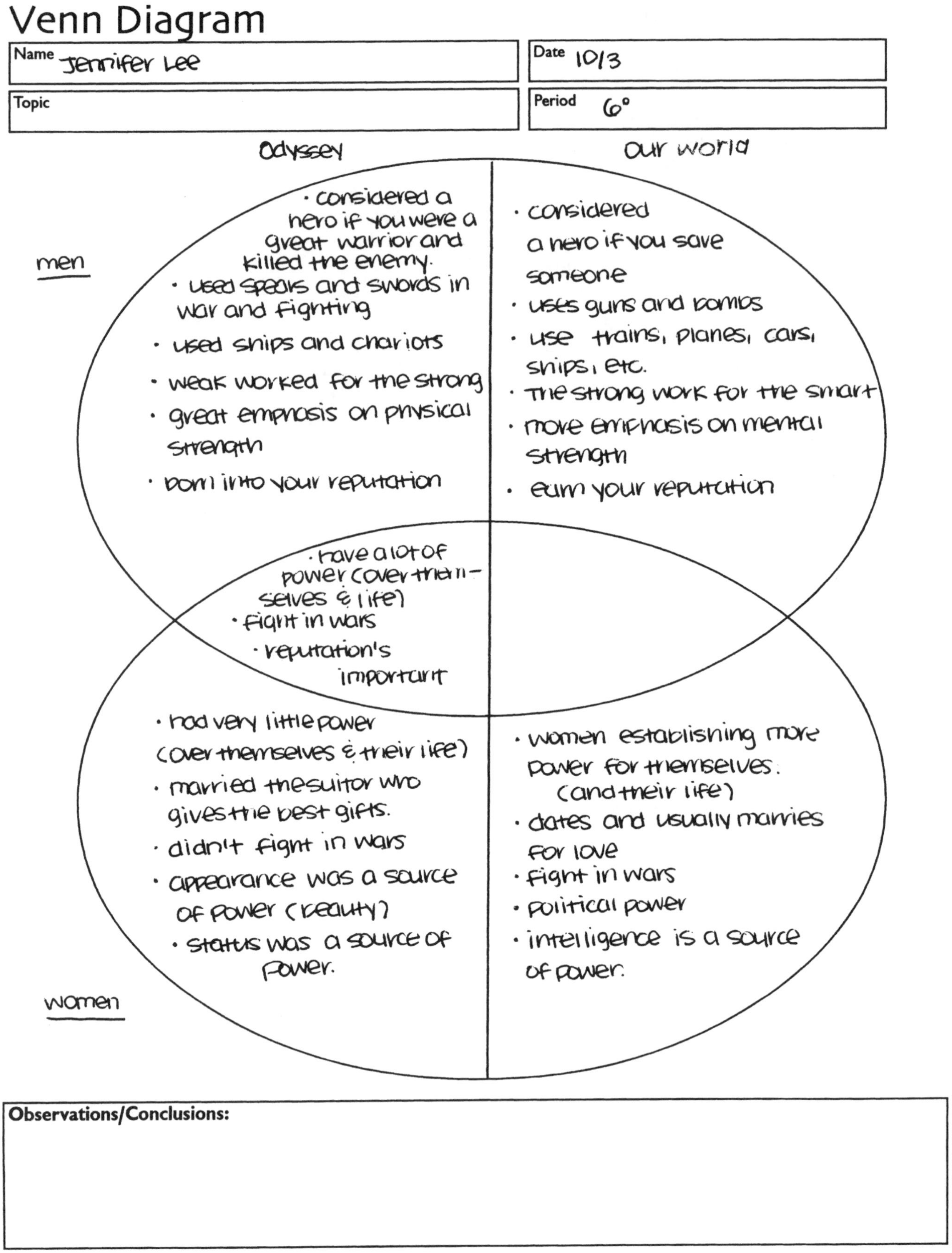

Venn Diagram

Name Jennifer Lee	Date 10/3
Topic	Period 6°

	Odyssey	Our world
men	· considered a hero if you were a great warrior and killed the enemy. · used spears and swords in war and fighting · used ships and chariots · weak worked for the strong · great emphasis on physical strength · born into your reputation	· considered a hero if you save someone · uses guns and bombs · use trains, planes, cars, ships, etc. · The strong work for the smart · more emphasis on mental strength · earn your reputation
men (overlap)	· have a lot of power (over them-selves & life) · fight in wars · reputation's important	
women	· had very little power (over themselves & their life) · married the suitor who gives the best gifts. · didn't fight in wars · appearance was a source of power (beauty) · status was a source of power.	· women establishing more power for themselves. (and their life) · dates and usually marries for love · fight in wars · political power · intelligence is a source of power.

Observations/Conclusions:

FIGURE 24.2 Venn Diagram comparing men and women in Homer's *Odyssey* and our society today

Dense Question Strategy

Overview: Good readers build meaningful links between what they read and think and the world in which they live. This assignment asks you to generate a basic question that the text can answer, then add to this some component that links what you are reading to your own experiences, thoughts, beliefs, and opinions. Eventually you create one single question, called a "dense question," about which you can write an essay. In this essay you would write about the intersection between your reading this semester, your life, and the world. Easy stuff! I have provided example questions related to *Catcher in the Rye*; you should be able to translate these into helpful samples for whatever book you are reading.

TYPE OF QUESTION	DESCRIPTION	EXAMPLE
TEXT	•-info found in text	•-Who is the narrator of the story?
READER	•-reader's experience, values, ideas	•-Have you ever felt fed up with everything •-and just wanted to take off, get away on •-your own?
WORLD or OTHER LIT.	•-knowledge of history, other cultures, •-other literature	•-What other character—in a book or a •-movie—would you compare the main •-character to?
SHADED:		
TEXT/READER	•-combines knowledge of text with •-reader's own experiences, values, ideas	•-What characteristics do you share with •-the main character?
TEXT/WORLD	•-combines knowledge of text with •-knowledge of history and cultures	•-In what ways is Holden similar to •-teenagers today? In what ways are today's •-teenagers different?
TEXT/OTHER LITERATURE	•-combines knowledge of text with •-knowledge of other pieces of literature	•-How does Holden's relationship with his •-sister compare with Esperanza's?
READER/WORLD	•-combines knowledge of reader's own •-experiences with knowledge of other •-cultures, people	•-In what ways are teenagers in other •-countries similar to American teens? In •-what ways are they different?
READER/OTHER LITERATURE	•-combines knowledge of reader's own •-experiences with other pieces of literature	•-In what ways are you similar and/or •-different from Holden and Esperanza?
DENSE QUESTION:		
TEXT/READER/WORLD -or- TEXT/READER/OTHER LIT.	•-combines knowledge of all three areas •-into one DENSE question	•-Why does Holden feel alienated and how •-is that related to what many of today's •-teens feel? Include in your answer a •-discussion of the extent to which you do •-or don't share these same feelings and why.

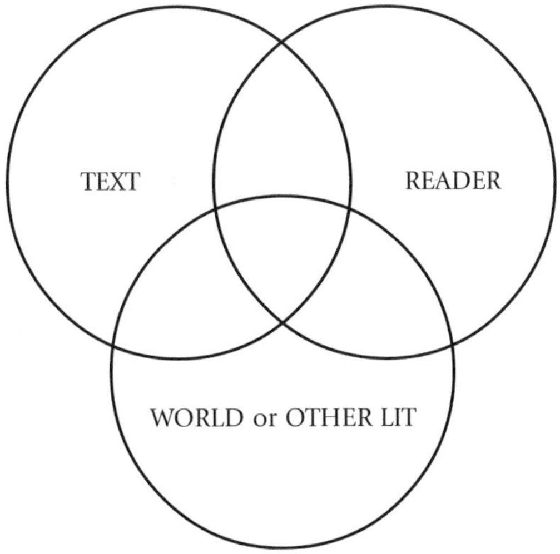

FIGURE 24.3 Venn Diagram: Dense Question Strategy

25 Visual Explanations

STANDARDS

- Reading
  - ☐ Analyze organizational patterns of information
  - ☐ Compare ideas, texts, or authors
  - ☐ Evaluate the arguments presented in a text
  - ☐ Extend ideas
  - ☐ Generate relevant questions
  - ☐ Identify and analyze recurring themes
  - ☐ Prepare to read
  - ☐ Synthesize information from multiple sources
- Writing
  - ☐ Establish a main or controlling idea
  - ☐ Organize information and ideas in logical, appropriate format
  - ☐ Prepare to write
  - ☐ Use sensory, concrete, or illustrative details to support claims
- Speaking
  - ☐ Analyze devices used in others' speeches
  - ☐ Compare events or ideas
  - ☐ Organize information for desired effect on audience
  - ☐ Prepare to speak
- Listening
  - ☐ Improve note-taking skills
  - ☐ Organize information
- Viewing
  - ☐ Gather details and examples for subsequent analysis of text
  - ☐ Identify organization of information
- Test Preparation
  - ☐ Comprehend information
  - ☐ Organize ideas
  - ☐ Prioritize information
  - ☐ Remember information

SUBJECT AREAS

- English language arts
- Health
- Humanities
- Mathematics
- Science
- Social studies

USES

- Ask useful questions
- Assess student performance
- Compare two or more items, aspects, or people
- Evaluate ideas
- Extend ideas beyond obvious
- Facilitate discussion
- Gather evidence to support claims
- Generate ideas
- Identify themes
- Make connections
- Narrow or refine subject
- Observe patterns
- Organize information
- Prepare to read
- Prepare to write
- Respond to reading
- Support critical reading
- Synthesize ideas
- Take notes while reading
- Visualize what is read

DESCRIPTION

In his books, information scientist Edwin Tufte (1996) alternately discusses images as verbs and as nouns. A map, for instance, is a noun; the act of mapping out your ideas or a course through time and space is, on the other hand, a verb. A visual explanation is just a means of using graphic elements—lines, shapes, symbols, icons, colors, patterns, and so on—to convey relationships or ideas. We use them in maps, diagrams, charts, and drawings. Football coaches use them to describe what they want to happen (or what did happen) out on the football field. As our society becomes more multilingual, more visual in its forms of communication, visual explanations will become more common and communication more effective.

The Visual Explanation tool is difficult to describe since it comes in all forms and serve many different functions. (See Figure 25.1 for some possibilities.) The question to ask, however, when deciding if a Visual Explanation would help is, "Would this reveal something that mere words do not or cannot?" Also, when "drawing the action," ask whether other features—line patterns, colors, shapes, or icons—would allow you to communicate more useful information in your Visual Explanation.

Rarely is the artistic merit of an explanation important. You are trying to convey an idea. Primary colors or stick figures are fine if they work. Visual Explanations are ways of thinking—in numbers, shapes, colors, or patterns—and communicating. They work well in all subject areas and are one of the many types of text students must be able to read—and create—if they are to be successful in this world.

NOTES AND EXAMPLES

Example One: Tupac's Mind

While reading *Macbeth*, students in my sophomore English class took time to wonder what goes through another person's mind as we watched Macbeth himself go crazy. In Figure 25.2, Jesse Moore reflects on what went through the mind of an artist he respected very much: Tupac Shakur. Such assignments help a student like Jesse build a bridge between his own interests and the books he is asked to read. This tool provided Jesse a viable means of explaining his own ideas using some of his graphic talent.

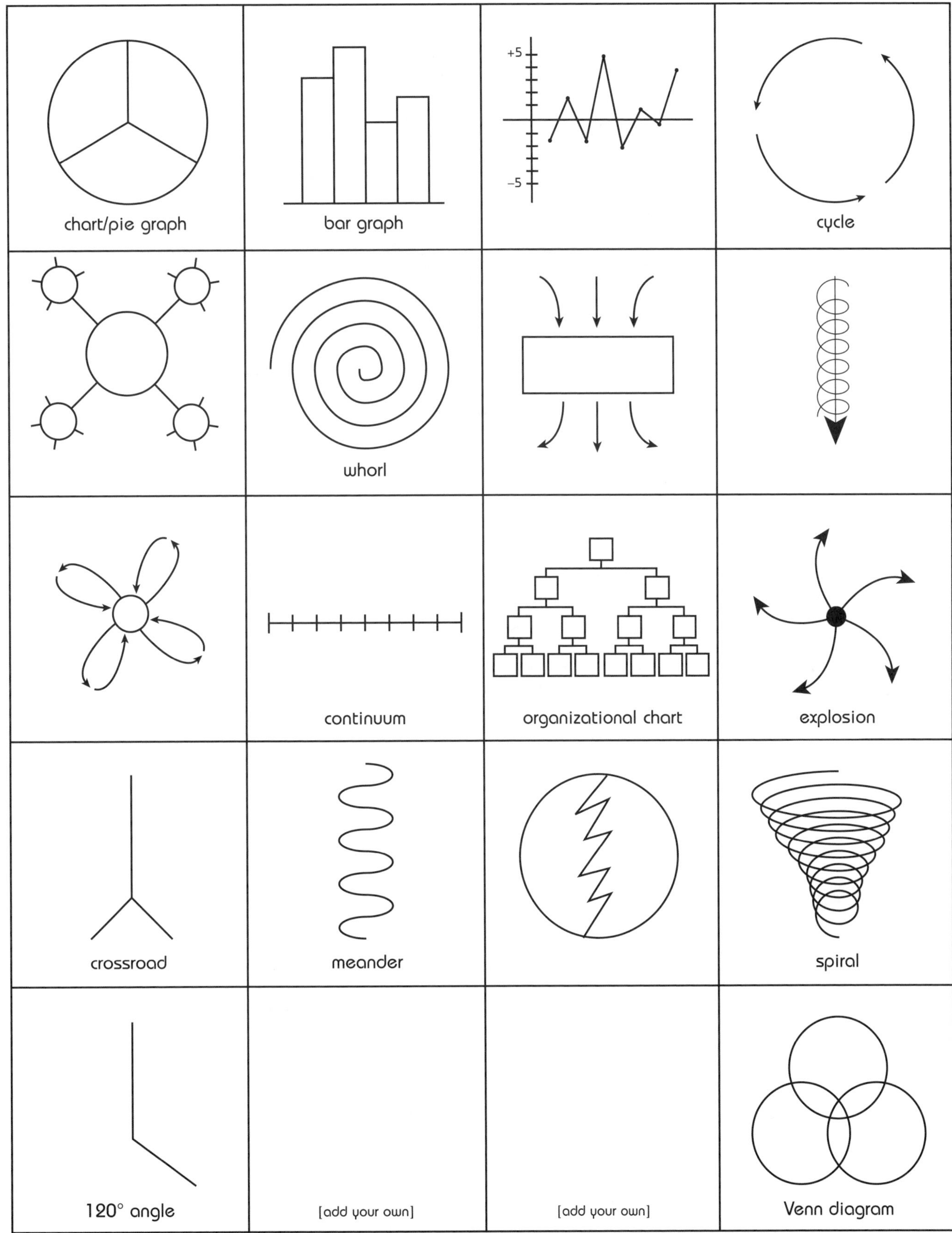

FIGURE 25.1 Visual Explanations: Gallery of Graphic Patterns

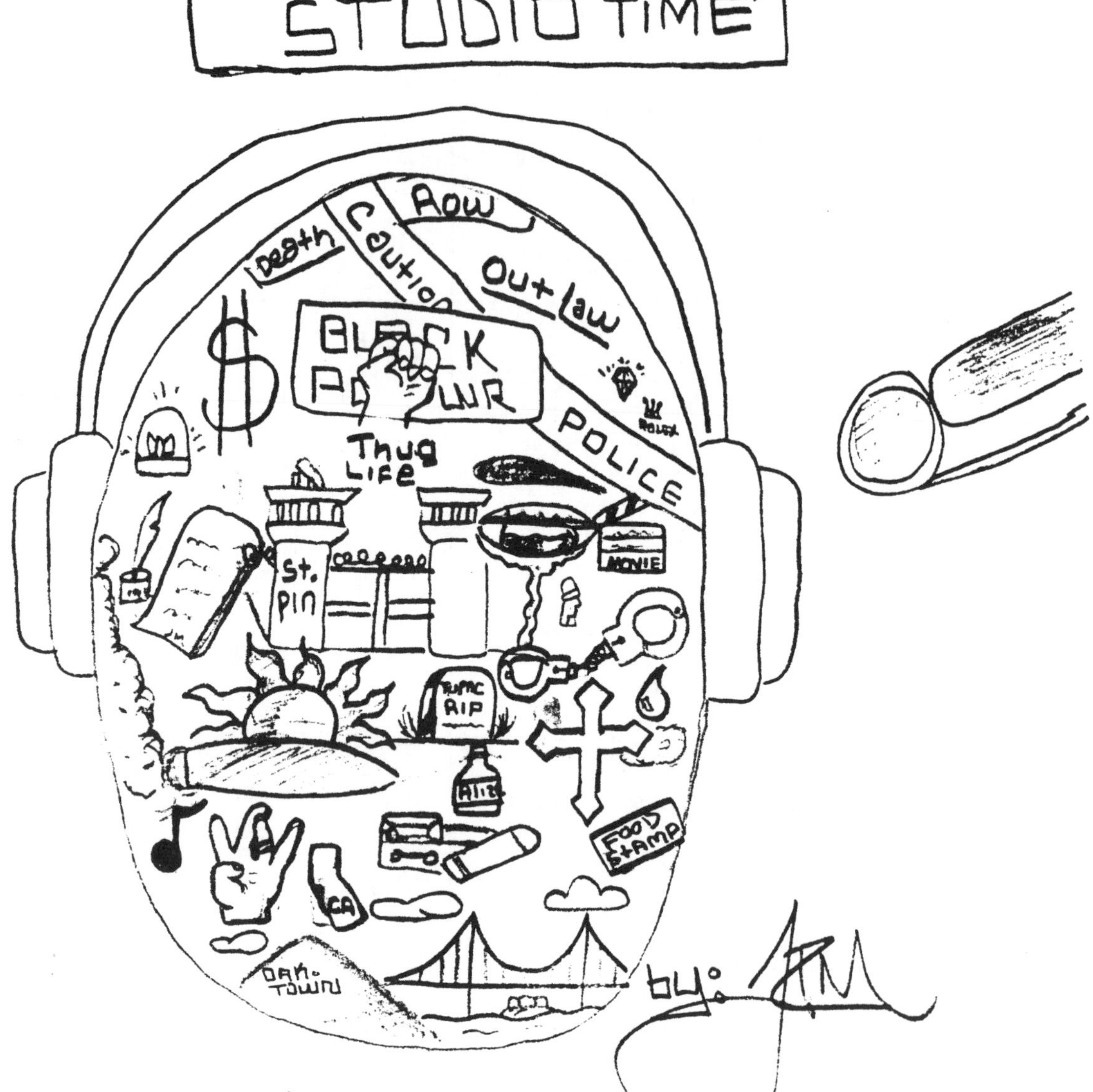
STUDIO TIME
Row
Death
Caution
Out law
BLACK POWR
Thug LIFE
POLICE
St. PIN
MOVIE
TUPAC RIP
FOOD STAMP
CA
OAK-TOWN
by: JM
Explain: This is a picture of what Tupac saw, dealt with, and said in his life. He loved his mom, who used to be a black panther (fist/Black Power flag); he saw people murdered (coufin); He has been to jail and prision (handcaufs/st. pin); Tupac always talked about being an outlaw from the west side (hand); Tupac was born in prison, and grew up in the getto with out a father (st. pin/Food stamp); Along with his love of music and poetry, he loved acting (Poetry paper, music note, Acting que)

FIGURE 25.2 Jesse Moore used this Visual Explanation to reflect on what went on in Tupac's mind in order to help him understand Macbeth's character.

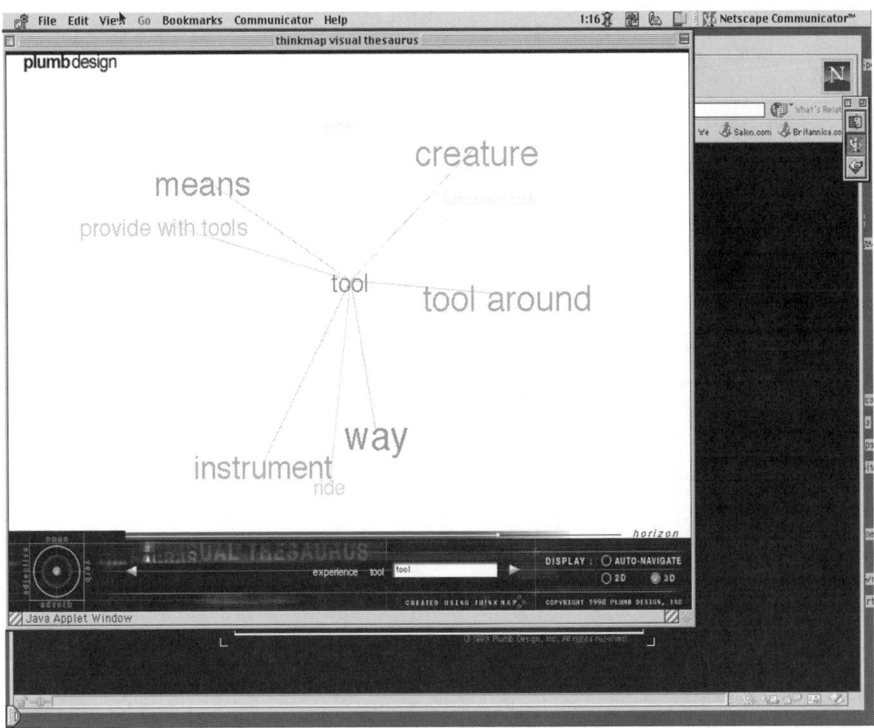

FIGURE 25.3 Visual Thesaurus. You can learn more about the *Plumb Design Visual Thesaurus* at <www.plumbdesign.com>. Image used with permission of Plumb Design.

Example Two: Mindmaps

The *Plumb Visual Thesaurus* (<www.plumbdesign.com>) is one of my favorite Web sites. In class, we type in a word and, with the site up on my TV monitor, watch it draw out a range of associations for the word. For example, in Figure 25.3, you can see what the site came up with when we entered the word *tool*. You can ask it to pick terms by part of speech and it can display them in various formats. Katy Wallace (see Figure 25.4) shows us the good old-fashioned way of using this technique. With pen and paper she generated a wonderful mess of interesting ideas about the subject of identity, then synthesized these ideas into a paragraph.

Example Three: Odysseus' Palace

When we reach the climactic scenes of Homer's *Odyssey*, students have a hard time seeing what a palace must have looked like in the time in which the story is set. I tell them to draw Odysseus' palace, based on only those details they can find in the book. This forces them to read closely and be sure that what they draw is what Homer wrote. It also develops their inferential skills because they must draw from different bits of information about what something looked like or how many doors there were, for example. (See Figure 25.5.)

Example Four: *Midsummer Night's Dream*

Tony found it difficult to keep track of the different characters and their relationships while reading Shakespeare's *Midsummer Night's Dream*, so drew out the relationships to help him visualize the connections. (See Figure 25.6.)

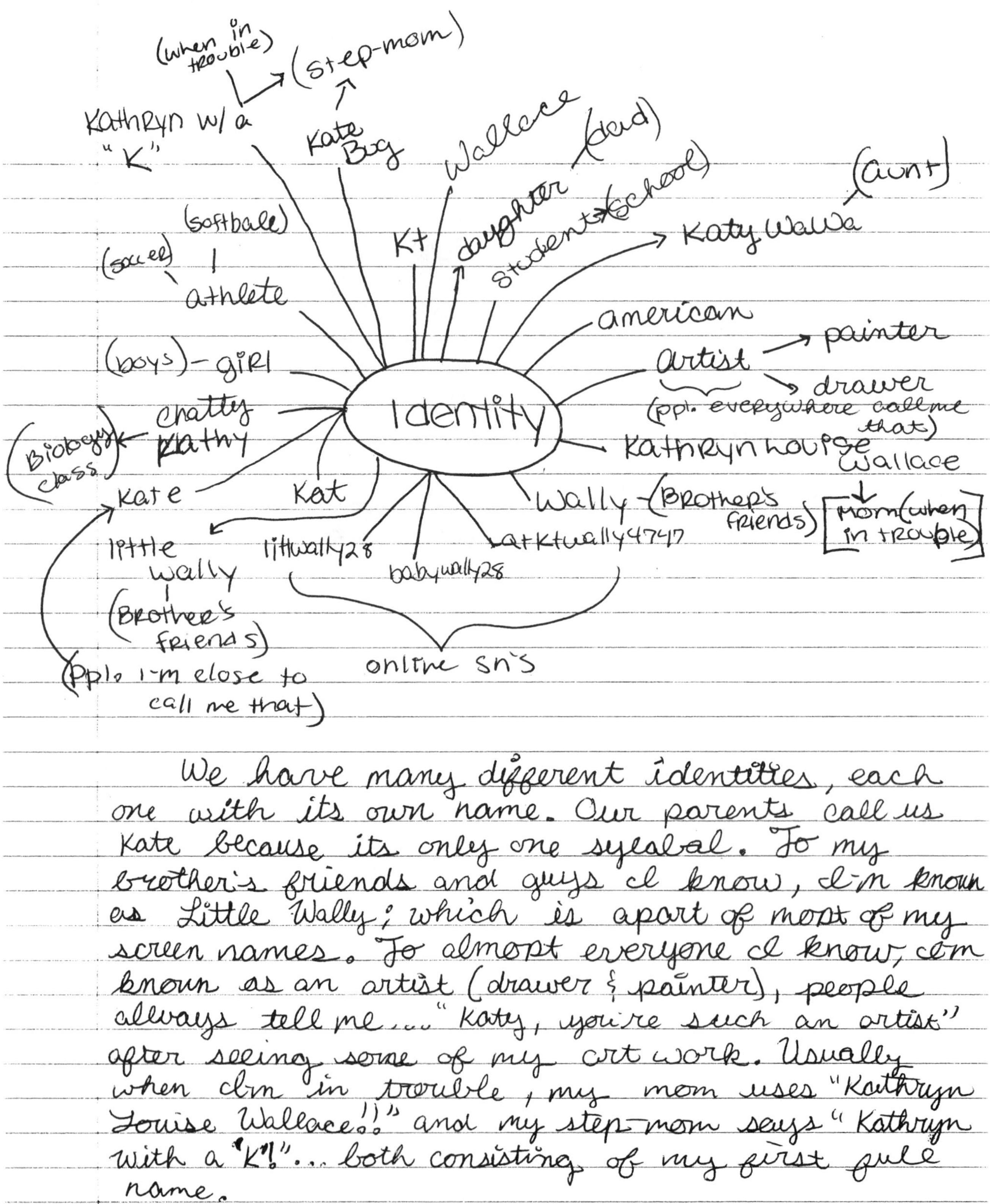
(when in trouble)
(step-mom)
Kathryn w/ a "K"
Kate Bug
Wallace
(dead)
(aunt)
Kt
daughter
student
school
Katy Walla
(softball)
(soccer)
athlete
american
painter
(boys) - girl
artist
drawer
(ppl. everywhere call me that)
chatty Kathy
Identity
(Biology class)
Kathryn Louise Wallace
mom (when in trouble)
kate
Kat
Wally
(Brother's friends)
little wally
(Brother's friends)
lilwally28
babywally28
katktwally4747
online sn's
(ppl. I'm close to call me that)
We have many different identities, each one with its own name. Our parents call us Kate because its only one syealbal. To my brother's friends and guys I know, I'm known as Little Wally; which is apart of most of my screen names. To almost everyone I know, I'm known as an artist (drawer & painter), people always tell me... "Katy, you're such an artist" after seeing some of my art work. Usually when I'm in trouble, my mom uses "Kathryn Louise Wallace!!" and my step-mom says "Kathryn with a "K"!"... both consisting of my first full name.

FIGURE 25.4 Katy Wallace generated a wide range of ideas about identity with this Visual Explanation prior to beginning a paper on that subject.

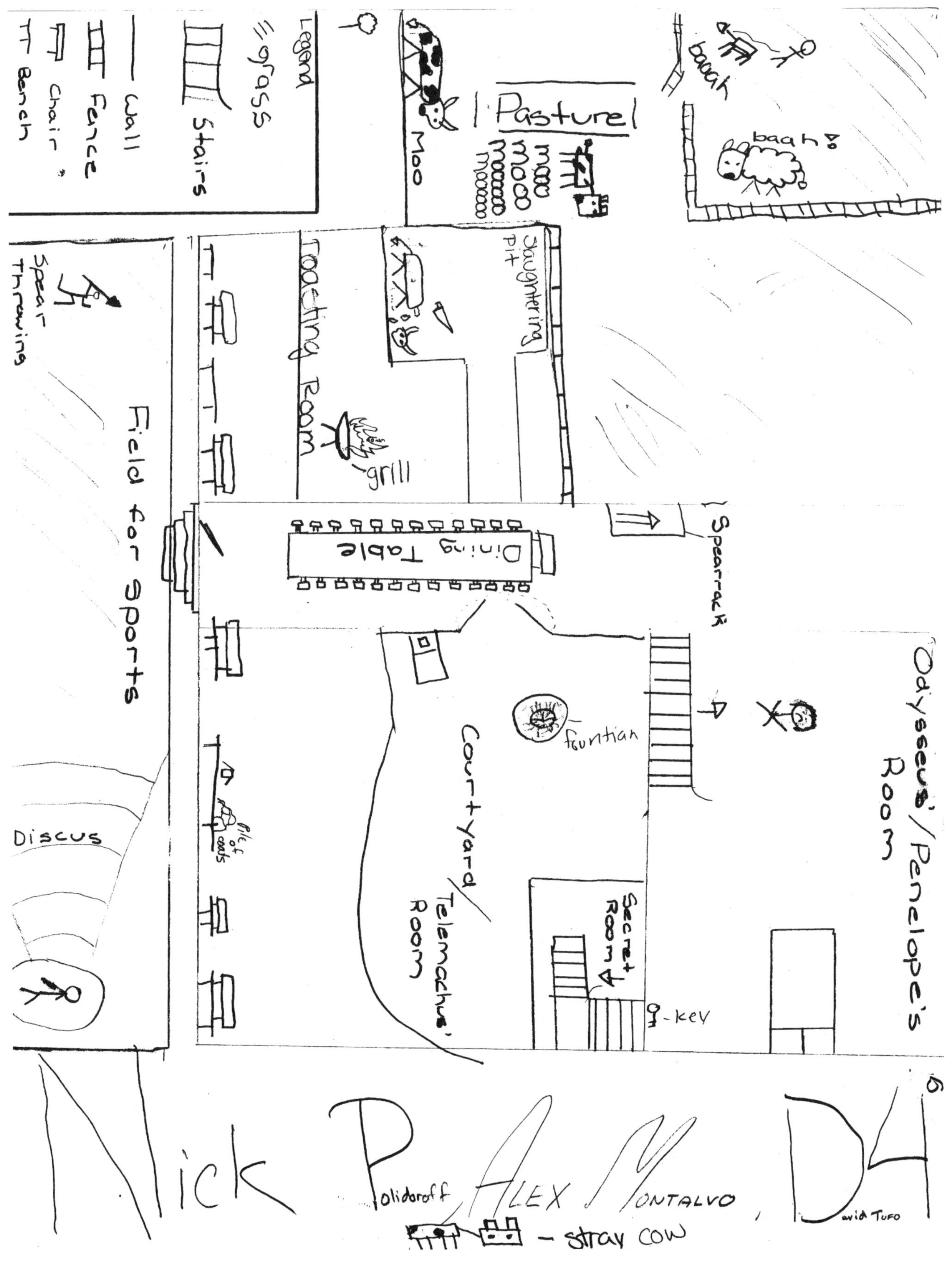

FIGURE 25.5 Students drew Odysseus' palace to help them visualize his return home.

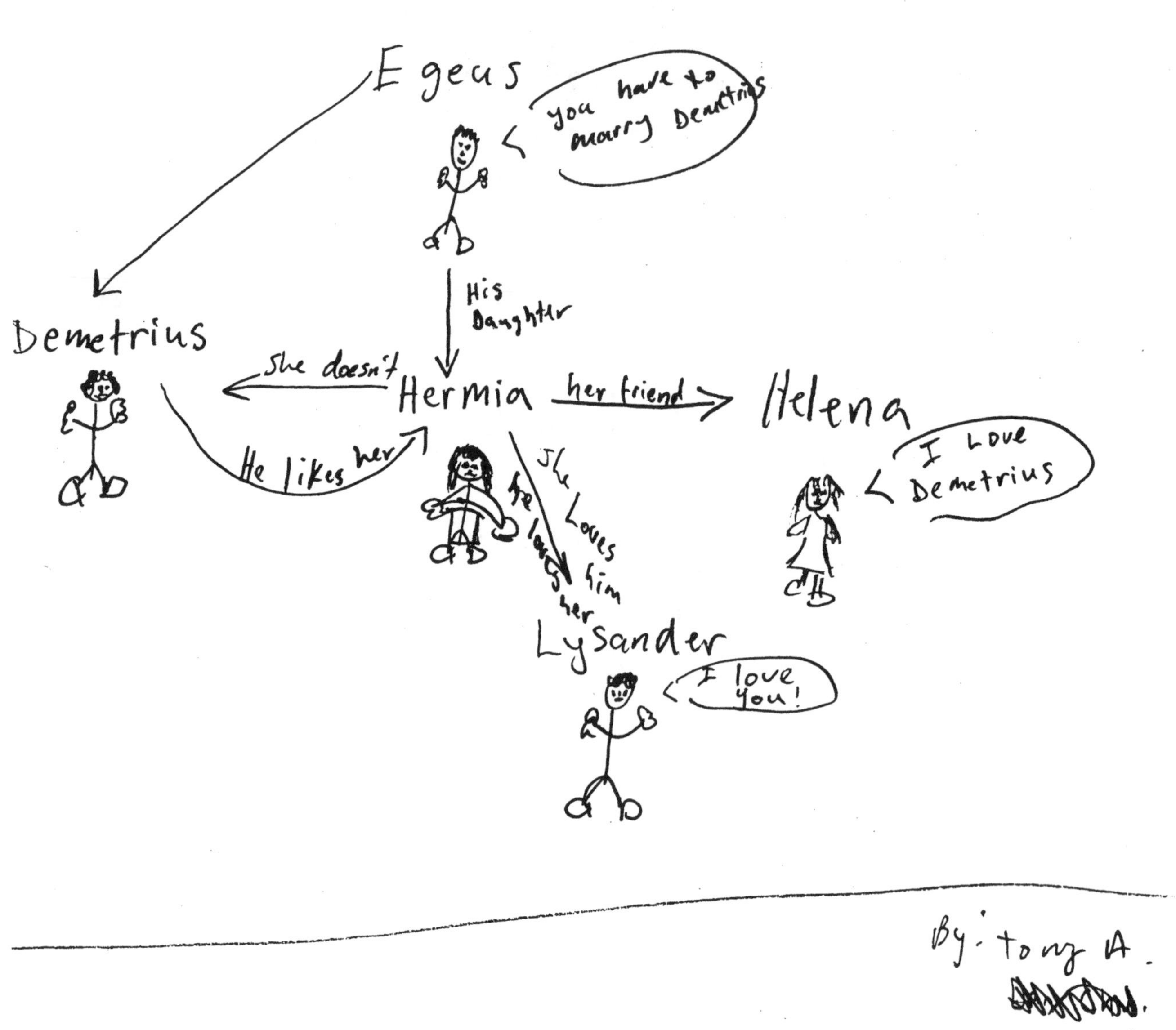

FIGURE 25.6 Tony Arteaga visually depicted the different relationships in *Midsummer Night's Dream.*

Example Five: Life Graph

Two students approached this assignment differently. (See Figures 25.7 and 25.8.) The idea was to generate ideas for different writing assignments while also building a bridge between their own emerging life and the life of a character in a book we were reading. Looking at life as a series of stages helps them see not only what the character is going through but what they themselves are going through. The graph shows them that not all events are equal in life, that some are, in fact, quite significant in the long run. I tell them to limit their events only to those that have compelling stories attached to them so that they can pick any spot on their graph and write a great story about it.

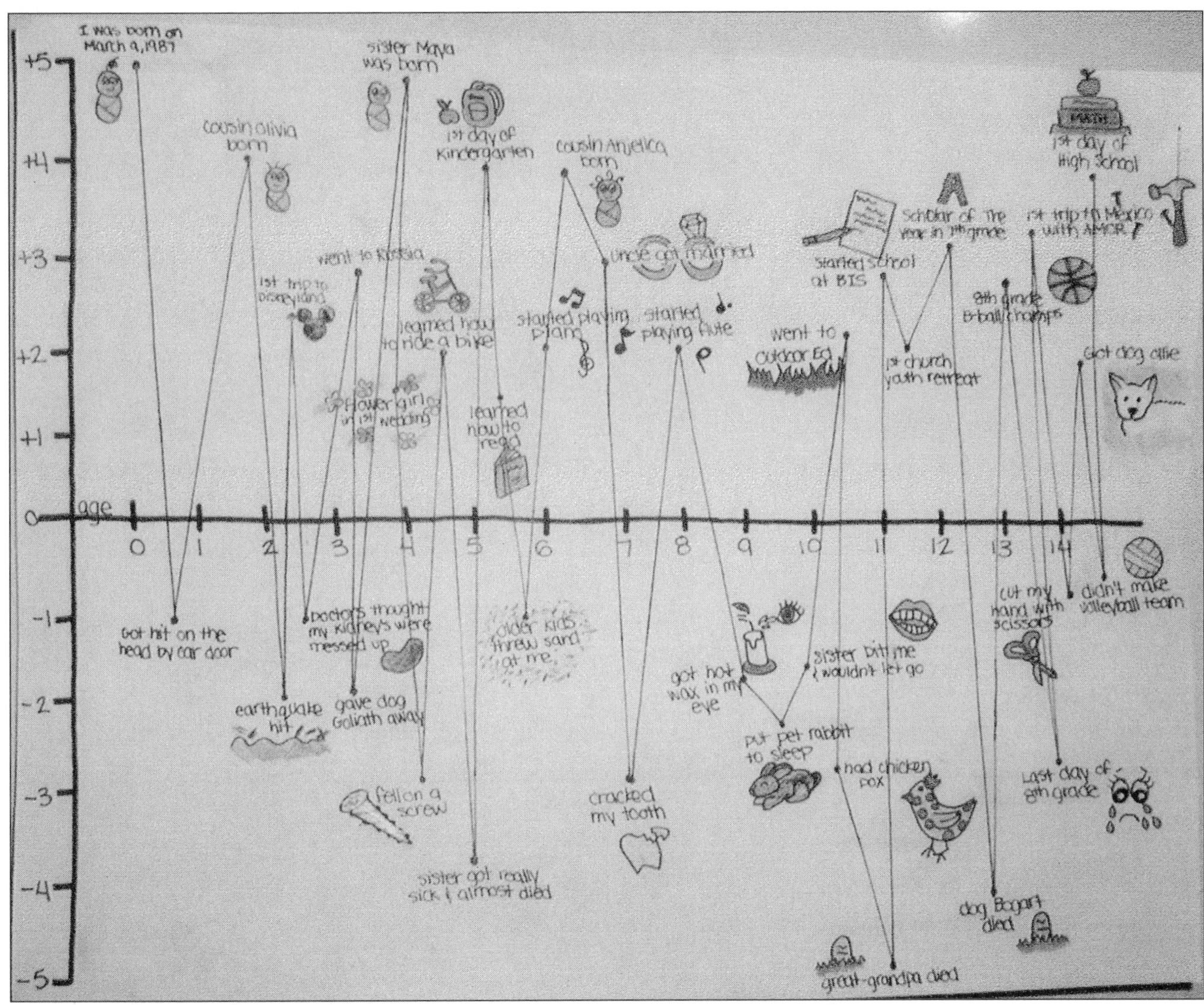

FIGURE 25.7 Cassie's Life Graph

Example Six: Homer's *Odyssey*

As they neared the end of *The Odyssey*, I wanted students to get the big picture and improve their understanding of how the story was organized. One group came up with a perfect way to explain the parallel journeys that both Odysseus and his son Telemachus take. (See Figure 25.9.) Their written explanation of the drawing further clarifies what they tried to accomplish in the drawing. They wrote:

> Our representation of *The Odyssey* is in the form of a sword. Yes, we may have produced it for its dashing looks and incredible physical appearance, but it also has a profound meaning. In the diagram, the sword helps juxtapose Odysseus and Telemachus, while describing the common main events along the blade of the sword. Above the sword are things Telemachus goes through during his life. There are also some words that describe Telemachus. Events having to do with Odysseus are located along the bottom side of the sword. You can also find character traits. Arrows go from some of the other traits that contradict each other.

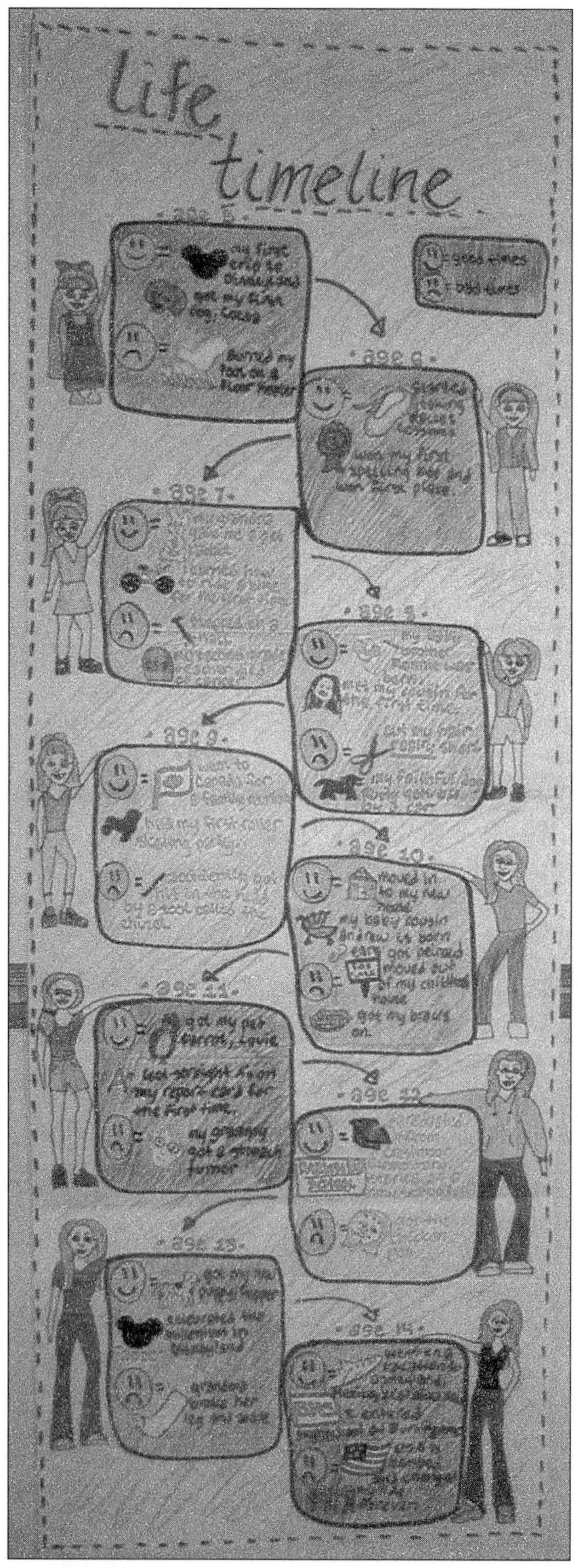

FIGURE 25.8 Melissa Glass approached the Life Graph assignment in a different way.

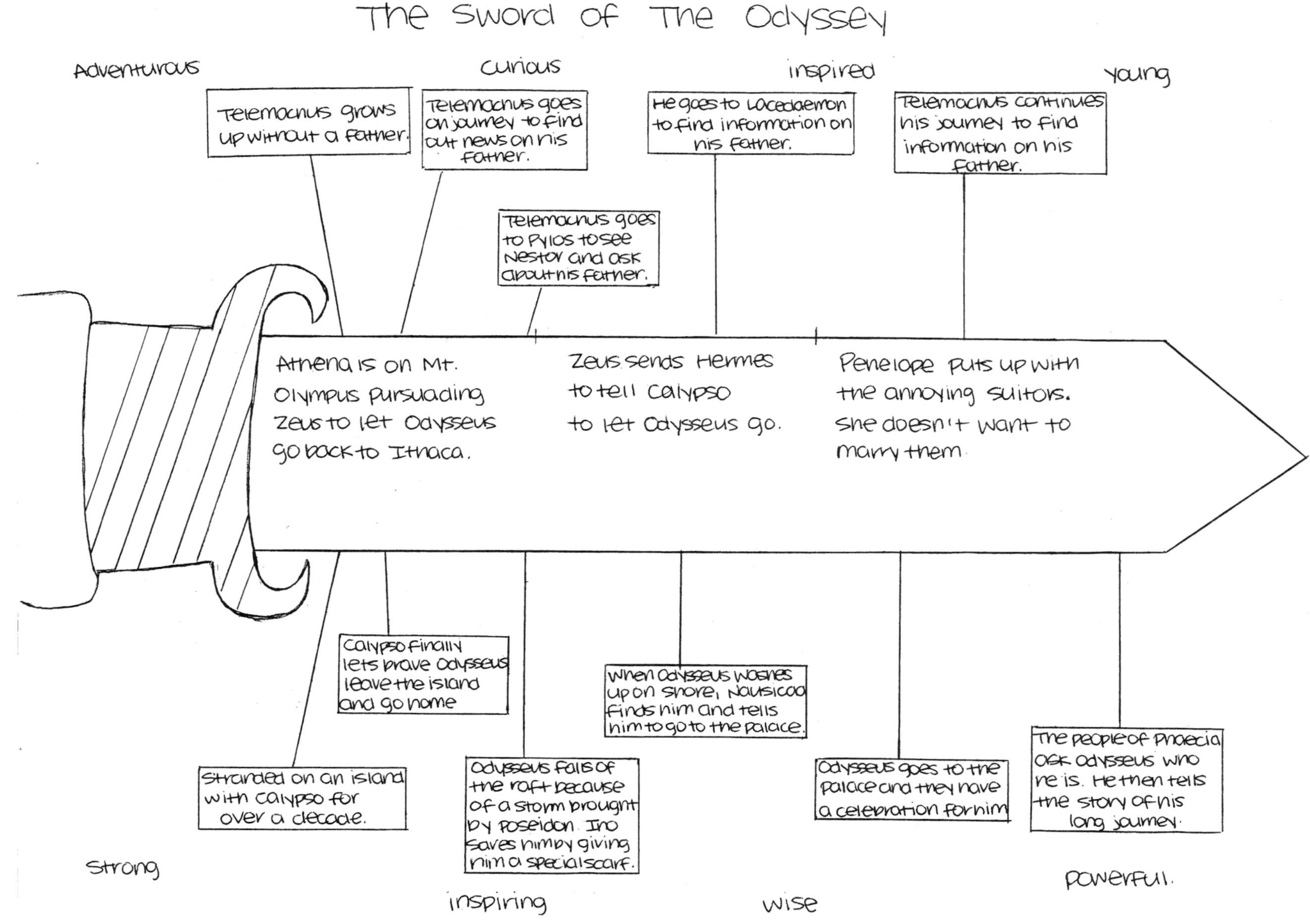

The Sword of The Odyssey
Adventurous
curious
inspired
young
Telemachus grows up without a father.
Telemachus goes on journey to find out news on his father.
Telemachus goes to Pylos to see Nestor and ask about his father.
He goes to Lacedaemon to find information on his father.
Telemachus continues his journey to find information on his father.
Athena is on Mt. Olympus pursuading Zeus to let Odysseus go back to Ithaca.
Zeus sends Hermes to tell Calypso to let Odysseus go.
Penelope puts up with the annoying suitors. She doesn't want to marry them.
Calypso finally lets brave Odysseus leave the island and go home
When Odysseus washes up on shore, Nausicaa finds him and tells him to go to the palace.
Stranded on an island with Calypso for over a decade.
Odysseus falls of the raft because of a storm brought by Poseidon. Ino saves him by giving him a special scarf.
Odysseus goes to the palace and they have a celebration for him
The people of Phaecia ask Odysseus who he is. He then tells the story of his long journey.
strong
inspiring
wise
powerful.

FIGURE 25.9 Students synthesized the different events in *The Odyssey* to help them understand the plot and the parallel journies of Odysseus and his son Telemachus.

26 Vocabulary Squares

STANDARDS

- Reading
  - ☐ Extend ideas
  - ☐ Generate relevant questions
  - ☐ Identify and analyze recurring themes
  - ☐ Prepare to read
- Language Study
  - ☐ Distinguish between denotative and connotative meaning
  - ☐ Examine and use different Greek and Latin roots of words
  - ☐ Know and use different parts of speech
- Test Preparation
  - ☐ Comprehend information
  - ☐ Organize ideas
  - ☐ Prioritize information
  - ☐ Remember information

SUBJECT AREAS

- English language arts
- Health
- Humanities
- Mathematics
- Science
- Social studies

USES

- Ask useful questions
- Assess student performance
- Develop academic literacy
- Extend ideas beyond obvious
- Generate ideas
- Make connections
- Prepare to read
- Respond to reading
- Synthesize ideas
- Visualize what is read

DESCRIPTION

Vocabulary Squares combine a range of strategies for improving students' vocabulary. It is one part of a language study program, not the only thing I do. Each of the six squares incorporates language study (etymology and parts of speech); vocabulary expansion (through synonyms, antonyms, and different conjugations); application (through use in an original sentence); and visual representation. Each of these aspects helps the student connect to and process the word in multiple ways. Teachers have the option of following up the completion of this assignment with a quiz or eventual test on the words.

The premise of the tool is that we learn vocabulary in context but only remember it if we can use it and get it to "stick" to what we already know. Too many teachers content themselves with assigning long lists of words or roots that are then found on massive tests that make success in classes elusive for students who don't test well. Also, students often receive lists of words from most of their classes. Some students can have as many as one hundred words they are expected to "memorize" each week between their English, science, and mathematics classes. Vocabulary squares assume that deeper study of a few words and the words related to them, including the history and meanings of the words, is superior to the interminable lists many students are assigned. One alternative to giving them the word is to give them the root word and have them find the information listed on the sheet. (See Figure 26.1.)

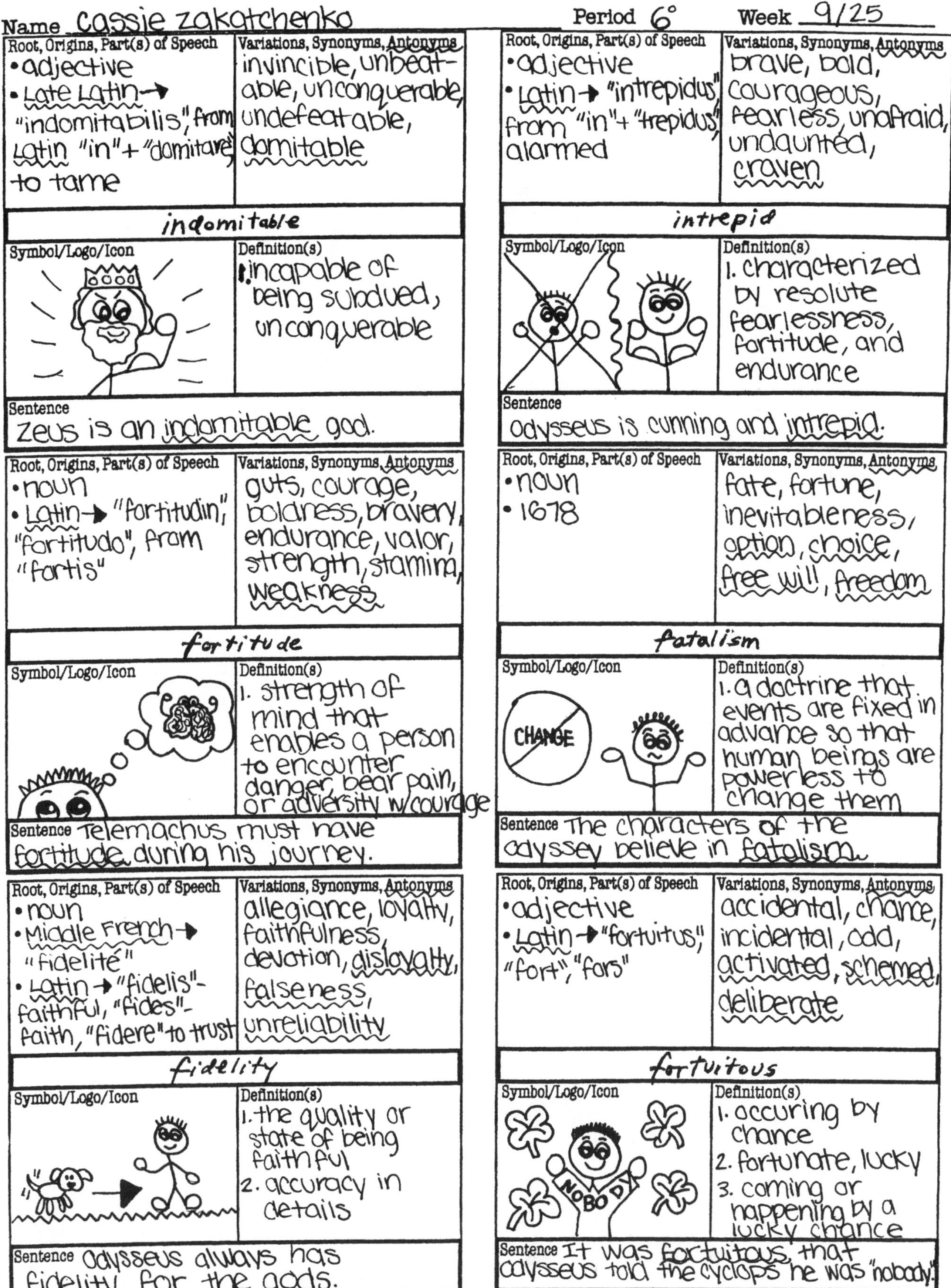

Name cassie zakatchenko Period 6° Week 9/25

indomitable

Root, Origins, Part(s) of Speech
- adjective
- Late Latin → "indomitabilis," from Latin "in" + "domitare," to tame

Variations, Synonyms, Antonyms
invincible, unbeatable, unconquerable, undefeatable, domitable

Symbol/Logo/Icon

Definition(s)
1. incapable of being subdued, unconquerable

Sentence Zeus is an indomitable god.

intrepid

Root, Origins, Part(s) of Speech
- adjective
- Latin → "intrepidus," from "in" + "trepidus," alarmed

Variations, Synonyms, Antonyms
brave, bold, courageous, fearless, unafraid, undaunted, craven

Symbol/Logo/Icon

Definition(s)
1. characterized by resolute fearlessness, fortitude, and endurance

Sentence Odysseus is cunning and intrepid.

fortitude

Root, Origins, Part(s) of Speech
- noun
- Latin → "fortitudin," "fortitudo," from "fortis"

Variations, Synonyms, Antonyms
guts, courage, boldness, bravery, endurance, valor, strength, stamina, weakness

Symbol/Logo/Icon

Definition(s)
1. strength of mind that enables a person to encounter danger, bear pain, or adversity w/courage

Sentence Telemachus must have fortitude during his journey.

fatalism

Root, Origins, Part(s) of Speech
- noun
- 1678

Variations, Synonyms, Antonyms
fate, fortune, inevitableness, option, choice, free will, freedom

Symbol/Logo/Icon
CHANGE

Definition(s)
1. a doctrine that events are fixed in advance so that human beings are powerless to change them

Sentence The characters of the odyssey believe in fatalism.

fidelity

Root, Origins, Part(s) of Speech
- noun
- Middle French → "fidelité"
- Latin → "fidelis" - faithful, "fides" - faith, "fidere" to trust

Variations, Synonyms, Antonyms
allegiance, loyalty, faithfulness, devotion, disloyalty, falseness, unreliability

Symbol/Logo/Icon

Definition(s)
1. the quality or state of being faithful
2. accuracy in details

Sentence Odysseus always has fidelity for the gods.

fortuitous

Root, Origins, Part(s) of Speech
- adjective
- Latin → "fortuitus," "fort," "fors"

Variations, Synonyms, Antonyms
accidental, chance, incidental, odd, activated, schemed, deliberate

Symbol/Logo/Icon
NOBODY

Definition(s)
1. occuring by chance
2. fortunate, lucky
3. coming or happening by a lucky chance

Sentence It was fortuitous that odysseus told the cyclops he was "nobody."

FIGURE 26.1 Sample Vocabulary Squares sheet

Bibliography

Note: Some titles included here are not directly cited but are perhaps the inspiration for ideas I have discussed in this book.

Allen, Janet. 1999. *Words Words Words: Teaching Vocabulary in Grades 4–12*. York, ME: Stenhouse.

Bateson, Mary Catherine. 1990. *Composing a Life*. New York: Plume.

Beck, Isabel L. ed., Margaret G. McKeown, and Rebecca L. Hamilton. 1997. *Questioning the Author: An Approach for Enhancing Student Engagement with Text*. Newark, DE: International Reading Association.

Bell, Madison Smart. 1997. *Narrative Design: A Writer's Guide to Structure*. New York: W. W. Norton.

Bloom, Benjamin, ed. 1956. *Taxonomy of Educational Objectives: The Classification of Educational Goals: Handbook I, Cognitive Domain*. New York; Toronto: Longmans; Green.

Booth, Wayne. 1995. *The Craft of Research: Chicago Guide to Writing, Editing, and Publishing*. Chicago: University of Chicago Press.

Brooks, Jacquiline Grennon, and Martin G. Brooks, 1999. *In Search of Understanding: The Case for Constructivist Classrooms*. Alexandria, VA: Association for Supervision and Curriculm Development.

Buehl, Doug. 2001. *Classroom Strategies for Interactive Learning*. Newark, DE: International Reading Association.

Burke, Jim. 1999. *The English Teacher's Companion: A Complete Guide to Classroom, Curriculum, and the Profession*. Portsmouth, NH: BoyntonCook.

———. 2000. *Reading Reminders: Tools, Tips and Techniques*. Portsmouth, NH: Boyton/Cook.

Burke, Jim, et al. 2002. *The Reader's Handbook*. Wilmington, MA: Great Source.

Caine, Renate Nummela, and Geoffrey Caine. 1994. *Making Connections: Teaching and the Human Brain*. Menlo Park, CA: Addison-Wesley.

Chamot, Anna Uhl, and J. Michael O'Malley. 1994. *The CALLA Handbook: Implementing the Cognitive Academic Language Learning Approach*. Reading, MA: Addison-Wesley.

Christenbury, Leila, and Patricia P. Kelly. 1983. *Questioning: A Path to Critical Thinking*. Urbana, IL: ERIC and National Council of Teachers of English.

Claggett, Fran, and Joan Brown. 1992. *Drawing Your Own Conclusions: Graphic Strategies for Reading, Writing, and Thinking*. Portsmouth, NH: Heinemann.

Coalition of Essential Schools. 1989. "Asking the Essential Questions: Curriculum Development." *HORACE* 5(5).

Csikszentmihalyi, Mihaly. 1991. *Flow: The Psychology of Optimal Experience*. New York: HarperPerennial.

Daniels, Harvey. 2001. *Literature Circles: Voice and Choice in the Student-Centered Classroom*. York, ME: Stenhouse.

Devlin, Keith. 2000. *The Math Gene: How Mathematical Thinking Evolved and Why Numbers Are Like Gossip*. New York: Basic Books.

Echevarria, Jana, and Anne Graves. 1998. *Sheltered Content Instruction: Teaching English Language Learners with Diverse Abilities*. Reading, MA: Addison-Wesley.

Ehrlich, Jeffrey, and Marc Mannheimer. 1990. *The Carpenter's Manifesto: A Total Guide That Takes All the Mystery Out of Carpentry for Everybody*. New York: Henry Holt.

Elbow, Peter. 1981. *Writing with Power: Techniques for Mastering the Writing Process*. New York: Oxford University Press.

Facione, Peter A., and Noreen C. Facione. 1996. "Holistic Critical Thinking Scoring Rubric." Millbrae, CA: California Press.

Gardner, Howard. 1983. *Frames of Mind: The Theory of Multiple Intelligences*. New York: Basic.

———. 1996. *Leading Minds: An Anatomy of Leadership*. New York: Basic.

———. 2000. *The Disciplined Mind: Beyond Facts and Standardized Tests, the K–12 Education That Every Child Deserves*. New York: Simon and Schuster.

Goleman, Daniel. 1995. *Emotional Intelligence*. New York: Bantam.

Kauffman, Stuart. 1995. *At Home in the Universe: The Search for the Laws of Self-Organization and Complexity*. New York: Oxford University Press.

Langer, Judith. 1999. "Beating the Odds: Teaching Middle and High School Students to Read and Write Well." Accessed 10 October, 2001. *http://cela.albany.edu/eie2/index.html*.

Levine, Mel. 1994. *Educational Care: A System for Understanding and Helping Children with Learning Problems at Home and in School*. Cambridge, MA: Educators Publishing.

Nielsen, Jakob. 1999. *Designing Web Usability: The Practice of Simplicity*. Indianapolis, IN: New Riders.

Norman, Donald. 1993. *Things That Make Us Smart: Defending Human Attributes in the Age of the Machine*. Cambridge, MA: Perseus.

Olson, Carol Booth, ed. 1996. *Reading, Thinking, and Writing About Multicultural Literature*. Glenview, IL: Scott Foresman.

Peitzman, Faye, and George Gadda. 1994. *With Different Eyes: Insights into Teaching Language Minority Students Across the Disciplines*. Reading, MA: Addison-Wesley.

Peterson, Art. 1996. *The Writer's Workout Book: 113 Stretches Toward Better Prose*. Berkeley: National Writing Project.

Postman, Neil. 1995. *The End of Education: Redefining the Value of School*. New York: Vintage.

———. 1999. *Building a Bridge to the Eighteenth Century: How the Past Can Improve Our Future*. New York: Alfred A. Knopf.

Robb, Laura, et al. 2001. *The Reader's Handbook*. Wilmington, MA: Great Source.

Robinson, Adam. 1993. *What Smart Students Know: Maximum Grades, Optimum Learning, Minimum Time*. New York: Three Rivers.

Schlossberg, Edwin. 1998. *Interactive Excellence: Defining and Developing New Standards for the Twenty-First Century*. New York: Ballantine.

Schmoker, Michael. 1999. *Results: The Key to Continuous School Improvement*. Alexandria, VA: Association of Supervision and Curriculum Development.

Schoenbach, Ruth, Cynthia Greenleaf, Christine Cziko, and Lori Hurwitz. 1999. *Reading for Understanding: A Guide to Improving Reading in Middle and High School Classrooms*. San Francisco: Jossey-Bass.

Scholes, Robert. 1998. *The Rise and Fall of English: Reconstructing English as a Discipline*. New Haven: Yale University Press.

Sebranek, Patrick, Dave Kemper, and Verne Meyer. 2001. *Writer's Inc. A Student Handbook for Writing and Learning*. Wilmington, MA: Great Source.

Sternberg, Robert J. 1997. *Thinking Styles*. New York: Cambridge University Press.

Strunk, William, and E. B. White. 1999. *The Elements of Style*. Boston: Allyn and Bacon.

Tovani, Cris. 2000. *I Read It, But I Don't Get It: Comprehension Strategies for Adolescent Readers*. York, ME: Stenhouse.

Tufte, Edward R. 1996. *Visual Explanations: Images and Quantities, Evidence and Narrative*. Cheshire, CT: Graphics.

Vygotsky, Lev. 1994. *Thought and Language*. Edited by A. Kosulin. Cambridge: MIT Press.

Zemelman, Steve, Harvey Daniels, and Arthur Hyde. 1998. *Best Practice: New Standards for Teaching and Learning in America's Schools.* Portsmouth, NH: Heinemann.

Designing a Standards-Based Curriculum

BEFORE: INSTRUCTIONAL DESIGN

Effective instruction requires a purpose and meaningful context that establishes not only what *but* why *students must learn the assigned materials. Rationales such as "To meet the standards" or "To pass the test" lack meaning and do not motivate.*

Content Standards

What should students know and be able to do by the end of this task, unit, or course?

CONSIDERATIONS

- Connections to previous and future skills and concepts
- Constraints of time and resources
- Availability of necessary materials and resources

Student Preparation

What must students know or be able to do to accomplish Content Standards goals?

CONSIDERATIONS

- Specialized or new vocabulary terms
- Background knowledge on the idea, historical period, or story
- Skills, capacities, habits, or techniques
- Connections to previously learned skills and concepts

Teacher Preparation

What skills, knowledge, or resources do you need to effectively teach this skill or concept?

CONSIDERATIONS

- What you need or want to teach *after* this unit
- What support and material resources are available help teach this skill or concept

Instructional Standards

What strategies and instructional designs are most effective and efficient in teaching this skill or concept?

CONSIDERATIONS

- Graphic organizers
- Note-making strategies
- Instructional strategies: reciprocal teaching, Literature Circles, direct instruction
- Class and student configurations (e.g., pairs, groups, whole class)
- Visual aids, multimodal, multisensory approaches

Curricular Conversations

How does this skill or concept relate to the larger themes in the course, curriculum, or lives of students?

CONSIDERATIONS

- Workplace connections
- Personal connections
- Cross-curricular connections

Standards Alignment

Which standard(s) will this task or unit help students master?

CONSIDERATIONS

- Curricular objectives and context of the lesson
- Current progress toward mastery of this standard
- Connections to and reinforcement of standards students have already met
- Standards you have not yet addressed or that students have not yet mastered
- Extent to which this task or unit prepares students to meet other standards, for example, district frameworks, ESLRs, Advanced Placement, exit exam, or SAT standards

Performance Standards

What evidence of student learning or mastery are you willing to accept?

CONSIDERATIONS

- Is there more than one way to show mastery of this skill or concept?
- Do students have ample opportunity and means by which to master this standard?
- Do students know what a successful performance looks like (e.g., through exemplars or modeling)?
- Do students know the criteria by which their performance will be evaluated up front (e.g., through exemplars, rubrics, directions, modeling)?
- Are the criteria for mastery consistent with those in other classes, schools, districts, and states?
- Are all skills and concepts equally important—and given equal weight—on all assessments?
- Is this method an effective/appropriate use of your time/attention?

DURING: IMPLEMENTATION AND EXPERIENCE

Effective design demands that we lay a solid but adaptable foundation that will ensure the success of the task or unit once it begins. While such attention to design asks a lot of the teacher at first, such questions and considerations become mental habits that lead to efficient and effective instructional design.

Teaching and Learning

This list offers a sequence of steps building on learners' knowledge and progress by extending their capacity and competence as they move toward mastery of a standard:

- *Introduce* the skill, concept, or task with clear instructions that students can hear, see, and read
- *Connect* the task, concept, or unit to what they have studied/will study
- *Assess* prior knowledge and current understanding of the skill or concept
- *Demonstrate* the task, explaining what you are thinking as you do so
- *Try* the task/have students explain their initial understanding of the concept
- *Evaluate* their performance; check for understanding
- *Correct* or clarify their performance as needed, based on observed results
- *Practice* the skill or continue study of the concept
- *Assess* level of mastery and need for more group/individualized instruction
- *Extend* students' understanding/mastery by increasing the task's difficulty.
- *Monitor* students' level of mastery and need for more group or individualized instruction
- *Reinforce* understanding and mastery as you move on to next task or concept

AFTER: EVALUATION AND PLANNING

Feedback and reinforcement are essential elements in any instructional design. In this last stage, teachers answer the question "What next?" before returning to the beginning and starting the process with a new task or concept.

Instructional Design

What does the performance data tell you the students need to do or learn next?

CONSIDERATIONS

- Did all students master the skill or concept?
- What is the next step—and why?
- Was your method the most effective means to teach this skill or concept?
- What changes should you make in the technique or assignment next time?

WHAT'S NEXT?

Return to the beginning and follow the sequence for teaching the next skill or concept.

Reproducible Tools for Classroom Use

Continuum Creator

Name ______________________ Date ______________

Assignment ______________________ Period ______________

Suggestions for Use: Looking at data or ideas along a continuum helps us understand the qualities of that information. For example, some foods are "tasty" but not "delicious"; some teams are "great" but not "excellent." A continuum allows us to identify different categories or degrees. A Continuum of Importance, for example, shows us what is "irrelevant" and what is "essential." If we can determine what is "important," we know what to look for when we are writing, reading, or taking notes.

Continuum of ______________________

Before

1. Title your continuum to establish what you are trying to analyze. Examples: Continuum of Importance, Continuum of Performance, Continuum of Understanding, Continuum of Quality, Continuum of Probability, or Continuum of Attitude.
2. Decide what questions you should ask to help you determine:
   - The categories, or what should go in the boxes (e.g., High, Medium, Low)
   - The criteria for what should go in each section (e.g., To determine if something is "irrelevant," I will ask the question, "If you took this out of the story, would anything change?")
   - The purpose/focus of this continuum. Example: This continuum answers the question "How can I tell what is important when reading a newspaper article? When studying for a test? When taking notes during a lecture?"
3. Determine the traits of each point along the continuum.
   - Example: A score of 6 on the Continuum of Understanding means you understand the surface details (e.g., what it is) but not its meaning or importance. A 10 on the Continuum of Performance means you did it all and did it to the highest standard.

During

1. As you read, write, listen, or watch, look for items appropriate for your continuum. For example, while reading about the history of Greece in your history textbook, determine if the information about who began the Trojan War is "important" according to your continuum. The same continuum would help you determine that it is not very important to know what the soldiers ate for dinner during the war; thus you should not include that in your notes.
2. Evaluate and revise your criteria as needed. If you realize that the criteria for importance are not useful, change them. For example, if your current criteria suggest that what the soldiers in the Trojan War ate *is* important, change them. This will help you take better notes, listen more effectively, and read with greater success.

After

Use your continuum to prepare to write an essay or study for a test. It might even be a good idea to create a new continuum that helps you determine the likelihood of something being on the test: No chance/Possible/Probable/Inevitable or 0/25/50/75/100%.

Character Card

Useful Literary Terms

- allusion
- analogy
- antagonist
- character
- conflict
- convention(s)
- diction
- exposition
- imagery
- irony
- motif
- narrator
- persona
- plot
- point of view
- protagonist
- setting
- theme(s)
- tone
- voice

Character Card

Useful Literary Terms

- allusion
- analogy
- antagonist
- character
- conflict
- convention(s)
- diction
- exposition
- imagery
- irony
- motif
- narrator
- persona
- plot
- point of view
- protagonist
- setting
- theme(s)
- tone
- voice

Character Card

Useful Literary Terms

- allusion
- analogy
- antagonist
- character
- conflict
- convention(s)
- diction
- exposition
- imagery
- irony
- motif
- narrator
- persona
- plot
- point of view
- protagonist
- setting
- theme(s)
- tone
- voice

Character Card

Useful Literary Terms

- allusion
- analogy
- antagonist
- character
- conflict
- convention(s)
- diction
- exposition
- imagery
- irony
- motif
- narrator
- persona
- plot
- point of view
- protagonist
- setting
- theme(s)
- tone
- voice

Core Skills

ASK QUESTIONS
- Who is involved?
- What are they doing? (Why?)
- What do they want very badly? (Why?)
- What is the situation or problem?
- Who is telling the story? (Why?)
- How is the story designed? (Why?)
- What is the source of tension?
- Can you trust the narrator?

MAKE CONNECTIONS
- I wonder why . . .
- What caused . . .
- I think . . .
- This is similar to . . .
- This is important because . . .
- This reminds me of . . .
- What I find confusing is . . .
- What will happen next is . . .
- I can relate to this because . . .

PREDICT
- What will happen next?
- Why do you think that?
- What effect will that have on the story or the characters?

SUMMARIZE
- What happened?
- What is essential to tell?
- What was the outcome?
- Who was involved?
- Why did this happen?
- Is that a detail or essential information?

STANDARDS/TEST CONNECTION
- The best word to describe the tone is . . .
- What device does the author use to . . .
- The writer organizes information: sequentially, spatially, comparatively . . .
- The main character feels/thinks . . .

SYNTHESIZE
- Three important points/ideas are . . .
- These are important because . . .
- What comes next . . .
- The author wants us to think . . .
- At this point the article/story is about . . .
- I still don't understand . . .
- What interested me most was . . .
- This means that . . .

Core Skills

ASK QUESTIONS
- Who is involved?
- What are they doing? (Why?)
- What do they want very badly? (Why?)
- What is the situation or problem?
- Who is telling the story? (Why?)
- How is the story designed? (Why?)
- What is the source of tension?
- Can you trust the narrator?

MAKE CONNECTIONS
- I wonder why . . .
- What caused . . .
- I think . . .
- This is similar to . . .
- This is important because . . .
- This reminds me of . . .
- What I find confusing is . . .
- What will happen next is . . .
- I can relate to this because . . .

PREDICT
- What will happen next?
- Why do you think that?
- What effect will that have on the story or the characters?

SUMMARIZE
- What happened?
- What is essential to tell?
- What was the outcome?
- Who was involved?
- Why did this happen?
- Is that a detail or essential information?

STANDARDS/TEST CONNECTION
- The best word to describe the tone is . . .
- What device does the author use to . . .
- The writer organizes information: sequentially, spatially, comparatively . . .
- The main character feels/thinks . . .

SYNTHESIZE
- Three important points/ideas are . . .
- These are important because . . .
- What comes next . . .
- The author wants us to think . . .
- At this point the article/story is about . . .
- I still don't understand . . .
- What interested me most was . . .
- This means that . . .

Core Skills

ASK QUESTIONS
- Who is involved?
- What are they doing? (Why?)
- What do they want very badly? (Why?)
- What is the situation or problem?
- Who is telling the story? (Why?)
- How is the story designed? (Why?)
- What is the source of tension?
- Can you trust the narrator?

MAKE CONNECTIONS
- I wonder why . . .
- What caused . . .
- I think . . .
- This is similar to . . .
- This is important because . . .
- This reminds me of . . .
- What I find confusing is . . .
- What will happen next is . . .
- I can relate to this because . . .

PREDICT
- What will happen next?
- Why do you think that?
- What effect will that have on the story or the characters?

SUMMARIZE
- What happened?
- What is essential to tell?
- What was the outcome?
- Who was involved?
- Why did this happen?
- Is that a detail or essential information?

STANDARDS/TEST CONNECTION
- The best word to describe the tone is . . .
- What device does the author use to . . .
- The writer organizes information: sequentially, spatially, comparatively . . .
- The main character feels/thinks . . .

SYNTHESIZE
- Three important points/ideas are . . .
- These are important because . . .
- What comes next . . .
- The author wants us to think . . .
- At this point the article/story is about . . .
- I still don't understand . . .
- What interested me most was . . .
- This means that . . .

Core Skills

ASK QUESTIONS
- Who is involved?
- What are they doing? (Why?)
- What do they want very badly? (Why?)
- What is the situation or problem?
- Who is telling the story? (Why?)
- How is the story designed? (Why?)
- What is the source of tension?
- Can you trust the narrator?

MAKE CONNECTIONS
- I wonder why . . .
- What caused . . .
- I think . . .
- This is similar to . . .
- This is important because . . .
- This reminds me of . . .
- What I find confusing is . . .
- What will happen next is . . .
- I can relate to this because . . .

PREDICT
- What will happen next?
- Why do you think that?
- What effect will that have on the story or the characters?

SUMMARIZE
- What happened?
- What is essential to tell?
- What was the outcome?
- Who was involved?
- Why did this happen?
- Is that a detail or essential information?

STANDARDS/TEST CONNECTION
- The best word to describe the tone is . . .
- What device does the author use to . . .
- The writer organizes information: sequentially, spatially, comparatively . . .
- The main character feels/thinks . . .

SYNTHESIZE
- Three important points/ideas are . . .
- These are important because . . .
- What comes next . . .
- The author wants us to think . . .
- At this point the article/story is about . . .
- I still don't understand . . .
- What interested me most was . . .
- This means that . . .

Reading: Think About It!

When reading remember to:

- ■ Ask questions of the text, yourself, and the author
- ■ Make connections to yourself, other texts, the world
- ■ Use different strategies to achieve and maintain focus while reading
- ■ Determine ahead of time why you are reading this text and how it should be read
- ■ Adjust your strategies as you read to help you understand and enjoy what you read

Evaluating how well you read

Evaluate and decide which of the following best describes your reading performance today. Explain *why* you gave yourself the score, also.

My reading was:

1. Excellent because I
   - ■ read the full 20 minutes
   - ■ read actively (e.g., used different strategies and techniques)
   - ■ understood what I read
2. Successful because I
   - ■ read almost the entire 20 minutes
   - ■ tried to use some strategies that mostly helped me read better
   - ■ understood most of what I read
3. Inconsistent because I
   - ■ read only about half the time
   - ■ used some strategies but they didn't help me much
   - ■ understood some of what I read
4. Unsuccessful because I
   - ■ read little or nothing
   - ■ did not read actively
   - ■ did not understand what I read
     - ■ I didn't understand because . . .

Develop your own questions

Develop your own question(s) or prompt(s) that you find helpful when thinking about how or what you read:

■ ______________________________

____

■ ______________________________

____

Reading: Think About It!

When reading remember to:

- ■ Ask questions of the text, yourself, and the author
- ■ Make connections to yourself, other texts, the world
- ■ Use different strategies to achieve and maintain focus while reading
- ■ Determine ahead of time why you are reading this text and how it should be read
- ■ Adjust your strategies as you read to help you understand and enjoy what you read

Evaluating how well you read

Evaluate and decide which of the following best describes your reading performance today. Explain *why* you gave yourself the score, also.

My reading was:

1. Excellent because I
   - ■ read the full 20 minutes
   - ■ read actively (e.g., used different strategies and techniques)
   - ■ understood what I read
2. Successful because I
   - ■ read almost the entire 20 minutes
   - ■ tried to use some strategies that mostly helped me read better
   - ■ understood most of what I read
3. Inconsistent because I
   - ■ read only about half the time
   - ■ used some strategies but they didn't help me much
   - ■ understood some of what I read
4. Unsuccessful because I
   - ■ read little or nothing
   - ■ did not read actively
   - ■ did not understand what I read
     - ■ I didn't understand because . . .

Develop your own questions

Develop your own question(s) or prompt(s) that you find helpful when thinking about how or what you read:

■ ______________________________

____

■ ______________________________

____

Reading: Think About It!

When reading remember to:

- ■ Ask questions of the text, yourself, and the author
- ■ Make connections to yourself, other texts, the world
- ■ Use different strategies to achieve and maintain focus while reading
- ■ Determine ahead of time why you are reading this text and how it should be read
- ■ Adjust your strategies as you read to help you understand and enjoy what you read

Evaluating how well you read

Evaluate and decide which of the following best describes your reading performance today. Explain *why* you gave yourself the score, also.

My reading was:

1. Excellent because I
   - ■ read the full 20 minutes
   - ■ read actively (e.g., used different strategies and techniques)
   - ■ understood what I read
2. Successful because I
   - ■ read almost the entire 20 minutes
   - ■ tried to use some strategies that mostly helped me read better
   - ■ understood most of what I read
3. Inconsistent because I
   - ■ read only about half the time
   - ■ used some strategies but they didn't help me much
   - ■ understood some of what I read
4. Unsuccessful because I
   - ■ read little or nothing
   - ■ did not read actively
   - ■ did not understand what I read
     - ■ I didn't understand because . . .

Develop your own questions

Develop your own question(s) or prompt(s) that you find helpful when thinking about how or what you read:

■ ______________________________

____

■ ______________________________

____

Reading: Think About It!

When reading remember to:

- ■ Ask questions of the text, yourself, and the author
- ■ Make connections to yourself, other texts, the world
- ■ Use different strategies to achieve and maintain focus while reading
- ■ Determine ahead of time why you are reading this text and how it should be read
- ■ Adjust your strategies as you read to help you understand and enjoy what you read

Evaluating how well you read

Evaluate and decide which of the following best describes your reading performance today. Explain *why* you gave yourself the score, also.

My reading was:

1. Excellent because I
   - ■ read the full 20 minutes
   - ■ read actively (e.g., used different strategies and techniques)
   - ■ understood what I read
2. Successful because I
   - ■ read almost the entire 20 minutes
   - ■ tried to use some strategies that mostly helped me read better
   - ■ understood most of what I read
3. Inconsistent because I
   - ■ read only about half the time
   - ■ used some strategies but they didn't help me much
   - ■ understood some of what I read
4. Unsuccessful because I
   - ■ read little or nothing
   - ■ did not read actively
   - ■ did not understand what I read
     - ■ I didn't understand because . . .

Develop your own questions

Develop your own question(s) or prompt(s) that you find helpful when thinking about how or what you read:

■ ______________________________

____

■ ______________________________

____

Reading: Think About It!

Thinking about *how* you read

- I was distracted by . . .
- I started to think about . . .
- I got stuck when . . .
- I was confused/focused today because . . .
- One strategy I used to help me read this better was . . .
- When I got distracted I tried to refocus myself by . . .
- These word(s) or phrases were new/ interesting to me . . . I think they mean . . .
- When reading I should . . .
- When I read today I realized that . . .
- I had a hard time understanding . . .
- I'll read better next time if I . . .

Thinking about *what* you read

- Why does the character/author . . .
- Why doesn't the character/author . . .
- What surprised me most was . . .
- I predict that . . .
- This author's writing style is . . .
- I noted that the author uses . . .
- The main character wants/is . . .
- If I could, I'd ask the author/character . . .
- The most interesting event/idea in this book is . . .
- I realized . . .
- The main conflict/idea in this book is . . .
- I wonder why . . .
- One theme that keeps coming up is . . .
- I found the following quote interesting . . .
- I __________ this book because . . .

Elaborating on what you think

- I think __________ because . . .
- A good example of __________ is . . .
- This remined me of __________ because . . .
- This was important because . . .
- One thing that suprised me was ________ because I always thought . . .
- The author is saying that . . .

Reading: Think About It!

Thinking about *how* you read

- I was distracted by . . .
- I started to think about . . .
- I got stuck when . . .
- I was confused/focused today because . . .
- One strategy I used to help me read this better was . . .
- When I got distracted I tried to refocus myself by . . .
- These word(s) or phrases were new/ interesting to me . . . I think they mean . . .
- When reading I should . . .
- When I read today I realized that . . .
- I had a hard time understanding . . .
- I'll read better next time if I . . .

Thinking about *what* you read

- Why does the character/author . . .
- Why doesn't the character/author . . .
- What surprised me most was . . .
- I predict that . . .
- This author's writing style is . . .
- I noted that the author uses . . .
- The main character wants/is . . .
- If I could, I'd ask the author/character . . .
- The most interesting event/idea in this book is . . .
- I realized . . .
- The main conflict/idea in this book is . . .
- I wonder why . . .
- One theme that keeps coming up is . . .
- I found the following quote interesting . . .
- I __________ this book because . . .

Elaborating on what you think

- I think __________ because . . .
- A good example of __________ is . . .
- This remined me of __________ because . . .
- This was important because . . .
- One thing that suprised me was ________ because I always thought . . .
- The author is saying that . . .

Reading: Think About It!

Thinking about *how* you read

- I was distracted by . . .
- I started to think about . . .
- I got stuck when . . .
- I was confused/focused today because . . .
- One strategy I used to help me read this better was . . .
- When I got distracted I tried to refocus myself by . . .
- These word(s) or phrases were new/ interesting to me . . . I think they mean . . .
- When reading I should . . .
- When I read today I realized that . . .
- I had a hard time understanding . . .
- I'll read better next time if I . . .

Thinking about *what* you read

- Why does the character/author . . .
- Why doesn't the character/author . . .
- What surprised me most was . . .
- I predict that . . .
- This author's writing style is . . .
- I noted that the author uses . . .
- The main character wants/is . . .
- If I could, I'd ask the author/character . . .
- The most interesting event/idea in this book is . . .
- I realized . . .
- The main conflict/idea in this book is . . .
- I wonder why . . .
- One theme that keeps coming up is . . .
- I found the following quote interesting . . .
- I __________ this book because . . .

Elaborating on what you think

- I think __________ because . . .
- A good example of __________ is . . .
- This remined me of __________ because . . .
- This was important because . . .
- One thing that suprised me was ________ because I always thought . . .
- The author is saying that . . .

Reading: Think About It!

Thinking about *how* you read

- I was distracted by . . .
- I started to think about . . .
- I got stuck when . . .
- I was confused/focused today because . . .
- One strategy I used to help me read this better was . . .
- When I got distracted I tried to refocus myself by . . .
- These word(s) or phrases were new/ interesting to me . . . I think they mean . . .
- When reading I should . . .
- When I read today I realized that . . .
- I had a hard time understanding . . .
- I'll read better next time if I . . .

Thinking about *what* you read

- Why does the character/author . . .
- Why doesn't the character/author . . .
- What surprised me most was . . .
- I predict that . . .
- This author's writing style is . . .
- I noted that the author uses . . .
- The main character wants/is . . .
- If I could, I'd ask the author/character . . .
- The most interesting event/idea in this book is . . .
- I realized . . .
- The main conflict/idea in this book is . . .
- I wonder why . . .
- One theme that keeps coming up is . . .
- I found the following quote interesting . . .
- I __________ this book because . . .

Elaborating on what you think

- I think __________ because . . .
- A good example of __________ is . . .
- This remined me of __________ because . . .
- This was important because . . .
- One thing that suprised me was ________ because I always thought . . .
- The author is saying that . . .

Literature Circle Roles

Discussion Director: Your role demands that you identify the important aspects of your assigned text and develop questions your group will want to discuss. Focus on the major themes or "big ideas" in the text and your reaction to those ideas. What interests you will most likely interest those in your group. You are also responsible for facilitating your group's discussion.

Illuminator: You find passages your group would like to/should hear read aloud. These passages should be memorable, interesting, puzzling, funny, or *important.* Your notes should include the quotations but also why you chose them and what you want to say about them. You can either read the passage aloud yourself or ask members of your group to read roles.

Illustrator: Your role is to draw what you read. This might mean drawing a scene as a cartoonlike sequence or an important scene so readers can better understand the action. You can draw maps or organizational trees to show how one person, place, or event related to the others. Explain how your drawing relates to the text. Label your drawings so we know who the characters are. Make your drawing on a separate sheet of paper.

Connector: Your job is to connect what you are reading with what you are studying or with the world outside of school. You can connect the story to events in your own life, news events, political events, or popular trends. Another important source of connections is books you've already read. The connections should be meaningful to you and those in your group.

Word Watcher: While reading the assigned section, you watch out for words worth knowing. These words might be interesting, new, important, or used in unusual ways. It is important to indicate the specific location of the words so the group can discuss these words in context.

Summarizer: Prepare a brief summary of the day's reading. In some cases, you might ask yourself what details, characters, or events are so important that they would be included on an exam. If it helps you to organize the information, consider making a numbered listed or a time line.

Literature Circle Roles

Discussion Director: Your role demands that you identify the important aspects of your assigned text and develop questions your group will want to discuss. Focus on the major themes or "big ideas" in the text and your reaction to those ideas. What interests you will most likely interest those in your group. You are also responsible for facilitating your group's discussion.

Illuminator: You find passages your group would like to/should hear read aloud. These passages should be memorable, interesting, puzzling, funny, or *important.* Your notes should include the quotations but also why you chose them and what you want to say about them. You can either read the passage aloud yourself or ask members of your group to read roles.

Illustrator: Your role is to draw what you read. This might mean drawing a scene as a cartoonlike sequence or an important scene so readers can better understand the action. You can draw maps or organizational trees to show how one person, place, or event related to the others. Explain how your drawing relates to the text. Label your drawings so we know who the characters are. Make your drawing on a separate sheet of paper.

Connector: Your job is to connect what you are reading with what you are studying or with the world outside of school. You can connect the story to events in your own life, news events, political events, or popular trends. Another important source of connections is books you've already read. The connections should be meaningful to you and those in your group.

Word Watcher: While reading the assigned section, you watch out for words worth knowing. These words might be interesting, new, important, or used in unusual ways. It is important to indicate the specific location of the words so the group can discuss these words in context.

Summarizer: Prepare a brief summary of the day's reading. In some cases, you might ask yourself what details, characters, or events are so important that they would be included on an exam. If it helps you to organize the information, consider making a numbered listed or a time line.

Literature Circle Roles

Discussion Director: Your role demands that you identify the important aspects of your assigned text and develop questions your group will want to discuss. Focus on the major themes or "big ideas" in the text and your reaction to those ideas. What interests you will most likely interest those in your group. You are also responsible for facilitating your group's discussion.

Illuminator: You find passages your group would like to/should hear read aloud. These passages should be memorable, interesting, puzzling, funny, or *important.* Your notes should include the quotations but also why you chose them and what you want to say about them. You can either read the passage aloud yourself or ask members of your group to read roles.

Illustrator: Your role is to draw what you read. This might mean drawing a scene as a cartoonlike sequence or an important scene so readers can better understand the action. You can draw maps or organizational trees to show how one person, place, or event related to the others. Explain how your drawing relates to the text. Label your drawings so we know who the characters are. Make your drawing on a separate sheet of paper.

Connector: Your job is to connect what you are reading with what you are studying or with the world outside of school. You can connect the story to events in your own life, news events, political events, or popular trends. Another important source of connections is books you've already read. The connections should be meaningful to you and those in your group.

Word Watcher: While reading the assigned section, you watch out for words worth knowing. These words might be interesting, new, important, or used in unusual ways. It is important to indicate the specific location of the words so the group can discuss these words in context.

Summarizer: Prepare a brief summary of the day's reading. In some cases, you might ask yourself what details, characters, or events are so important that they would be included on an exam. If it helps you to organize the information, consider making a numbered listed or a time line.

Literature Circle Roles

Discussion Director: Your role demands that you identify the important aspects of your assigned text and develop questions your group will want to discuss. Focus on the major themes or "big ideas" in the text and your reaction to those ideas. What interests you will most likely interest those in your group. You are also responsible for facilitating your group's discussion.

Illuminator: You find passages your group would like to/should hear read aloud. These passages should be memorable, interesting, puzzling, funny, or *important.* Your notes should include the quotations but also why you chose them and what you want to say about them. You can either read the passage aloud yourself or ask members of your group to read roles.

Illustrator: Your role is to draw what you read. This might mean drawing a scene as a cartoonlike sequence or an important scene so readers can better understand the action. You can draw maps or organizational trees to show how one person, place, or event related to the others. Explain how your drawing relates to the text. Label your drawings so we know who the characters are. Make your drawing on a separate sheet of paper.

Connector: Your job is to connect what you are reading with what you are studying or with the world outside of school. You can connect the story to events in your own life, news events, political events, or popular trends. Another important source of connections is books you've already read. The connections should be meaningful to you and those in your group.

Word Watcher: While reading the assigned section, you watch out for words worth knowing. These words might be interesting, new, important, or used in unusual ways. It is important to indicate the specific location of the words so the group can discuss these words in context.

Summarizer: Prepare a brief summary of the day's reading. In some cases, you might ask yourself what details, characters, or events are so important that they would be included on an exam. If it helps you to organize the information, consider making a numbered listed or a time line.

Literature Circle Roles

Dicussion Director/Illuminator Questions
- What were you thinking about as you read?
- What did the text make you think about?
- What do you think this text/passage was about?
- How might others think about this text/passage?
- What would you ask the writer if you could?
- What are the most important ideas/moments?
- What do you think will happen next—and why?
- What was the most important change in this section?

Illustrator Questions
- Ask your group, "What does this picture mean?"
- Why did you choose this scene to illustrate?
- How does this drawing relate to the story?
- Why did you choose to draw it the way you did?
- Who and/or what is in this picture?
- What did drawing it help you see?
- What did this passage make you think about?
- What are you trying to accomplish in this drawing?

Connector Questions
- What connections can you make to your own life?
- What/who else could you compare this story to?
- What other books might you compare to this one?
- What other characters or authors come to mind?
- What's the most interesting or important connection?
- How does this section relate to the ones before it?

Word Watcher Questions
- Which words are used frequently?
- Which words are used in unusual ways?
- What words seem to have special meaning?
- What new words did you find in this section?
- What part of speech is this word?
- What is the connotative meaning of this word?
- What is the denotative meaning of this word?

Summarizer Questions
- What are the most important events in the section?
- What makes them so important?
- How do these events affect the plot of characters?
- What changes did you notice when you read?
- What questions about this might appear on an exam?
- What might be a good essay topic for this section?

Literature Circle Roles

Dicussion Director/Illuminator Questions
- What were you thinking about as you read?
- What did the text make you think about?
- What do you think this text/passage was about?
- How might others think about this text/passage?
- What would you ask the writer if you could?
- What are the most important ideas/moments?
- What do you think will happen next—and why?
- What was the most important change in this section?

Illustrator Questions
- Ask your group, "What does this picture mean?"
- Why did you choose this scene to illustrate?
- How does this drawing relate to the story?
- Why did you choose to draw it the way you did?
- Who and/or what is in this picture?
- What did drawing it help you see?
- What did this passage make you think about?
- What are you trying to accomplish in this drawing?

Connector Questions
- What connections can you make to your own life?
- What/who else could you compare this story to?
- What other books might you compare to this one?
- What other characters or authors come to mind?
- What's the most interesting or important connection?
- How does this section relate to the ones before it?

Word Watcher Questions
- Which words are used frequently?
- Which words are used in unusual ways?
- What words seem to have special meaning?
- What new words did you find in this section?
- What part of speech is this word?
- What is the connotative meaning of this word?
- What is the denotative meaning of this word?

Summarizer Questions
- What are the most important events in the section?
- What makes them so important?
- How do these events affect the plot of characters?
- What changes did you notice when you read?
- What questions about this might appear on an exam?
- What might be a good essay topic for this section?

Literature Circle Roles

Dicussion Director/Illuminator Questions
- What were you thinking about as you read?
- What did the text make you think about?
- What do you think this text/passage was about?
- How might others think about this text/passage?
- What would you ask the writer if you could?
- What are the most important ideas/moments?
- What do you think will happen next—and why?
- What was the most important change in this section?

Illustrator Questions
- Ask your group, "What does this picture mean?"
- Why did you choose this scene to illustrate?
- How does this drawing relate to the story?
- Why did you choose to draw it the way you did?
- Who and/or what is in this picture?
- What did drawing it help you see?
- What did this passage make you think about?
- What are you trying to accomplish in this drawing?

Connector Questions
- What connections can you make to your own life?
- What/who else could you compare this story to?
- What other books might you compare to this one?
- What other characters or authors come to mind?
- What's the most interesting or important connection?
- How does this section relate to the ones before it?

Word Watcher Questions
- Which words are used frequently?
- Which words are used in unusual ways?
- What words seem to have special meaning?
- What new words did you find in this section?
- What part of speech is this word?
- What is the connotative meaning of this word?
- What is the denotative meaning of this word?

Summarizer Questions
- What are the most important events in the section?
- What makes them so important?
- How do these events affect the plot of characters?
- What changes did you notice when you read?
- What questions about this might appear on an exam?
- What might be a good essay topic for this section?

Literature Circle Roles

Dicussion Director/Illuminator Questions
- What were you thinking about as you read?
- What did the text make you think about?
- What do you think this text/passage was about?
- How might others think about this text/passage?
- What would you ask the writer if you could?
- What are the most important ideas/moments?
- What do you think will happen next—and why?
- What was the most important change in this section?

Illustrator Questions
- Ask your group, "What does this picture mean?"
- Why did you choose this scene to illustrate?
- How does this drawing relate to the story?
- Why did you choose to draw it the way you did?
- Who and/or what is in this picture?
- What did drawing it help you see?
- What did this passage make you think about?
- What are you trying to accomplish in this drawing?

Connector Questions
- What connections can you make to your own life?
- What/who else could you compare this story to?
- What other books might you compare to this one?
- What other characters or authors come to mind?
- What's the most interesting or important connection?
- How does this section relate to the ones before it?

Word Watcher Questions
- Which words are used frequently?
- Which words are used in unusual ways?
- What words seem to have special meaning?
- What new words did you find in this section?
- What part of speech is this word?
- What is the connotative meaning of this word?
- What is the denotative meaning of this word?

Summarizer Questions
- What are the most important events in the section?
- What makes them so important?
- How do these events affect the plot of characters?
- What changes did you notice when you read?
- What questions about this might appear on an exam?
- What might be a good essay topic for this section?

Conversational Roundtable

Name ______________________ Date ______________

Topic ______________________ Period ______________

Suggestions for Use: Ask yourself what the focus of your paper, discussion, or inquiry is. Is it a character, a theme, an idea, a country, a trend, or a place? Then examine it from four different perspectives, or identify four different aspects of the topic. Once you have identified the four areas, find and list any appropriate quotations, examples, evidence, or details.

Decision Tree

Name ______________________________ Date ______________

Topic ______________________________ Period ______________

Suggestions for Use: Use this Decision Tree diagram to examine the possible outcomes of different decisions. You might consider the different consequences of a character's possible choices, or you might consider how it would change the story to tell it from different points of view. In Health, History, or Business, you might consider the ramifications of different choices. Provide arguments for and against each decision.

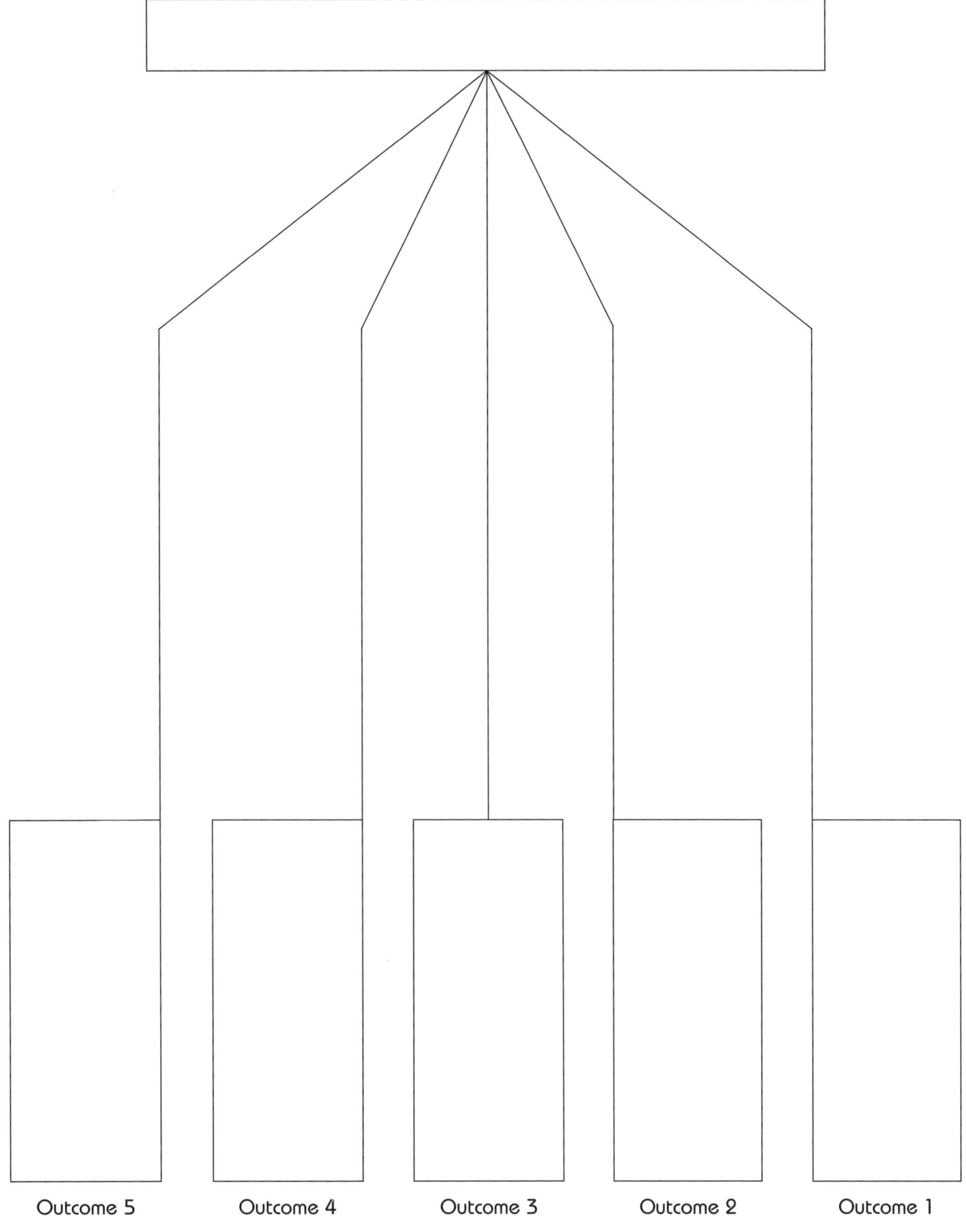

Episodic Notes (Three-Square)

Name ______________________ Date ____________

Topic ______________________ Period ____________

Purpose: Identify most important moments; show cause-effect and organization (sequence).

1. Determine the three most crucial stages, scenes, or moments in the story or process.
2. Draw in the box what happens and what you "see" in the text. Be as specific as possible.
3. Remember, these are *notes,* not works of art: try to capture the action and important details of the moment.
4. Explain (in the notes section) what is happening and why it is important.

Caption ______________________

Caption ______________________

Caption ______________________

Episodic Notes (Six-Square)

Name ______________________ Date ______________

Topic ______________________ Period ______________

Purpose: Identify most important moments; show cause-effect and organization (sequence).

1. Determine the most crucial stages, scenes, or moments in the story or process.
2. Draw in the box what happens and what you "see" in the text. Be as specific as possible.
3. Remember, these are *notes,* not works of art: try to capture the action and important details of the moment.
4. Explain (in the notes section) what is happening and why it is important.

Idea Cards

Name ______________________________ Date ______________

Interactive Notes

Name ____________________ Date ____________________

Topic ____________________ Period ____________________

Directions: Use Interactive Notes to help you read informational or literary texts. Interactive Notes guide you through a reading process to help you develop your ideas and express them in academic language. You may put questions, comments, connections, or favorite lines in any column; then use the prompts (or create your own) to help you write.

BEFORE
Prepare to Read

- List: √ title(s)
  √ headings
  √ captions
  √ objectives
  √ themes
  √ words to know
- Ask questions
- Make predictions
- Set a purpose
- Decide what matters most

DURING
Question and Comment

- I wonder why . . .
- What caused . . .
- I think . . .
- This is similar to . . .
- This is important because . . .
- What do they mean by . . .
- What I find confusing is . . .
- What will happen next is . . .
- I can relate to this because . . .
- This reminds me of . . .
- As I read, I keep wanting to ask . . .

AFTER
Summarize and Synthesize

- Three important points/ideas are . . .
- These are important because . . .
- What comes next . . .
- The author wants us to think . . .
- At this point the article/story is about . . .
- I still don't understand . . .
- What interested me most was . . .
- The author's purpose here is to . . .
- A good word to describe (e.g., this story's tone) is . . . because . . .
- This idea/story is similar to . . .

Linear Array

Name ______________________ Date __________

Topic ______________________ Period __________

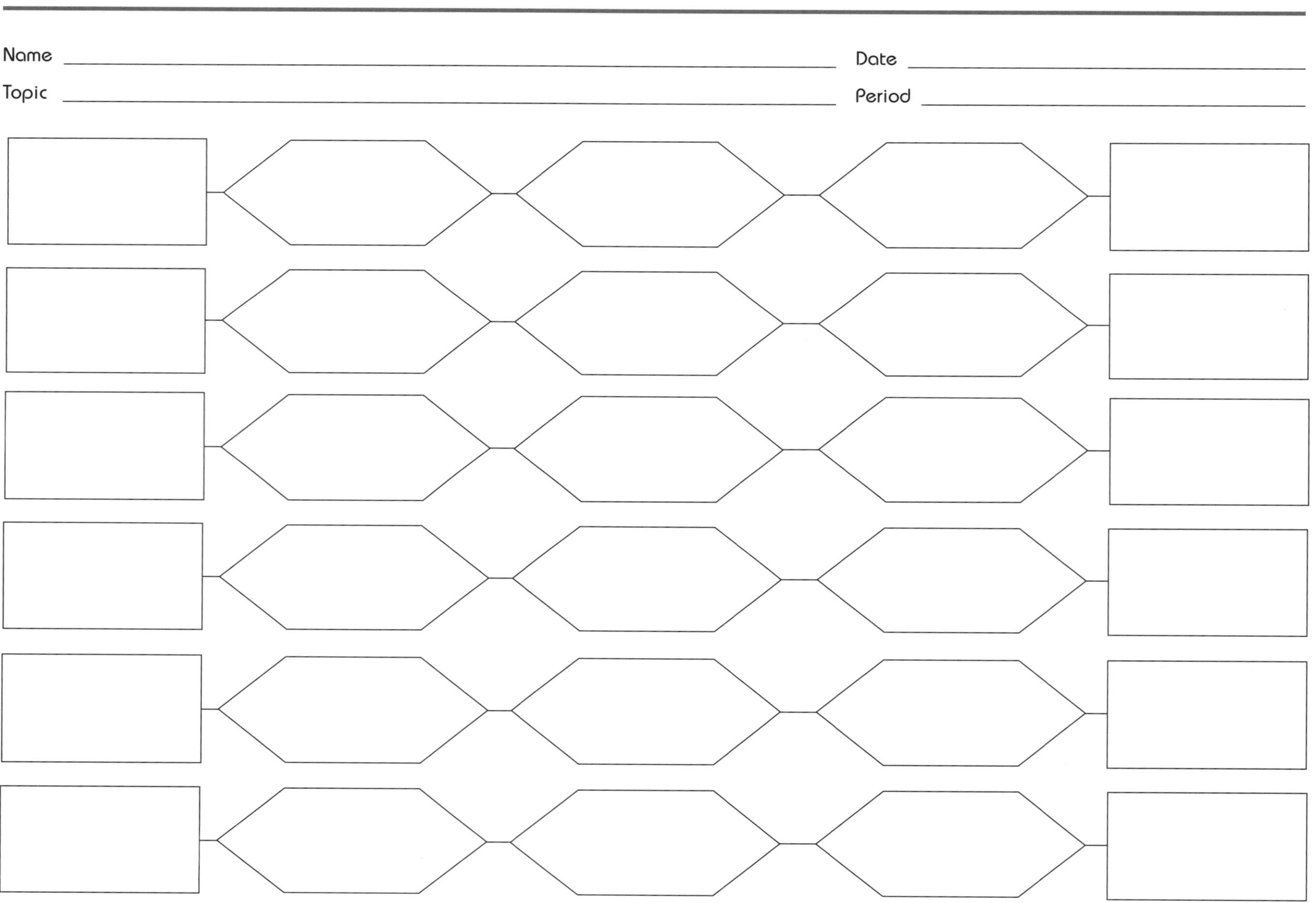

Literature Circle Notes: Overview of the Roles

Discussion Director: Your role demands that you identify the important aspects of your assigned text and develop questions your group will want to discuss. Focus on the major themes or "big ideas" in the text and your reaction to those ideas. What interests you will most likely interest those in your group. You are also responsible for facilitating your group's discussion.

Sample Questions
- What were you thinking about as you read?
- What did the text make you think about?
- What do you think this text/passage was about?
- How might other people (of different backgrounds) think about this text/passage?
- What *one* question would you ask the writer if you got the chance? Why?
- What are the most important ideas/moments in this text/section?
- What do you think will happen next—and why?
- What was the most important change in this section? How and why did it happen?

Illuminator: You find passages your group would like to/should hear read aloud. These passages should be memorable, interesting, puzzling, funny, or *important*. Your notes should include the quotations but also why you chose them and what you want to say about them. You can either read the passage aloud yourself or ask members of your group to read roles.

Sample Questions
- What is happening in this passage?
- Why did you choose this passage?
- What does this passage mean, or what is it discussing?
- How should you present this passage?
- Who is speaking or what is happening in this passage?
- What is the most unique aspect of this passage—and why is it unique?
- What did this quotation/passage make you think about when you read it?
- What makes this passage so confusing, important, or interesting?

Illustrator: Your role is to draw what you read. This might mean drawing a scene as a cartoonlike sequence or an important scene so readers can better understand the action. You can draw maps or organizational trees to show how one person, place, or event relates to the others. Explain how your drawing relates to the text. Label your drawings so we know who the characters are. Make your drawing on a separate sheet of paper.

Sample Questions
- Ask members of your group, "What do you think this picture means?"
- Why did you choose this scene to illustrate?
- How does this drawing relate to the story?
- Why did you choose to draw it the way you did?
- What do we see—i.e., who and/or what is in this picture?
- What, if anything, did drawing it help you see that you had not noticed before?
- What did this quotation/passage make you think about when you read it?
- What are you trying to accomplish through this drawing?

Connector: Your job is to connect what you are reading with what you are studying or with the world outside of school. You can connect the story to events in your own life, news events, political events, or popular trends. Another important source of connections is books you've already read. The connections should be meaningful to you and those in your group.

Sample Questions
- What connections can you make to your own life?
- What other places or people could you compare this story to?
- What other books or stories might you compare to this one?
- What other characters or authors might you compare to this one?
- What is the most interesting or important connection that comes to mind?
- How does this section relate to those that came before it?

Word Watcher: While reading the assigned section, you watch out for words worth knowing. These words might be interesting, new, important, or used in unusual ways. It is important to indicate the specific location of the words so the group can discuss these words in context.

Sample Questions
- Which words are used frequently?
- Which words are used in unusual ways?
- What words seem to have special meaning to the characters or author?
- What new words did you find in this section?
- What part of speech is this word?
- What is the connotative meaning of this word?
- What is the denotative meaning of this word?

Summarizer: Prepare a brief summary of the day's reading. Use the questions to the right to help you decide what to include. In some cases, you might ask yourself what details, characters, or events are so important that they would be included on an exam. If it helps you to organize the information, consider making a numbered list or a time line.

Sample Questions
- What are the most important events in the section you read?
- What makes them so important?
- What effect do these events have on the plot or the other characters?
- What changes—in plot, character, or tone—did you notice when you read?
- What questions about the section you read might appear on an exam?
- What might be a good essay topic for this section of the story?

Literature Circle Notes: Discussion Director

Name ____ Date ____________________

Discussion Director: Your role demands that you identify the important aspects of your assigned text and develop questions your group will want to discuss. Focus on the major themes or "big ideas" in the text and your reaction to those ideas. What interests you will most likely interest those in your group. You are also responsible for facilitating your group's discussion.

Sample Questions

- What were you thinking about as you read?
- What did the text make you think about?
- What do you think this text/passage was about?
- How might other people (of different backgrounds) think about this text/passage?
- What *one* question would you ask the writer if you got the chance? Why?
- What are the most important ideas/moments in this text/section?
- What do you think will happen next—and why?
- What was the most important change in this section? How and why did it happen?

Write your discussion questions here; write your responses to them in the main note-taking area to the right. >>>>

Assignment for Today: page ________ — page ________

Topic to be carried over to tomorrow:

Assignment for Tomorrow: page ________ — page ________

Here you should review, retell, or reflect on what you read so far. (Use the back if necessary.)

Literature Circle Notes: Illuminator

Name ______________________________ Date ______________

Illuminator: You find passages your group would like to/should hear read aloud. These passages should be memorable, interesting, puzzling, funny, or *important*. Your notes should include the quotations but also why you chose them and what you want to say about them. You can either read the passage aloud yourself or ask members of your group to read roles.

Sample Questions

- What is happening in this passage?
- Why did you choose this passage?
- What does this passage mean, or what is it discussing?
- How should you present this passage?
- Who is speaking or what is happening in this passage?
- What is the most unique aspect of this passage—and why is it unique?
- What did this quotation/passage make you think about when you read it?
- What makes this passage so confusing, important, or interesting?

Write the page and paragraph number in this column. Unless the quote is really long, you should also write the quote in this column; write your responses to it in the main note-taking area to the right.>>>>

Assignment for Today: page ________ — page ________

Topic to be carried over to tomorrow:

Assignment for Tomorrow: page ________ — page ________

Here you should review, retell, or reflect on what you read so far. (Use the back if necessary.)

Literature Circle Notes: Illustrator

Name ______________________________ Date ______________

Illustrator: Your role is to draw what you read. This might mean drawing a scene as a cartoonlike sequence or an important scene so readers can better understand the action. You can draw maps or organizational trees to show how one person, place, or event relates to the others. Use the notes area to explain how your drawing relates to the text. Label your drawings so we know who the characters are. **Make your drawing on the back of this page or on a separate sheet of paper.**

Sample Questions

- Ask members of your group, "What do you think this picture means?"
- Why did you choose this scene to illustrate?
- How does this drawing relate to the story?
- Why did you choose to draw it the way you did?
- What do we see—i.e., who and/or what is in this picture?
- What, if anything, did drawing it help you see that you had not noticed before?
- What did this quotation/passage make you think about when you read it?
- What are you trying to accomplish through this drawing?

Your drawing should be on the back or on a separate sheet of paper; your notes and explanation should be on the right.>>>>

Assignment for Today: page ________ — page ________

Topic to be carried over to tomorrow:

Assignment for Tomorrow: page ________ — page ________

Here you should review, retell, or reflect on what you read so far. (Use the back if necessary.)

Literature Circle Notes: Connector

Name ____________________ Date ____________

Connector: Your job is to connect what you are reading with what you are studying in this or other classes. You can also connect the story with events in your own life or the world outside school as depicted in the news or other media. Another valuable source of connections is books you've already read this year. Connections should be meaningful to you and those in your group.

Sample Questions

- What connections can you make between the text and your life?
- What other places or people could you compare this story to?
- What other books or stories might you compare to this one?
- What other characters or authors might you compare to this one?
- What current trends or events are related to this section of the book?
- What is the most interesting or important connection that comes to mind?
- What is the connection that no one else but you can discover?
- How does this section relate to those that came before it?

Write your discussion questions here; write your responses to them in the main note-taking area to the right.>>>>

Assignment for Today: page ________ — page ________

Topic to be carried over to tomorrow:

Assignment for Tomorrow: page ________ — page ________

Here you should review, retell, or reflect on what you read so far. (Use the back if necessary.)

Literature Circle Notes: Word Watcher

Name ______________________________ Date ______________

Word Watcher: While reading the assigned section, you watch out for words worth knowing. These words might be interesting, new, important, or used in unusual ways. It is important to indicate the specific location of the words so the group can discuss these words in context.

Sample Questions

- Which words are used frequently?
- Which words are used in unusual ways?
- What words seem to have special meaning to the characters or author?
- What new words did you find in this section?
- What part of speech is this word?
- What is the connotative meaning of this word?
- What is the denotative meaning of this word?

In this column, write the word as well as page and paragraph numbers. Write the definition and any explanation about why you chose the word in the notes section to the right.>>>>

Assignment for Today: page ________ — page ________

Topic to be carried over to tomorrow:

Assignment for Tomorrow: page ________ — page ________

Here you should review, retell, or reflect on what you read so far. (Use the back if necessary.)

Literature Circle Notes: Summarizer

Name ______________________________ Date ______________

Summarizer: Prepare a brief summary of the day's reading. Use the questions to the right to help you decide what to include. In some cases, you might ask yourself what details, characters, or events are so important that they would be included on an exam. If it helps you to organize the information, consider making a numbered list or a time line.

Sample Questions

- What are the most important events in the section you read?
- What makes them so important?
- What effect do these events have on the plot or the other characters?
- What changes—in plot, character, or tone—did you notice when you read?
- What questions about the section you read might appear on an exam?
- What might be a good essay topic for this section of the story?

Write your discussion questions here; write your responses to them in the main note-taking area to the right.>>>>

____

Assignment for Today: page ________ — page ________

Topic to be carried over to tomorrow:

Assignment for Tomorrow: page ________ — page ________

Here you should review, retell, or reflect on what you read so far. (Use the back if necessary.)

Outline Notes

Name ____________________ Date ____________

Topic ____________________ Period ____________

Main Idea/Subject ____________________

Supporting Idea 1. ____________________

Details/Examples A. ____________________

B. ____________________

C. ____________________

D. ____________________

E. ____________________

Supporting Idea 2. ____________________

Details/Examples A. ____________________

B. ____________________

C. ____________________

D. ____________________

E. ____________________

Supporting Idea 3. ____________________

Details/Examples A. ____________________

B. ____________________

C. ____________________

D. ____________________

E. ____________________

Supporting Idea 4. ____________________

Details/Examples A. ____________________

B. ____________________

C. ____________________

D. ____________________

E. ____________________

Summary/Observations

Speech Outline Notes

Name ______________________ Date ______________

Topic ______________________ Period ______________

Main Idea/Subject ______________________

(What is the question your speech is trying to answer?)

Introduction ______________________

Consider:

- Asking a thought-provoking question
- Beginning with a good/funny story
- Opening with a demonstration
- Making a strong statement
- Using a prop or visual

A. ______________________

B. ______________________

C. ______________________

D. ______________________

E. ______________________

Body of My Speech ______________________

Details/Examples A. ______________________

- ______________________

B. ______________________

- ______________________

C. ______________________

- ______________________

D. ______________________

- ______________________

E. ______________________

- ______________________

Remember to:

- Organize your speech in order of importance, chronological order, comparison/contrast, cause/effect, order of location, or problem/solution
- Use interesting details, examples, or stories
- Consider your audience's needs and questions

Conclusion ______________________

Details/Examples A. ______________________

B. ______________________

C. ______________________

D. ______________________

E. ______________________

Remember to:

- Tell one last interesting fact or story
- Explain why the topic is important
- Sum up the most important ideas in your speech
- Make a strong statement

Pyramid Notes

Name ______________________________ Date ______________

Topic ______________________________ Period ______________

Notes ____

____

____

____

____

____

____

____

Cornell Notes

Name ______________________________ Date ______________

Topic ______________________________ Period ______________

Q Notes

Name ______________________ Date ______________

Topic ______________________ Period ______________

Overview: Q Notes combine two well-known and powerful methods: SQ3R and Cornell Notes. I call them "Q Notes" because you can only write **Q**-uestions in the left-hand margin; when you prepare for a **Q**-uiz, the **Q**-uestions serve as CUES to remind you what you must know. When using these notes to study, fold the **right edge** of the paper over so that it lines up with the dotted line. You should then only be able to see your questions in the **Q**-column. Use these to **Q**-uiz yourself.

Directions: Turn the titles, subheadings, and topic sentences into questions in this column.

Directions: In this area, write the answers to the questions. Use bullets or dashes to help organize your ideas. Also, use symbols and abbreviations to help you take notes more efficiently.

Here you should review, retell, or reflect on what you read so far.

Reporter's Notes

Name ______________________________ Date ______________

Topic ______________________________ Period ______________

Reporter's Notes help you get the crucial information—not "just the facts, Ma'am," but the meaning of the facts, too. These are the questions all reporters ask when they write their articles. These are the questions that good readers ask. Not all questions are always appropriate; you decide if it's okay to leave one or more blank, but be sure you can explain why that information is absent.

WHO (is involved or affected)	**Most Important WHO**
WHAT (happened)	**Most Important WHAT**
WHERE (did it happen)	**Most Important WHERE**
WHEN (did it happen)	**Most Important WHEN**
HOW (did they do it or did others respond)	**Most Important HOW**
WHY (did they do this, react this way)	**Most Important WHY**
SO WHAT? (Why is this event/info/idea important?)	**Most Important SO WHAT?**

Sensory Notes

Name ______________________ Date ____________

Topic ______________________ Period ____________

Directions: Sensory Notes are a tool and technique designed to help you pay closer attention to details while you read. Effective readers use all their senses while they read. Use this sheet to take notes on what you see, hear, smell, feel—and think—as you read. Be specific and, if possible, write down the page numbers for future reference.

I SEE . . .	**Most Important Image**
I HEAR . . .	**Most Important Sound**
I FEEL . . .	**Most Important Sensation**
I SMELL . . .	**Most Important Scent**
I THINK. . .	**Most Important Thought**

Spreadsheet Notes (Three-Column)

Name ______________________ Date ______________

Topic ______________________ Period ______________

Summary/Response

Spreadsheet Notes (Four-Column)

Name ____________________ Date _______________ Period _______________

Topic/Chapter:

	Subject (Who or What)	**Where**	**When**	**Why (Important)**
	Cosimo de Medici	Italy (Florence)	1389–1464	Major patron of the arts during the Renaissance

Spreadsheet Notes (Multicolumn)

Name ______________________ Date ______________

Topic ______________________ Period ______________

Who's Who? The Character Directory

Title ______________________ Name ______________________ Period ______________

Directions: When deciding which characters to include in the directory below, you must distinguish between major and minor characters. If you organize all the characters along a continuum of importance, some would be at one end (e.g., a zero: not important) while others would be at the other end (e.g., a ten: essential, or most important). Before adding a character's name to the directory, ask yourself whether they are important enough, and if so, why they are so important.

Character's Name	Relationship/Role	Location	Description/Notes

Story Notes

Name ______________________ Date ______________

Topic ______________________ Period ______________

Main Characters (Tip: Before listing them, determine what makes someone a "main character.")

Setting (Tip: Setting includes not just time, but place and atmosphere.)

Primary Conflicts/Central Problems

Main Events (Tip: Before listing them, determine the criteria for a "main event.")

Climax

Resolution

Observations/Conclusions (Tip: Consider important themes, surprises, and connections to your life, other books, or classes.)

Plot Notes

Name ______________________ Date ______________

Topic ______________________ Period ______________

1. **Exposition:** Background information establishing the setting and describing the situation in which the main characters find themselves.
2. **Rising action:** Characters face or try to solve a problem. This results in conflicts within themselves or with others; these conflicts grow more intense and complicated as the story unfolds.
3. **Climax:** Eventually the story reaches a crucial moment when the character must act.
4. **Falling action:** Sometimes called the denouement, this part of the story explores the consequences of the climactic decision. The reader feels the tension in the story begin to ease up.
5. **Resolution:** The story's central problem is finally solved, leaving the reader with a sense of completion, though the main character may not feel the same way.

Climax

Rising Action

Falling Action

Exposition (Beginning)

Resolution (Ending)

Exposition (Beginning)	Rising Action	Climax	Falling Action	Resolution (Ending)

What's Most Important?	Most Important?	What's Most Important?

Observations: Possible themes, important characters, notes on the author's style

Summary Notes

Name ______________________ Date ______________

Topic ______________________ Period ______________

BEFORE

1. Determine your purpose.
2. Preview the document.
3. Prepare to take notes.

DURING

4. Take notes to help you answer these questions:
   - Who is involved?
   - What events, ideas, or people does the author emphasize?
   - What are the causes?
   - What are the consequences or implications?
5. Establish criteria to determine what is important enough to include in the summary.
6. Evaluate information as you read to determine if it meets your criteria for importance.

AFTER

7. Write your summary, which should:
   - Identify the title, author, and topic in the first sentence
   - State the main idea in the second sentence
   - Be shorter than the original article
   - Begin with a sentence that states the topic (see sample)
   - Include a second sentence that states the author's main idea
   - Include 3–5 sentences in which you explain—*in your own words*—the author's point of view
   - Include one or two interesting quotations or details
   - Not alter the author's meaning
   - Organize the ideas in the order in which they appear in the article
   - Use transitions such as "According to" + the author's name to show that you are summarizing someone else's ideas
   - Include enough information so that someone who has not read the article will understand the ideas

Sample verbs: The author:

- argues
- asserts
- concludes
- considers
- discusses
- emphasizes
- examines
- explores
- focuses on
- implies
- mentions
- notes
- points out
- says
- states
- suggests

Sample summary written by Jackie Ardon

In "Surviving a Year of Sleepless Nights," Jenny Hung **discusses** *success and how it may not be so good.* Hung **points out** *that having fun is better than having success and glory.* Jenny Hung survived a painful year because of having too many honors classes, getting straight A's, and having a GPA of 4.43. Why would any of this be bad? It's because she wasn't happy. She describes working so hard for something she didn't really want. **At one point she says,** "There was even a month in winter when I was so self-conscious of my raccoon eyes that I wore sunglasses to school." She says she often stayed up late doing work and studying for tests for her classes. After what she had been through, she decided that it was not her life, and chose her classes carefully once sophomore year came around.

Summary Sheet

Name ______________________ Unit/Subject ______________

Period ____________ Date ____________ Class ______________

QUICK PICKS names • dates • words	OVERVIEW: Summarize the topic or chapter in one sentence.		

Synthesis Notes

Name ______________________________ Date ______________

Directions: Use this page to gather and organize the crucial information about the story. Use the right-hand column to identify one aspect or character that seems vital to the story. You might determine what is most crucial by asking, "Which of all these (e.g., characters) makes the biggest difference in the story?" Some sections *might* be empty when you finish.

Story Title (and possible meaning)	Most Important Aspect (Explain)
Characters (name, description, roles)	Most Important Aspect (Explain)
Setting (where, when, atmostphere)	Most Important Aspect (Explain)
Themes (ides(s) central to the story; include examples)	Most Important Aspect (Explain)
Plot (what happens)	Most Important Aspect (Explain)
Style (use of language, imagery, symbolism, dialogue)	Most Important Aspect (Explain)
Point of View (tense, reliability, focus, narrator, in time)	Most Important Aspect (Explain)
Design (linear, episodic; use of special form—e.g., letter, journal)	Most Important Aspect (Explain)
Tone (what the story sounds like)	Most Important Aspect (Explain)

T Notes

Name ______________________ Date ______________

Subject ______________________ Period ______________

Here (and on the back) you should write your obsevations, draw your conclusions, write your summary.

Target Notes

Name ______________________ Date ______________

Subject ______________________ Period ______________

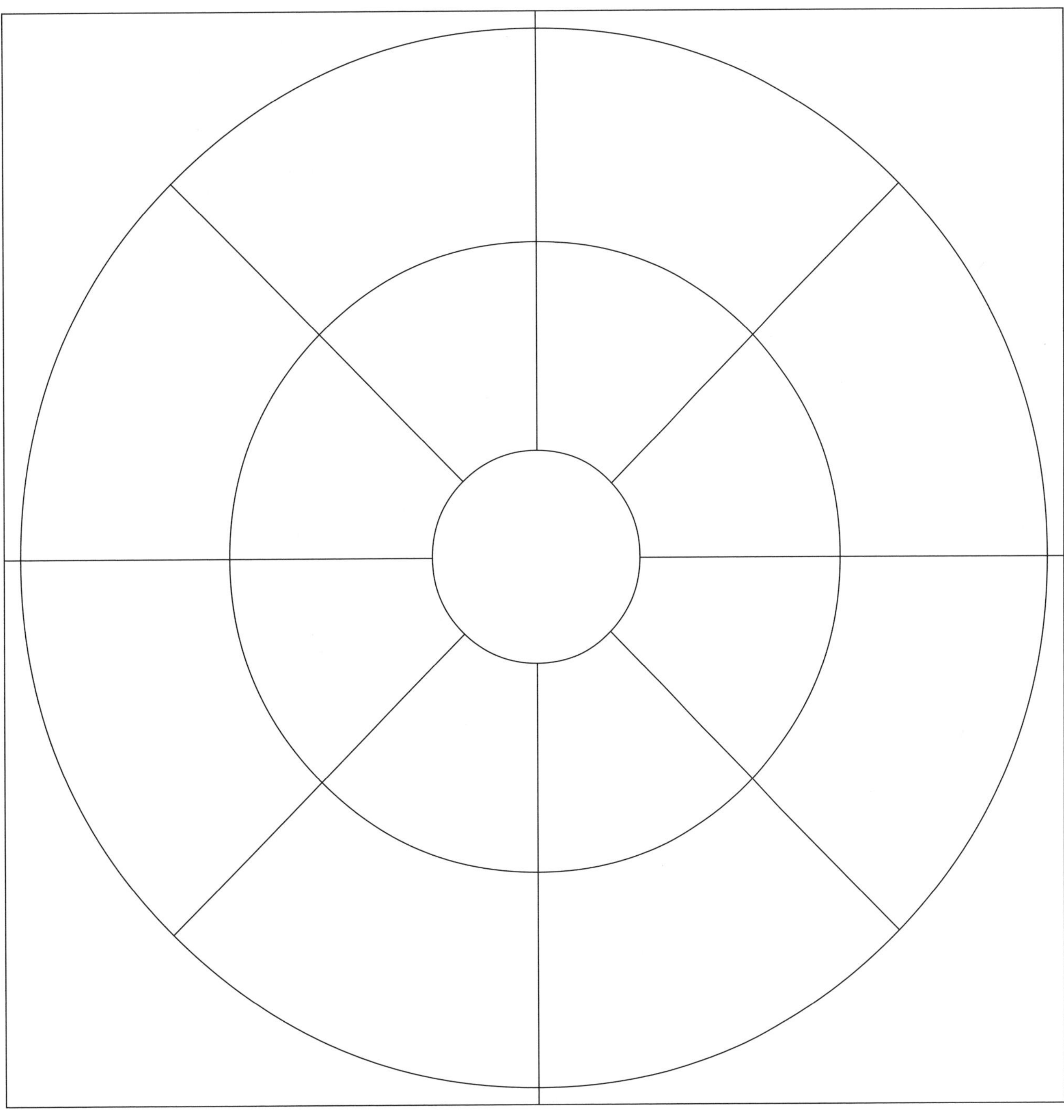

Think in Threes

Name ______________________ Date ____________

Project ______________________ Page ____________

Time Line Notes

Name ______________________________ Date ______________

Directions: Each line represents the next stage in a sequence. In a novel this might mean the next scene or chapter; in history it might mean the next event or year. In the box underneath each line you should explain why this happened, what it means, why it is important, or what it will cause to happen next.

1.

2.

3.

4.

5.

6.

7.

8.

9.

10.

11.

12.

Notes/Observations:

Venn Diagram (Two-Domain)

Name ______________________ Date __________

Topic ______________________ Period __________

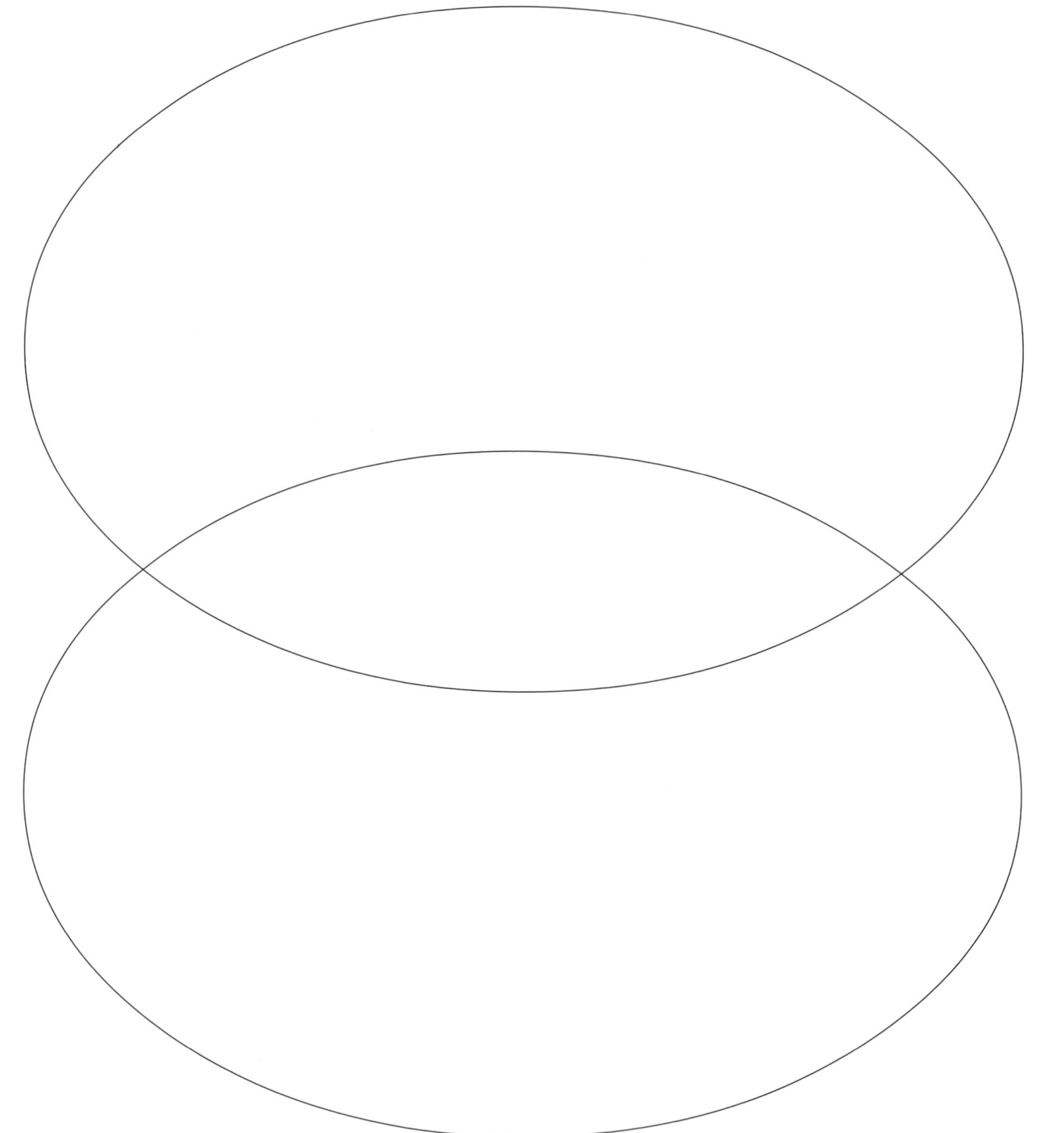

Observations/Conclusions:

Venn Diagram (Three-Domain)

Name ______________________ Date ______________

Topic ______________________ Period ______________

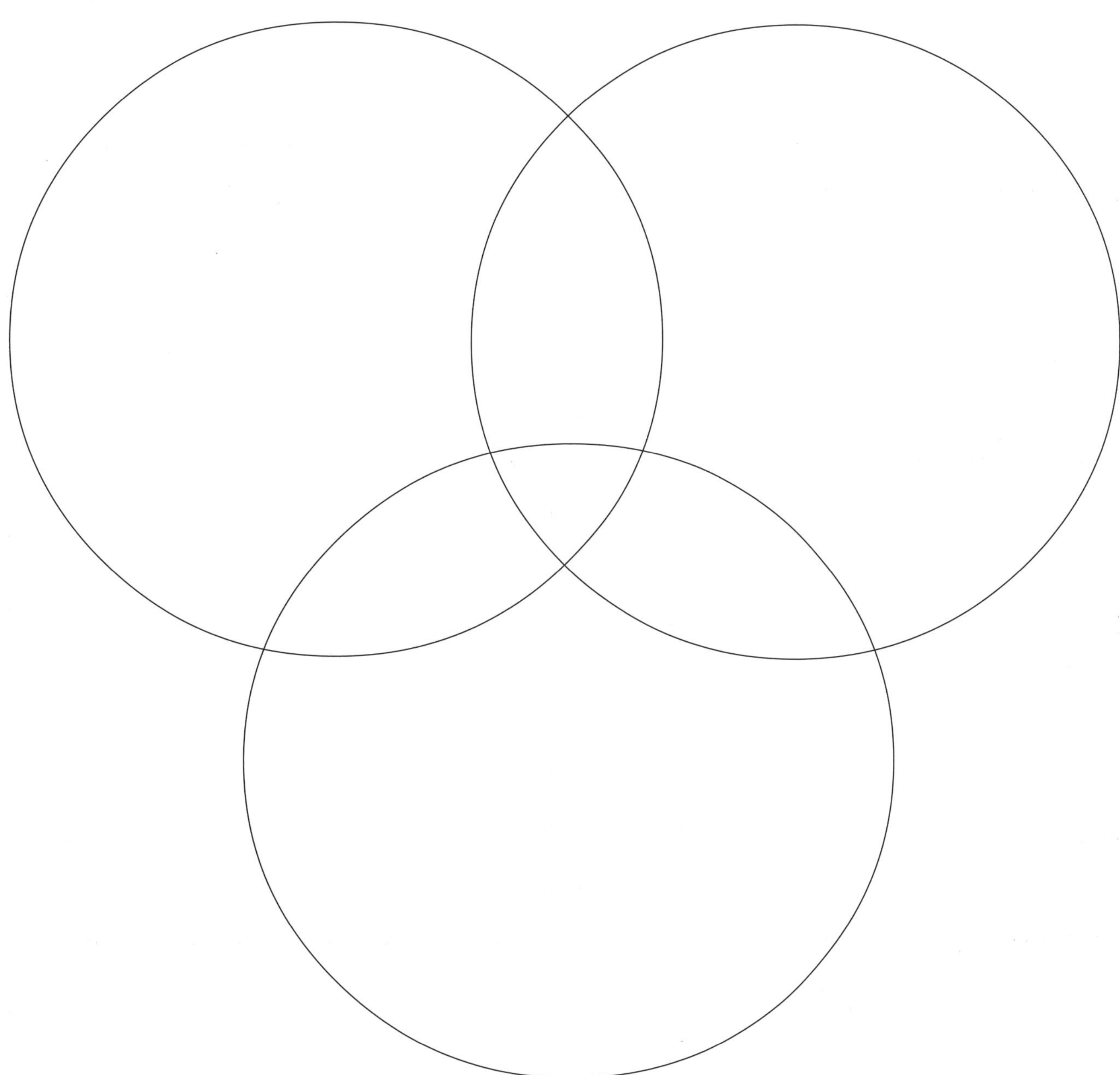

Observations/Conclusions:

Vocabulary Squares

Name ______________________ Period ____________ Week ____________

Directions: Please base your sentences on your current reading assignment unless otherwise directed.

Etymology and Part(s) of Speech	Variations, Synonyms, Antonyms
Symbol/Logo/Icon	Definition(s)
Sentence	

Etymology and Part(s) of Speech	Variations, Synonyms, Antonyms
Symbol/Logo/Icon	Definition(s)
Sentence	

Etymology and Part(s) of Speech	Variations, Synonyms, Antonyms
Symbol/Logo/Icon	Definition(s)
Sentence	

Etymology and Part(s) of Speech	Variations, Synonyms, Antonyms
Symbol/Logo/Icon	Definition(s)
Sentence	

Etymology and Part(s) of Speech	Variations, Synonyms, Antonyms
Symbol/Logo/Icon	Definition(s)
Sentence	

Etymology and Part(s) of Speech	Variations, Synonyms, Antonyms
Symbol/Logo/Icon	Definition(s)
Sentence	

Index